IMMIGRANT AGENCY

IMMIGRANT AGENCY

Hmong American Movements and the Politics of Racialized Incorporation

YANG SAO XIONG

RUTGERS UNIVERSITY PRESS

New Brunswick, Camden, and Newark, New Jersey, and London

Library of Congress Cataloging-in-Publication Data
Names: Xiong, Yang Sao, author.
Title: Immigrant agency : Hmong American movements and the politics of
    racialized incorporation / Yang Sao Xiong.
Description: New Brunswick : Rutgers University Press, [2022] | Includes
    bibliographical references and index.
Identifiers: LCCN 2021021435 | ISBN 9781978824041 (paperback) |
    ISBN 9781978824058 (hardback) | ISBN 9781978824065 (epub) |
    ISBN 9781978824072 (mobi) | ISBN 9781978824089 (pdf)
Subjects: LCSH: Hmong Americans–Social conditions. | Hmong Americans—
    Political activity. | Hmong (Asian people)–United States. | Social movements–
    United States.
Classification: LCC E184.H55 X66 2022 | DDC 305.895/972073—dc23
LC record available at https://lccn.loc.gov/2021021435

A British Cataloging-in-Publication record for this book is available from the British
Library.

References to internet websites (URLs) were accurate at the time of writing. Neither
the author nor Rutgers University Press is responsible for URLs that may have expired
or changed since the manuscript was prepared.

♾ The paper used in this publication meets the requirements of the American National
Standard for Information Sciences—Permanence of Paper for Printed Library
Materials, ANSI Z39.48-1992.

www.rutgersuniversitypress.org

Manufactured in the United States of America

For my mother and father, wife, and children.

CONTENTS

CONTENTS

TABLES AND FIGURES

TABLES AND FIGURES

MAPS

ABBREVIATIONS

AB 78	Assembly Bill 78 (California)
ACS	American Community Survey
AFDC	Aid to Families with Dependent Children
ALC	Asian Law Caucus
APIs	Asians and Pacific Islanders
AREERA	Agricultural Research, Extension, and Education Reform Act of 1998
CCLS	Central California Legal Services
CHAC	Chico Hmong Advisory Council
CIA	Central Intelligence Agency
CPA	Comprehensive Plan of Action for Indochinese Refugees
D	Democrat
DFL	Democratic Farmer Labor Party
FCNA	Fresno Center for New Americans
FUSD	Fresno Unified School District
HSA	Hmong Student Association
HSIC	Hmong Students Inter-Collegiate Coalition
HVNA	Hmong Veterans' Naturalization Act
INA	Immigration and Nationality Act
Lao PDR	Lao People's Democratic Republic
LPR	lawful permanent resident
LVA	Lao Veterans of America
MFI	Mong Federation, Inc.
MSA	metropolitan statistical area
MSF	military service frame
NAPALC	National Asian Pacific American Legal Consortium
PRWORA	Personal Responsibility and Work Opportunity Reconciliation Act of 1996
PUMS	public use microdata sample
R	Republican
SECA	Strategic Ethnic Collective Action
SGU	special guerrilla unit
SMO	social movement organization
SSA	Social Security Administration
SSI	Supplemental Security Income
TANF	Temporary Assistance for Needy Families
UNHCR	United Nations High Commissioner for Refugees
USAID	U.S. Agency for International Development

IMMIGRANT AGENCY

1 · IMMIGRANT AGENCY

Try to imagine, for a moment, that you are living in a state of war and that you and your family have been struggling to survive for the past seven years. Then, all of a sudden, things changed dramatically, for the worst. Every eight minutes, several 500- to 750-pound bombs dropped from the sky, landing who knows where. Upon impact these bombs shredded everything in their paths within hundreds of meters. Imagine that a planeload of bombs continued to drop every eight minutes around the clock every day for the next nine years.

During the American-Vietnam War, the U.S. military dropped over two million tons of ordnance on Laos during 580,000 bombing missions—the equivalent of a planeload of bombs dropped every eight minutes, twenty-four hours a day, for nine years. War, forced displacement, and statelessness were the lived experiences of millions of Laotians, including hundreds of thousands of Hmong.

This is a story about human courage and agency in the face of great despair and seemingly insurmountable odds, a remarkable tale of how Hmong political refugees from war-torn Laos not only managed to come to the United States when the government had no plans to ever admit them, but also how they, in a relatively short period of time and against tremendous odds, became one of the most politically engaged groups within American society. As a child of Hmong political refugees who was raised in refugee camps and educated in the United States, I take this story seriously because I am accountable to the people who have lived this history and whose lives continue to be impacted by it.

This is also a story about how the United States has treated and mistreated immigrants and refugees, particularly Hmong former refugees since the end of the Cold War. As a country, the United States does very little to actively incorporate immigrants and refugees into its political system. However, as a racial state, the country actively engages in actions that prevent immigrants and refugees from entering its borders, limit their access to rights and resources, undermine their political standing, and curtail their access to political representation and power. In some ways, the U.S. treatment and betrayal of its Hmong allies is unique; in many ways, it reveals underlying processes of how the racial state perpetuates the political marginalization of immigrants and refugees.

Although political incorporation is often seen as something that states do, immigrants exert agency in incorporating themselves. However, they do so in conditions not of their choosing and far from racially neutral. This book takes seriously the call by scholars to take account of structural racism and racialization in the field of immigration studies (Bonilla-Silva 1997; Brown and Jones 2015; Jung 2009; Romero 2008; Saenz and Douglas 2015; Treitler 2015). While other scholars have called for "bringing the state back" into the study of immigrant incorporation (Bloemraad 2006), both race and the state need to be examined together if we are to better understand the power of structures and the potentials and limits of human agency. One way of centering race while taking account of the role of the state in the study of immigrant political incorporation is to examine how the racial state racializes and positions immigrant groups upon their arrival and how immigrant groups exert agency in resisting racialization as they engage in political struggles for social justice and inclusion. Another way is to examine how the racial state, through public policies, engages in ongoing racialization alongside incorporation in order to curtail immigrant groups' political standing, perpetuate their political marginalization, and maintain racial and political inequality in society. This book contributes to both these tasks by examining how Hmong social actors and groups, in response to perceived political opportunities, political threats, or both, engage in collective action and strategically interact with the U.S. political system and other groups in American society in order to seek political incorporation in U.S. society.

During the past thirty-five years, Hmong Americans, in response to political threats or political opportunities or both, have exerted agency in making sustained claims on the U.S. political system and getting their interests represented in public policies. Through strategic ethnic collective actions, Hmong Americans have been able to distinguish themselves as a unique immigrant group, respond effectively to political threats, and obtain tangible benefits. Through time and through past protest experiences, Hmong former refugees have come to learn how they are racialized as a group, what types of claims the state is more responsive to, how to mobilize resources and people, whom to ally with, and how to recognize and utilize political opportunities to influence decision makers. For example, in response to the political threat posed by federal welfare reforms in the mid-1990s, Hmong strategically positioned themselves alongside other Asian and immigrant groups. Specifically, they allied with and received substantial support from the Asian Law Caucus (ALC), a pan-Asian organization, but resisted an "Asian" identity; they marched and rallied alongside thousands of immigrants but chose not to simply fight for "immigrant" rights. Instead, Hmong drew on their collective political narratives of the Secret War in Laos and the U.S. involvement in that war to frame their claims in a way that persuaded the United States to consider its own "national honor" and interests. Through such strategic positioning and framing of group identity, Hmong were able to persuade the U.S. government to grant them tangible benefits. However, even when it granted Hmong benefits, the U.S. government racialized and othered Hmong, undermining their political standing within the political system.

This book is especially timely and important given ongoing global crises of war and the forced displacement and international migration of millions of people around the globe. The thirteen million refugees from Syria and six million refugees from Afghanistan are the latest victims of war. As political refugees start new lives all over again as strangers in peculiar new lands, they face not only the immediate problems of social-cultural adjustment and economic instability but also the perennial problems of ethnic and racial discrimination and political marginalization. Understanding the experiences of Hmong former refugees, their political agency in the United States, and how the United States racialized them can shed fresh light on the possibilities as well as challenges for vulnerable immigrant and refugee populations as they try to enter into, participate in, and influence the political system of their host society. This book examines not only Hmong's courage and agency but also how the United States utilizes its power to perpetuate immigrants' political marginalization.

Throughout this book, I use the term "state" to refer to the "set of political, military, judicial, and bureaucratic organizations that exert political authority and coercive control over people living within the borders of well-defined territories" (Amenta et al. 2002, 49). I use the term "state actors" to refer to individuals who represent or engage in actions, such as policy making, on behalf of the state. I use "state segments" to refer to a group of state actors or different branches or bureaucracies of the state. The U.S. Congress, the legislative branch of the U.S. government, is an example of a state segment. The U.S. Department of Veterans Affairs, the Department of State, and the Department of Agriculture are also state segments.

The state's strong tendency to protect capitalist interests (Block 1977) is intertwined with its interest in protecting White privilege and power. Historically, the United States has racially subjected various colonized peoples such as Native Americans and Puerto Ricans and noncolonized peoples such as Blacks and Asians and usurped foreign sovereignties and their peoples (Jung and Kwon 2013, 934). The interests of the White majority have been naturalized as national and state interests (Oliver 2017). The United States is a racial state in the sense that it is both "increasingly the pre-eminent site of racial conflict" (Omi and Winant 1994, 82) and a "repressive, white-controlled and white-interest-oriented modern state that regularly generates racial conflict, enforces racial divisions, and attempts to exploit, exclude or eliminate certain racial groups through homogenizing or marginalizing processes" (Feagin and Elias 2013, 945). As a racial state, the United States has historically incorporated some groups (e.g., Northern and Western Europeans) but disincorporated others (e.g., Mexicans, Chinese, Japanese Americans) (Ngai 1998; Omi and Winant 1994; Rogers 2006).

Although Whites are not the only ones capable of defining racial meanings or practicing racism—non-Whites also have agency in defining and resisting racial meanings and partaking in racism (and antiracism)—Whites have been the major beneficiaries of systemic racism (Omi and Winant 2013). That the United States is interested in protecting capitalist interests and upholding the system of White supremacy has tremendous implications for immigrant political incorporation.

Instead of incorporating all groups, the U.S. capitalist and racial state has often used its power to enact policies and practices that disincorporate particular groups—that is, marginalize or exclude certain groups from rights, resources, or representation and curtail or reverse the gains of groups that have achieved a limited degree of political incorporation.[1] For instance, prior to the federal Welfare Reform Act of 1996, immigrants with legal status, such as Hmong refugees and lawful permanent residents, were generally eligible to receive public benefits on the same basis as U.S. citizens. However, when welfare reform was enacted, it barred non-U.S. citizens from receiving public benefits such as Supplemental Security Income (SSI) and food stamps. Refugees' eligibility for public benefits was limited to the first seven years of their arrival unless they could obtain naturalization. In this way, welfare reform continued the U.S. government's practice of excluding undocumented immigrants from benefits and reversed the rights of legal immigrants who had previously been eligible for public benefits. But the state's disincorporation of groups can also occur in much more subtle ways.

Racialization is one of the most enduring and powerful ways through which the U.S. racial state disincorporates groups. Following Hochman (2019, 1245), I take racialization to be "the process through which *racialized groups,* rather than 'races' are formed." U.S. society in general and its political system in particular, far from being color-blind in their treatment—whether inclusion or exclusion—of individuals and groups, treat them according to their perceived racial differences. Racial difference, in turn, is socially constructed and maintained through practices of racialization (Omi and Winant 1994). Racialization is a useful analytical concept in the study of immigrant political incorporation for what it *does.* As a process, racialization operates independent of and alongside the process of political incorporation. Racialization matters for immigrant political incorporation in at least two ways: (1) the state, through policies and practices, racializes immigrant groups upon their arrival and reracializes them from time to time, placing them in particular positions within the U.S. racial hierarchy; and (2) because state institutions or actors who racialize groups need not use explicitly racist labels or language, racialization is a powerful way by which the state curtails immigrant groups' political standing and, by extension, perpetuates their political marginalization and racial subjugation without appearing overtly racist.

In this book, I use the term "racialized immigrant incorporation" to refer to the process in which the state subtly disincorporates an immigrant group by racializing it even when it grants such a group limited policy concessions. By racializing an immigrant group, the state curtails its political standing and delimits its political incorporation. Because state racialization can occur both in the absence of de jure discrimination and alongside processes of political incorporation, making it a pervasive, albeit subtle, process, it is important that studies of immigrant political incorporation take account not only of the extent to which a group's interests are effectively represented in public policies (the traditional definition of political incorporation) but also of the extent to which a group is racialized as either a legitimate group with political standing or one that is illegitimate and has little or no political standing within the nation. The concept of racialized immigrant incorporation recognizes that an immigrant group's capacity to make sustained claims on the political system—a more recent definition of political incorporation—is both conditioned by its unique contexts of exit and reception and shaped by its ascribed position in the racial hierarchy.

UNDERSTANDING IMMIGRANT POLITICAL INCORPORATION

In a recent book on explaining immigrant political incorporation, Jennifer Hochschild and John Mollenkopf (2009b, 19) present readers with the following illustration: "Traits well beyond a person's legal immigration status affects his or her ability to enter, and likelihood of entering, the political arena. For example, even if both are legal permanent residents of the host country, an English-speaking South Asian with a college degree moving to Canada under its point system is much more likely be politically incorporated than is a Hmong refugee with less than a high school education moving to the United States as part of a family reunification plan." As I elaborate below, Hochschild and Mollenkopf recognize that an immigrant's or immigrant group's degree of political incorporation is shaped by the resources that they possess as well as by the opportunities and constraints of the contexts of reception. I cite Hochschild and Mollenkopf's example not only because it mentions the Hmong, the multigenerational ethnic community whose politics in the United States is the focus of this book, but also because it hints at the puzzling questions that my study addresses.

Unlike most other post-1965 immigrants to the United States, foreign-born Hmong came as political refugees from Laos. Like other Southeast Asian refugees, Hmong refugees' migration to the United States was the direct result of the United States' failed foreign policy and military intervention in Southeast Asia. But in the aftermath of the American-Vietnam War in 1975, the U.S. government had no plans to resettle Hmong in the United States, even though in that same year the U.S. Congress was anxiously considering how to resettle over a hundred thousand Vietnamese and Cambodian refugees. Indeed, declassified government documents reveal that in the autumn of 1975 the U.S. government secretly planned to resettle Laotian Hmong refugees permanently in Thailand, with or without Thai approval (see chapter 2). Fortunately, as the result of the efforts of well-positioned refugee advocates, the first major wave of Hmong refugees quietly made it to the United States in the spring of 1976.

Secondary waves of Hmong refugees arrived in the United States between 1980 and 1995. Unlike the first wave of Hmong refugees who were more likely to be educated and to speak some English, Hmong refugees who arrived in the second and later waves came with very little financial and social capital. With most of their existing skills largely devalued in the host society, many able-bodied, working-age Hmong men and women were unable to secure gainful employment to support themselves or their families. Unemployment and underemployment coupled with increasing costs of living had the net effect of making Hmong Americans one of the most economically disadvantaged groups in American society. Ample research has documented Hmong Americans' struggle with poverty since their arrival to the United States (Downing et al. 1984; Reder et al. 1984; Rumbaut and Ima 1988; Xiong 2013).

Besides economic disadvantages, Hmong are also disadvantaged by their racialization, initially as "Indochinese" and subsequently as "Asians." Within the existing racial structure of the United States, Asians have been racially triangulated. Political scientist Claire Jean Kim argues that since the mid-1960s Whites have used political reasons to both valorize Asian Americans as superior relative to Blacks and position Asian Americans as foreigners compared to Whites and Blacks. Namely, Whites valorize Asians in order to dominate both Asians and Blacks but especially Blacks. In order to exclude Asian Americans politically and civically, they construct Asians as "immutably foreign and unassimilable with Whites on cultural and/or racial grounds" (Kim 1999, 107). These processes of "relative valorization and civic ostracism" (in short, "racial triangulation") reinforce White dominance and privilege and affect Asian Americans' opportunities to obtain public goods.

Scholars who study political incorporation are interested in to what extent people are able to make sustained claims on the polity and sometimes have their interests effectively represented in public policy (Browning, Marshall, and Tabb 1984, 1986; Hochschild and Mollenkopf 2009a; Hochschild et al. 2013). But what does it take for people to be able to make sustained claims on the polity and get their interests effectively represented in public policy? Scholars have highlighted the roles of resources and political opportunity structures in shaping groups' political incorporation (Bloemraad 2006; Ireland 1994; Koopmans 2004; Maxwell 2008). In a now classic book, *Protest Is Not Enough: The Struggle of Blacks and Hispanics for Equality in Urban Politics,* Browning, Marshall, and Tabb (1984) argue that a group's organization and structure of resources affect its mobilization capacity and strategic choices (e.g., between protest and electoral strategies). By the structure of resources, they mean the resources both inside and outside of the group, such as the size of the group, its socioeconomic resources, its political experiences, and the amount of support for minority interests among the rest of the population.

Judging by Hmong's population size and socioeconomic resources in the late 1980s, one might assume that their capacity to engage in politics during that period was very weak. In 1990, the Hmong population in the United States was 94,439 according to the U.S. census. They were dispersed across multiple states but were concentrated in three states: California, Minnesota, and Wisconsin. Throughout the 1980s and 1990s, Hmong's poverty rate (64 percent) was several times that of the U.S. population (14 percent). In 1990, only 3 percent of the Hmong American population twenty-five years and older had obtained a bachelor's degree or higher, compared to 26 percent of all U.S. adults (more details on Hmong's socioeconomic status are described below). However, resource-based models of political incorporation do not reliably predict Hmong's ability to engage in politics.

Although Hmong refugees arrived with very little financial and material capital, Hmong brought with them certain political experiences, particularly their experience as a group who took up arms against other political factions during the Secret War in Laos, engaged in resistance movements for decades after the war, and survived for years or decades in the harsh refugee camps under Thai control. As we will see in later chapters, these shared political experiences proved crucial to Hmong's ability to mobilize collective consensus among Hmong individuals, construct political narratives and frame political claims, and motivate corrective action from goal granters on socially defined problems during concrete political struggles.

AN ALTERNATIVE MODEL OF IMMIGRANT POLITICAL INCORPORATION

To better understand immigrants' political incorporation, we need to conceptualize political incorporation as a complex, contentious, and interactive process and pay closer attention to their agency (i.e., their strategic choices) within this process. Specifically, we should think of immigrant political incorporation as an ongoing, dynamic, multi-pronged process involving minimally both the immigrant group's concerted efforts to influence public policy, especially in getting their self-interest represented in public policy, and obtaining legitimate political standing within the political system and the state's efforts at disincorporating them. In struggling for political incorporation, individuals and groups make choices between sets of actions given the dilemmas and structural constraints they confront in concrete political circumstances (Jasper 2004). They may, for instance, construct and deploy particular collective identities and not others as part of claims making in concrete political struggles and institutional contexts (Okamoto 2014; Oliver 2017; Polletta and Jasper 2001).

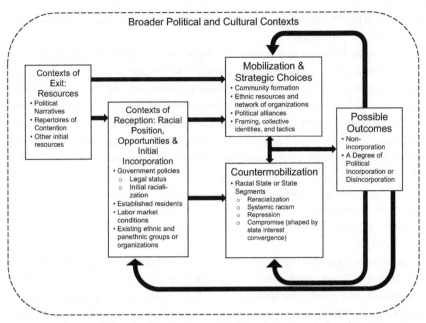

FIGURE 1.1. Strategic Ethnic Collective Action Model of Immigrant Political Incorporation

Accepting the view that social actors make choices about identities, tactics, and allies often in circumstances not of their choosing (Meyer 2004b), I take immigrant political incorporation to be a process that entails immigrants, the state or state segments, and others selecting and applying strategic choices that affect immigrants' political standing and, by extension, their capacity to make sustained claims on the political system. My Strategic Ethnic Collective Action (SECA) model of immigrant political incorporation privileges immigrant groups' collective action and strategic choices but recognizes the role of immigrants' contexts of exit and reception in shaping their resources, racial position, opportunities (or constraints), and strategic choices. Collective action involves both the factors that constrain action, such as resources and political opportunity structures, and those that social actors can choose and change over time, such as group identities, alliances, and tactics (McAdam 1982; McCarthy and Zald 1977; Snow and Benford 1988; Taylor and Van Dyke 2004; Van Dyke and McCammon 2010). Figure 1.1 is a visual representation of the SECA conceptual model.

Contexts of Exit, Discursive Resources, and Repertoires of Contention

Immigrant groups' capacity for collective mobilization and the extent of their initial political incorporation (or disincorporation) may be very different depending on each group's contexts of exit and reception. Immigration scholars have rightfully rejected the classic assumption that immigrants experience a single path to full assimilation. These scholars recognize, instead, that immigrants and subsequent generations of immigrants can experience multiple social and economic outcomes—upward, downward, or lateral social mobility—depending on their group's specific "modes of incorporation," which in turn are shaped by their contexts of exit and reception (Portes and Rumbaut 1990; Portes and Zhou 1993). Although most past research that utilizes the concepts of immigrants' contexts of exit and reception has used them to explain immigrants' socioeconomic outcomes, I contend that these concepts, with some modifications, are useful in the study of immigrant politics and political incorporation. However, I make no assumption that immigrants' contexts of exit and reception can by themselves determine immigrants' political outcomes (their degrees of political incorporation or disincorporation). Instead, I assume that immigrants are imbedded in multiple contexts (local, state, regional, national; host and homeland contexts; and broader political contexts), that these contexts can differently facilitate or constrain immigrants' resources and opportunities, and that immigrants' political outcomes are contingent on the interactions between their collective mobilizations and the state's or other groups' countermobilizations.

Contexts of exit usually refer to the socioeconomic conditions of immigrants in their country of origin that affect their social class backgrounds, and the circumstances under which an immigrant group exited its country of origin (Portes and Rumbaut 1990; Portes and Zhou 1993). For the purpose of immigrant political incorporation, I broaden this concept to include the conditions and circumstances in immigrants' initial country of resettlement and, in the case of refugees, their first country of asylum. After all, some immigrants and refugees have lived and worked in more than two countries; their stay in intermediate countries such as initial countries of resettlement or asylum also can shape the experiences and resources they bring to their final country of settlement. Contexts of exit shape the kinds and amounts of material, financial, and human capital (education credentials, job skills, language skills, etc.) that immigrants and their families arrive with (Portes and Rumbaut 1990). People displaced from their home country by war, for instance, tend to arrive with less financial and human capital than other voluntary professional immigrants. The circumstances that lead immigrants to exit their home country will also shape whether immigrants will be regarded by others as refugees or non-refugees, settlers or sojourners, legitimate or illegitimate immigrants, and so on. Immigrants' legal status upon arrival, in turn, impacts their eligibility to acquire formal membership such as U.S. citizenship within their host society. Surprisingly, past research on immigrants has paid scant attention to the ways that contexts of exit shape groups' discursive resources and repertoires of contention.

However, besides shaping the material and financial resources and human capital that new immigrants bring with them, immigrants' contexts of exit such as wars, military alliances, and forced displacements can powerfully shape an immigrant group's cultural or discursive resources such as collective political narratives (Fine 1995; Williams 1995) as well as their repertoires of contention (Tilly 2008). Collective political narratives are the common stories that people within a group tell about people, events, and unanticipated crises or troubles. Social movement actors can draw on a group's extant political narratives to both mobilize group solidarity and make political claims on different targets. Collective political narratives tied to an ethnic immigrant group's unique historical relationship with its host state can affect the types of collective political identities that immigrant social actors construct, the types of claims that they pursue in the host country, and the extent to which the host government may be persuaded to respond to a set of claims. Repertoires of contention refer to all the forms of collective action with which a group of people is familiar and that its members can adapt and use when they want to oppose a decision or condition that they consider unjust or threatening (Tilly 1977, 2008). An immigrant group's premigration experiences, such as their direct involvement or exposure to the actions and circumstances of warfare, could shape the range of repertoires that they acquire. Some of these acquired repertoires are "modular" repertoires— that is, they are transferable and can be deployable by a variety of actors against a variety of targets in new contentious contexts (Tarrow 1993). Immigrant groups can draw on their preexisting collective political narratives and modular repertoires of contention to make claims (i.e., consciously articulate demands) of different types on different individuals and groups, including the political system of their new host society.

Contexts of Reception, Legal Status, Racial Position, Opportunities, and Strategic Choices

Contexts of reception refer to the set of contexts that receive or exclude immigrants upon their arrival in the new country. Contexts of reception include the political relations between sending and receiving countries, the political contexts or policies of the receiving country, the conditions of its labor markets, majority and minority groups, and the presence and characteristics of communities who share the ethnic background of the immigrant group (Portes and Zhou 1993, 82–83). For the purpose of immigrant political incorporation, I broaden the contexts of reception to include the prevailing social hierarchies in the receiving country and nongovernmental public institutions, such as education institutions that take part in reproducing or maintaining these hierarchies. In the context of the United States, racial, class, and gender hierarchies are pervasive and highly consequential for immigrants and nonimmigrants. This book emphasizes the existence of "systemic racism" in the United States while recognizing that systemic racism intersects with classism and sexism to create and maintain social closure and inequalities across and within U.S. social institutions, especially political institutions (Murphy 1988; Tilly 1998). Systemic racism refers to "the foundational, large-scale and inescapable hierarchical system of US racial oppression devised and maintained by whites and directed at people of colour" (Feagin and Elias 2013, 936). Besides the state, public institutions such as the mass media and educational institutions can racialize immigrant groups, positioning them in particular places within the U.S. racial hierarchy.

While contexts of exit condition a group's initial resources, collective political narratives, and protest repertoires, contexts of reception affect the group's initial legal status, its initial racialized identity and position within the racial hierarchy, its access to existing established groups or organizations, and its potential to form ethnic communities. As a key component of political contexts, government policies (hereinafter state policies) determine immigrants' initial legal status and continue to determine their access to rights, benefits, and resources long after immigrants' initial reception. In the United States, state policies also determine immigrants' initial racialization through the creation of official racial categories and differential assignment of consequences on racialized groups (Hochschild and Weaver 2007). Because race powerfully organizes individuals' and groups' life chances, I expect that an immigrant group's initial racialization by the state and/or established residents will influence the group's initial political incorporation. For example, a group's racialization upon arrival could affect its initial political standing, relationship with other existing racialized groups, and ability to form interethnic and interracial alliances. State policies can be both sponsors of action and the targets of action (Amenta et al. 2002; Kriesi et al. 1995b). State policies may become the targets of action when they are perceived as political threats—that is, actions that exclude or threaten to exclude particular groups from receiving public goods or rights. As Amenta et al. (2002, 67) point out, "State policies can encourage, discourage, shape, or transform challengers because policies influence the flow of collective benefits to identifiable groups. In addition, by designating officially sanctioned and legitimated beneficiaries and by power of categorization, policies also help to define and redefine social groups." Besides shaping the goals and interests of groups and their access to public goods, state policies also impact immigrants' potential to form visible and cohesive ethnic immigrant communities. Specifically, the state policies regulating immigrants' admission and resettlement can influence whether and where ethnic immigrant communities can emerge. In the late 1970s and early 1980s, the U.S. policies of dispersing Southeast Asian refugees across multiple states and cities led to geographically isolated and fragmented neighborhoods of refugees. It was not until the mid-1980s that cohesive Southeast Asian communities emerged as a byproduct of family reunification made possible through secondary migration (Mortland and Ledgerwood 1987).

Initial Racialization. Immigrants are defined not simply by legal status but also by race. Upon arrival or soon thereafter, the racial state, dominant groups, and others racialize immigrants—that is, sort them into racial categories as part of their ongoing ideological processes of boundary construction and racial formation (Omi and Winant 1994; Massey 2009; Saperstein, Penner, and Light 2013). The specific racial position of some recent immigrant groups may be initially ambiguous. Although scholars have theorized about the structure of the U.S. racial hierarchy and some have come up with "typologies" of where various racialized groups are positioned relative to one another during particular historical periods (Gans 1999; Bonilla-Silva 2004; Gold 2004; Feagin and Elias 2013), it may be more useful in the study of immigrant political incorporation to not assume a priori any particular hierarchical arrangement—aside from the assumption that groups racialized as White within the U.S. racial hierarchy have unearned power above and beyond what other groups racialized as other than White have—until more thorough research has been done to clarify the context-dependent relative power of racialized groups and the interactions or lack of interactions among all or at least most racialized groups within any socially constructed racial hierarchy.

However, over time, as institutions, organizations, and groups create racial categories, put people in racial categories, and assign differential consequences to them, groups such as Hmong refugees come to recognize how they are racialized and positioned within the hierarchical racial structure of the United States. Besides government institutions and policies, public institutions such as the media can shape groups' political standing by defining them in particular ways (Xiong and Thornton 2021). Although hierarchical, racial axes may be multidimensional. For example, Asians as a racial category are often positioned between Whites and Blacks and are also defined as permanent foreigners (Kim 1999). Because racialization powerfully organizes individuals' and groups' life chances in the United States, the political incorporation of an immigrant group in this context is intertwined with that group's racialized identity and perceived position in the U.S. racial hierarchy. As time goes by and as immigrant groups interact with the political system, they may be reracialized, and depending on how a group is reracialized, it can affect their subsequent political standing and, by extension, their capacity to influence the political system.

Established Residents. However, the state and state segments are not the only entities with which immigrants interact as they pursue political incorporation. Immigrants also interact with established residents or members of majority or minority groups who regard themselves or are regarded by others as legitimate residents of an area. Like newcomers, established residents also care about having their interests represented in public policy. Established residents could receive immigrants positively, negatively, or indifferently, and the way that they treat immigrants can influence public opinion about immigrants. As we have seen throughout much of U.S. history, majority groups, namely Whites, have frequently stereotyped certain groups of immigrants—Chinese, Mexicans, Japanese, etc.—as being dangerous to American society and put pressures on their elected officials to enact laws restricting these groups' immigration to the United States and barring those who are already here from rights that other Americans enjoy. Because elected officials rely on the majority of voters to be reelected, if there is enough public pressure especially from majority groups, elected officials might cater policies according to the interests of established residents. Besides this, established residents can also constrain immigrants' political incorporation by preventing ethnic communities from forming, by disaggregating existing ethnic communities or diluting their concentrated power, and by discouraging new immigrants from moving into an area. For example, established residents have used housing discrimination to deny immigrants access to certain neighborhoods, maintaining racial segregation (Massey and Denton 1993). Middle-class established residents have gentrified neighborhoods, pushing racialized minorities out of their own communities (Gale 1984). Some residents have used restrictive municipal regulations to deflect immigration to a locale (Light 2006). Finally, some established residents have organized anti-immigrant movements to threaten existing immigrant communities and discourage new immigration (Perea 1997). Although the majority in the United States are Whites, other minorities also matter to immigrants as they forge alliances in pursuit of political incorporation (see below).

Labor Market Conditions. The conditions of the labor market, including the availability of jobs, the variety of occupations, and the level of job competition, affect immigrants' ability to secure gainful employment. Gainful employment, in turn, affects immigrants' ability to generate fixed resources (e.g., resources one needs for survival or functioning that cannot easily be allocated for other things) and discretionary resources (e.g., time and money that one can easily allocate toward social movement purposes) (McCarthy and Zald 1977). The more discretionary resources that an immigrant group has access to, the greater its capacity to engage in collective actions.

Ethnic Community Formation, Ethnic Resources, and Network of Organizations. The formation of ethnic community is a critical condition both for immigrants' ability to create, access, and/or mobilize politically relevant resources and for their standing as a legitimate claimant in the public arena. In response to disadvantages, discrimination, or exclusion, immigrant groups may form and turn to coethnic communities for linguistic, social, and economic support (Portes and Zhou 1992, 1993). A critical mass of coethnics who reside, work, and play in the same community provide the conditions for ethnic institutions such as ethnic media, businesses, and civic associations or organizations to develop, increasing the group's overall organizational capacity, which in turn can support collective mobilization. I define organizational capacity broadly as the set of resources (human skills, material and financial assets, discursive resources), communication networks, and social relationships that enables social actors to mobilize collective action.

As many researchers have shown, access to resources affects individuals' and groups' ability to engage in individual and collective political actions (McCarthy and Zald 1977; Wolfinger and Rosenstone 1980; Wong, Lien, and Conway 2005). Ethnic resources are an ethnic group's internally derived forms of human, material, and financial resources (such as civic skills, sense of efficacy, time, money, facilities, labor power), social and demographic resources (population and electorate size, social capital generating networks), and discursive resources (collective political narratives and other ideological resources). In addition to ethnic resources, members of ethnic communities often seek and mobilize resources that exist outside of the ethnic community. These exogenous resources may include formal civic or legal organizations, state representatives, the mass media, political actors, and so on.

Existing Ethnic and Panethnic Groups and Political Alliances. Besides interacting with the state and majority groups, immigrants also interact with other minorities or minority-led organizations within the contexts of reception. Interethnic or interracial coalitions might already exist in some places where immigrants resettle, but most coalitions must be built or rebuilt. The more vulnerable an immigrant group is, the more it will need the assistance of other more established ethnic groups or organizations during political contestations. While some established residents are hostile to newcomers, others of all races and ethnicities welcome and assist them. When a newcomer group needs political assistance, other more established groups or organizations may come to its aid for altruistic reasons, for reasons of shared race or ethnicity or for other instrumental reasons. Immigrant groups' alliances with more established groups or organizations increase their ability to make sustained claims on the political system. Unlike European immigrants who were often targeted for mobilization by local political machines and parties, non-White immigrant groups often rely on their own community-based civic organizations to mobilize politically (Wong 2006). Within immigrant minority communities, more politically experienced and connected organizations can sometimes serve as "bridging organizations" to less politically experienced, less connected organizations, creating access points for immigrants into the mainstream political system (Chung 2007).

The set of contexts of reception are dynamic rather than static. I expect that an immigrant group's initial public reception, initial legal status, and initial racialization will influence its initial degree of political incorporation. However, as some conditions within the contexts of reception (e.g., public policies, labor market conditions, access to institutional and state allies) change over time while other conditions, such as the racial hierarchy, remain largely unchanged, they can create contingencies such as advantages or disadvantages and political opportunities or threats for immigrants. These contingencies, in turn, can affect immigrants' opportunities and motivation for mobilizing collective action and the strategic choices they make as they interact with the political system and other groups.

Mobilization and Countermobilization. Immigrants could engage in collective action in response to perceived political opportunities or threats or both (Goldstone and Tilly 2001; Okamoto 2003; Zepeda-Millán 2017). To increase the chances that their efforts will have the desired impact, immigrant groups must strategically mobilize collective consensus and action as well as anticipate and overcome countermobilization. Countermobilizations or organized efforts in opposition to immigrant political mobilization could take many forms depending on who is leading the countermobilization (whether established residents or the state) and could include overt as well as covert forms of repression. If the state decides to take action on a challenger's social problem, the result of that action could have no or little effect (nonincorporation), adverse effect (a degree of disincorporation), positive effect (a degree of incorporation), or mixed effect (a combination of incorporation and disincorporation).[2] Depending on whether the outcome or policy is more negative or positive, it could have feedback effects on both sides of the incorporation equation—effects on an immigrant group's legal status, their socioeconomic resources, and their organizational capacity to mobilize—and effects on the majority and majority institutions and state mobilization. Changes to state policies may, for example, make it easier or harder for immigrants to become naturalized, to find and keep stable jobs, or to obtain funding for existing community-based organizations. But they can also strengthen the state's ability to control, gather surveillance on, or repress immigrants.

The interactions between immigrant groups, extant minority and majority groups, and the racial state take place in nested political and cultural contexts. Contexts are nested in the sense that narrower contexts, such as local contexts, are embedded in and usually shaped by broader contexts, such as state, national, and supranational contexts. Supranational or international contexts can structure or constrain the political options available to actors within national contexts (Meyer 2003). Nested political contexts encompass local, state, or national policies and broader bi- and multilateral policies, any of which could pose as a political opportunity or a political threat to immigrants. Broader geopolitical contexts and relations between the host and home country may affect immigrants and their interests long after they arrive in the United States and may change over time. As homeland contexts change over time, immigrant groups might engage in political activities aimed at affecting government or nongovernment targets or issues in immigrants' former homelands (Collet and Lien 2009; Kivisto 2003; Østergaard-Nielsen 2003). Changes in bilateral trade relations and/or political relations between countries can have an immediate impact on how the host state treats its immigrants.

Operating alongside or in conjunction with state policies, the mass media and their framing of issues or agendas constitute a major component of the cultural contexts (Gamson and Meyer 1996). Racial discourses and the racialization of groups compose essential components of the U.S. cultural contexts. Over time, groups like Hmong refugees come to learn which types of political claims are made by whom within the society and which types of claims resonate with the existing cultural contexts and have a better chance of being taken seriously by goal granters.

To the extent that a substantial number of people within an immigrant group have been accorded some of the same rights that formal citizens of the host society have and are able to access some of the same public goods, we might say that such group has achieved an initial, limited degree of political incorporation. However, because immigrants' circumstances, initial legal status, and initial racial position can change, their initial political incorporation neither ensures future political incorporation nor prevents future political disincorporation.

To summarize, the SECA model of immigrant political incorporation privileges ethnic collective mobilization as a key mechanism in ethnic immigrant groups' political incorporation in the United States. In this model, an immigrant group's ability to mobilize collective action is dependent on its unique contexts of exit and reception. Contexts of exit condition a group's collective political narratives and initial resources, while contexts of reception affect the group's initial legal status, its initial racialized identity and position, and its access to material, financial, human, and discursive resources. Contexts of reception also affect an immigrant group's potential to form resourceful and visible ethnic immigrant communities. Community formation, in turn, can provide organizational capacity, increasing the group's capacity to access politically relevant resources inside as well as outside of the community.

GUIDING QUESTIONS

Informed by the SECA model of immigrant political incorporation, my study addresses two questions: (1) How are Hmong former refugees, who are among the poorest, least educated, least recognized, and least likely to be outreached to by partisan political organizations, able to make sustained claims on and have their interests represented in public policies in the United States? (2) How do Hmong's strategic choices and the state's responses to them illuminate the more general processes of racialized immigrant political incorporation?

CASES

Hmong's political agency is most clearly demonstrated in three major social movements: ordinary Hmong men and women's movement against federal welfare reforms in the 1990s, Hmong veterans' movement to obtain U.S. citizenship between the 1990s and 2000s, and Hmong professionals' movement to incorporate Hmong history into California's public school curriculum in the 2000s. In each of these social movements, Hmong mobilized a network of ethnic organizations, utilized a number of institutional and state allies, created political opportunities, and strategically framed their group identity and claims. Through these strategic actions, Hmong were able to mobilize collective consensus around the problems they defined as well as motivate corrective action on these problems. In the process, Hmong obtained tangible benefits for themselves—public benefits, naturalization accommodations, and representation in the school curriculum. However, even as the U.S. government or, in the case of Hmong's movement for curricular representation, the California government granted Hmong political rights, they racialized Hmong as a tribe, othered them as special guerrilla unit aliens, or racialized them as Southeast Asians.

I chose to study these three social movements for two reasons. The first reason has to do with timing. I chose social movements that occurred after 1990 for, by the early 1990s, with the fall of the Berlin Wall, there had been a significant shift (from colder to warmer relations) in U.S. political relations with countries such as the Soviet Union and China. This shift in the supranational political context led to an alteration in the United States' stance toward Hmong former refugees. Whereas during the Secret War in Laos (1960–1975) and in the first decade following the American-Vietnam War (1975–1985) the United States was secretly supportive of Hmong, whom they used to defend and further U.S. interests in Laos and Southeast Asia (see chapter 2 for more details), by the late 1980s the U.S. attitude toward and treatment of its former Hmong allies became hostile. For instance, in 1987 the United States became a signatory and funder to the Comprehensive Plan of Action for Indochinese Refugees, a multilateral policy that ended up repatriating tens of thousands of Hmong and other Southeast Asian refugees from Thailand back to Laos, Vietnam, and Cambodia (United Nations High Commissioner for Refugees 1996).

Moreover, in the early 1990s, immigrants and nonimmigrants witnessed a new cycle of anti-immigrant movements and policies in U.S. society. California's infamous Proposition 187, the so-called Save Our State initiative, was passed by a majority (59 percent) of its voters in November 1994. Two years later, the U.S. Congress passed and President Clinton signed into law both the Personal Responsibility and Work Opportunity Reconciliation Act and the Illegal Immigration Reform and Immigration Responsibility Act. The U.S. government's response to the events of September 11, 2001, led to additional policies, such as the USA PATRIOT Act of 2001, which intensified border enforcement and sharply increased deportations (Massey and Pren 2012). It is within this set of anti-immigrant contexts that the three Hmong American social movements emerged. Given that political contexts can either facilitate or constrain social movements, one of my interests was to understand how Hmong Americans were able to mobilize effectively to have their interests represented in public policy in spite of these political contexts.

Second, I selected these three social movements as illustrative cases of Hmong's concerted efforts to have their interests represented in public policy. Between 1990 and 2005, these were among the very few Hmong-led social movements whose goals were to change or create new public policy, and whose primary targets were the national or state government or their institutions, and whose intended beneficiaries were U.S.-based Hmong. I deliberately excluded cases of Hmong-led social movements that were aimed at achieving other kinds of outcomes, such as movements that were aimed at changing public opinion about domestic violence. I also excluded Hmong-led social movements aimed at preventing a foreign policy (as opposed to a domestic-oriented public policy) such as Hmong's 2004 mobilization against the United States granting of normal trade relations status to the Lao People's Democratic Republic; Hmong protesters in that movement perceived this foreign policy to be harmful primarily to their compatriots in Laos. I excluded cases in which Hmong sought changes in nonstate organizations' policy or practices, such as their 1998 protest against the KQRS Morning Show for its racist remarks about Hmong (Xiong 2016, 15). Finally, I excluded cases in which interest groups sought public policy for the purpose of changing some aspect of Hmong cultural practice. An example of this was the diffused action around the 2006 Hmong cultural marriage bill, sponsored by former senator Wes Skoglund of Minnesota and supported by some Hmong Americans. That bill, had it passed, would have changed the traditional role of Hmong marriage intermediaries (called *mej koob*) from intermediaries to legal solemnizers of marriage.

HMONG AMERICAN COMMUNITIES

Although Hmong American communities can be found in most of the fifty states and the District of Columbia, most Hmong Americans are concentrated in just three states: California, Minnesota, and Wisconsin. As shown in table 1.1, this pattern has held quite constant since the 1990 census. In 1990, the Hmong population in California, Minnesota, and Wisconsin constituted 52 percent, 19 percent, and 18 percent of the Hmong American population in the United States, respectively. During the mid-1990s, many Hmong Americans from these states, partly in response to federal welfare reforms (chapter 4), migrated to states such as North Carolina, Georgia, Oklahoma, and Arkansas. Although Hmong's migration to other states reduced their concentration in California, Minnesota, and Wisconsin, by 2010, about 80 percent of Hmong still resided in these states.

Whether in California, Minnesota, or Wisconsin, the Hmong population makes up less than 1 percent of each state's total population. However, the three states differ significantly in terms of the relative Hmong population: specifically, Hmong as a proportion of the state's Asian American population. Whereas California's Hmong make up a mere 1.5 percent of its Asian American population (about 5,557,000 in 2010), Minnesota's Hmong constituted 26 percent of its Asian American population (247,000). In Wisconsin, Hmong constituted 31 percent of the Asian American population (152,000). Whereas in California Hmong are dwarfed by several major Asian subgroups, in both Minnesota and

TABLE 1.1   Distribution of Hmong Americans by Select States, 1990–2010

State	1990 Number	1990 Percent	2000 Number	2000 Percent	2010 Number	2010 Percent	Percentage change between 1990 and 2000	Percentage change between 2000 and 2010
California	49,343	52.2	65,095	38.4	86,989	35.1	31.9	33.6
Minnesota	17,764	18.8	41,800	24.7	63,619	25.7	135.3	52.2
Wisconsin	16,980	18.0	33,791	19.9	47,127	19.0	99.0	39.5
Michigan	2,304	2.4	5,383	3.2	5,580	2.3	133.6	3.7
Colorado	1,207	1.3	3,000	1.8	3,611	1.5	148.6	20.4
Rhode Island	1,185	1.3	1,001	0.6	909	0.4	−15.5	−9.2
Washington	853	0.9	1,294	0.8	2,186	0.9	51.7	68.9
Oregon	595	0.6	2,101	1.2	2,722	1.1	253.1	29.6
North Carolina	544	0.6	7,093	4.2	10,433	4.2	1203.9	47.1
Kansas	543	0.6	1,004	0.6	1,645	0.7	84.9	63.8
Georgia	386	0.4	1,468	0.9	3,460	1.4	280.3	135.7
Massachusetts	134	0.1	1,127	0.7	992	0.4	741.0	−12.0
All other states	2,601	2.8	5,271	3.1	18,323	7.4	102.7	247.6
United States	94,439	100.0	169,428	100.0	247,596	100.0	79.4	46.1

NOTE: Hmong alone.
SOURCE: U.S. Bureau of the Census, 100 Percent Population Estimates 1990, 2000, and 2010.

Wisconsin, Hmong are the largest Asian subgroup. According to the 2005–2009 American Community Survey, the largest Asian subgroups in Minnesota are Hmong (48,949), Asian Indians (32,979), and Vietnamese (21,445). In Wisconsin, the largest Asian subgroups are Hmong (40,672), Asian Indians (19,362), and Chinese (16,492). In California, the largest Asian subgroups are Chinese (1,164,102), Filipinos (1,131,966), and Vietnamese (535,683). In Minnesota, Asians form the third largest minority group (3.6 percent), behind Hispanics (4 percent) and African Americans (4.3 percent). Similarly, in Wisconsin, Asians (2.1 percent) form the second largest group behind Hispanics (4.9 percent) and African Americans (5.9 percent). However, in California, Asians (12.4 percent) form the second largest group, behind only Hispanics, who constitute 36 percent of the state's population.

A substantial proportion of Hmong Americans are U.S. citizens. Specifically, 55 percent of Hmong Americans are U.S. citizens by birth, 24 percent are naturalized citizens, and 21 percent are noncitizens. When foreign-born naturalized persons are combined with native-born citizens, about 79 percent of Hmong Americans hold formal U.S. citizenship. As table 1.2 shows, Hmong's legal status is similar across the three major states in which they are concentrated.

With respect to educational attainment, California and Wisconsin appear on par with one another (table 1.3). However, the average educational attainment of

TABLE 1.2   Legal Status of Hmong Americans by Top Three States

	Population	Percentage non-U.S. citizen	Percentage naturalized U.S. citizen	Percentage U.S. citizen by birth[a]	Total U.S. citizen	Percentage eligible to vote[b]
Hmong in United States	195,614	20.8	24.0	55.3	79.2	38.4
California	66,846	21.7	21.4	56.8	78.3	36.7
Minnesota	48,949	23.5	25.5	51.0	76.5	36.7
Wisconsin	40,672	17.3	28.2	54.5	82.7	41.6
All other states	39,147	19.3	22.1	58.7	80.7	40.2

[a] Includes all persons born in the United States, U.S. territories, or abroad to U.S. parents.
[b] Includes all persons who are U.S. citizens and 18 years or older.
SOURCE: U.S. Census Bureau, American Community Survey PUMS, 2005–2009, weighted samples.

TABLE 1.3   Demographic Characteristics of Hmong Americans by Top Three States

	Population	Percentage of state population	Percentage of Asians in state	Percentage with BA or higher[a]	Median household income	Percentage with own home	Percentage below poverty
Hmong in United States	195,614	—	—	12.6	$47,900	54.9	27.9
California	66,846	0.2	1.5	12.3	$41,000	36.0	35.7
Minnesota	48,949	0.9	26.0	13.6	$44,700	58.5	30.4
Wisconsin	40,672	0.7	35.1	12.2	$57,000	65.3	20.1
All other states	39,147	—	—	12.3	$51,800	70.6	19.5

[a] Includes only persons 25 years or older.
SOURCE: U.S. Census Bureau, American Community Survey PUMS, 2005–2009, weighted samples.

Minnesota's Hmong population of twenty-five years and older is slightly higher than that of their counterparts in California and Wisconsin. On all three indicators of income shown, Hmong Californians fared the worst compared to the Hmong of Minnesota and Wisconsin. Minnesota falls between California and Wisconsin in terms of median household income, home ownership, and poverty.

Within each state, Hmong are more concentrated in some cities than in others. In California, Hmong are dispersed across nearly all counties of the Central Valley—a flat, agriculture-rich region that includes eighteen counties, stretching from Kern County in the south to Shasta County in the north (Umbach 1997).[3] According to U.S. census 2010 data, almost three-fourths of all Hmong Californians lived in just three metropolitan statistical areas (MSA) within the Central Valley: Fresno (30,648), Sacramento-Arden-Arcade-Roseville (25,794), and Merced (6,920). Maps 1.1 and 1.2 show the relative concentrations of Hmong Americans in the Fresno and Sacramento areas, respectively. The maps show Hmong as a

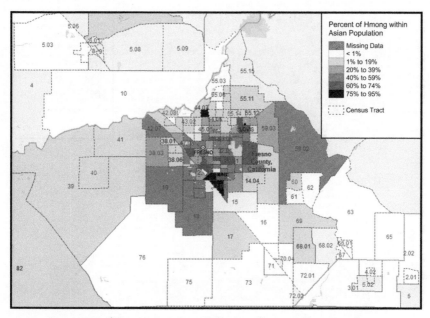

MAP 1.1. Proportion of Hmong Americans Relative to the Asian Alone Population in Fresno, California, by Census Tract, 2000. (Source: Social Explorer, based on data from U.S. Census Bureau, Census 2000)

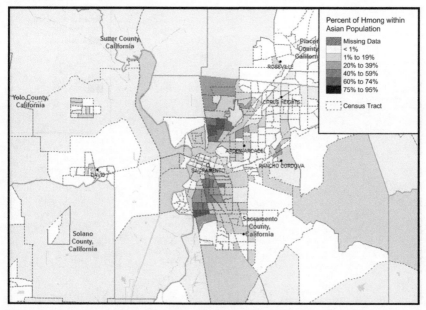

MAP 1.2. Proportion of Hmong Americans Relative to the Asian Alone Population in Sacramento, California, by Census Tract, 2000. (Source: Social Explorer, based on data from U.S. Census Bureau, Census 2000)

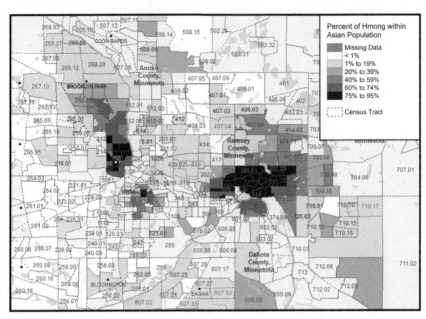

MAP 1.3. Proportion of Hmong Americans Relative to the Asian Alone Population in Saint Paul and Minneapolis, Minnesota, by Census Tract, 2000. (Source: Social Explorer, based on data from U.S. Census Bureau, Census 2000)

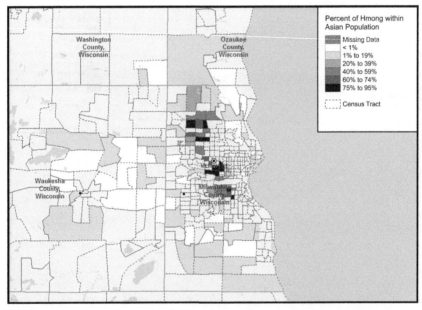

MAP 1.4. Proportion of Hmong Americans Relative to the Asian Alone Population in Milwaukee, Wisconsin, by Census Tract, 2000. (Source: Social Explorer, based on data from U.S. Census Bureau, Census 2000)

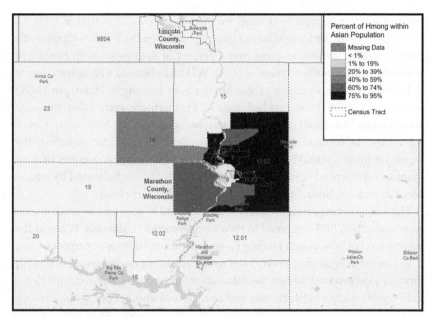

MAP 1.5. Proportion of Hmong Americans Relative to the Asian Alone Population in Wausau, Wisconsin, by Census Tract, 2000. (Source: Social Explorer, based on data from U.S. Census Bureau, Census 2000)

proportion of the Asian alone population in individual census tracts. For instance, black shaded tracts represent those in which Hmong Americans make up between 75 and 95 percent of the Asian American population. In Sacramento, Hmong are concentrated to the north and to the south of the downtown-capitol area. As we will return to shortly, in Fresno Hmong are concentrated in the inner city.

In Minnesota, about 40,100 Hmong, or 80 percent of the ethnic group, live in the Saint Paul–Minneapolis MSA. They are much more concentrated in Saint Paul than in Minneapolis, however. Saint Paul alone is home to 28,591 Hmong, making them the largest Asian subgroup (68 percent) in the city. Finally, within the state of Wisconsin, about half of all Hmong persons live in three MSAs: Milwaukee-Racine (8,078), Appleton-Oshkosh-Neenah (4,741), and Wausau (4,453). Maps 1.3, 1.4, and 1.5 show the relative concentrations of Hmong in the Saint Paul–Minneapolis, Milwaukee, and Wausau areas, respectively. In general, Hmong are concentrated in the cores of these urban areas.

HMONG AMERICANS' SOCIOECONOMIC STATUS

Although useful, table 1.3 provides us with information about Hmong Americans' socioeconomic status (SES) only at the state level. To better understand Hmong Americans' more local contexts of reception and the changes in their levels of group resources over time, we turn to table 1.4. The data in table 1.4 show that, among the foreign-born Hmong population, SES differs significantly across counties. In 1990, whereas over 9 percent of the foreign-born Hmong in Milwaukee and Marathon counties (both WI) had obtained a bachelor's degree or higher, less than 1 percent of the foreign-born Hmong in Hennepin (MN) and Sheboygan (WI) counties had done so. Furthermore, even within the same state, median household incomes differ across counties (e.g., Sheboygan County's $15,053 as compared to Marathon County's $33,573). Nevertheless, the important finding is that between 1990 and 2000, Hmong communities of most counties experienced significant improvements in SES, as measured by educational attainment, household median income, and poverty level.

However, Hmong communities of Minnesota and Wisconsin saw much greater improvements in SES compared to their counterparts in California. Whereas the poverty level of Wisconsin's Hmong community dropped from 75 percent in 1989 to 25 percent in 1999, the poverty level remained almost unchanged in California (from 54 to 53 percent). In fact, the data indicate that poverty worsened in Merced and Fresno counties between 1990 and 2000. It took another decade for Hmong Californians to see appreciable improvements in SES, especially in terms of poverty (poverty declined from 53 percent in 1999 to 36 percent in 2009). What could explain why Hmong's SES improved in Minnesota and Wisconsin but not in California?

From the census data, we can surmise that the labor market in Minnesota and Wisconsin probably provided more manufacturing job opportunities for their Hmong populations. Tables 1.5 and 1.6 use census 1990 data to provide information about the distribution of employed, foreign-born Hmong across industries and occupations. The evidence shows that both Hmong men and women are highly concentrated in the manufacturing industry of Minnesota and Wisconsin (52 and 38 percent, respectively), as compared to 19 percent in California. In the Twin Cities area, major manufacturing corporations such as 3M, Honeywell, Cargill, General Mills, and Sara Lee Foods are within reach of the skilled and to some extent unskilled work force. In contrast, Fresno and Merced have fewer comparable manufacturing companies, even though companies such as Foster Farms employ a number of Hmong people.

Although a larger proportion of the Hmong of Minnesota and Wisconsin are employed in occupations within the operators, fabricators, and laborers category than in the managerial and professional services category, manufacturing jobs at major companies probably provide greater stability in terms of wages and health benefits than service or retail occupations do. Furthermore, the costs of living in the major metropolitan areas of Minnesota and Wisconsin are generally lower than those of California's metro areas.[4] The greater availability of manufacturing jobs and the lower cost of living probably contribute to the improvement in Hmong's SES in Minnesota and Wisconsin.

TABLE 1.4 Legal and Economic Characteristics of Foreign-Born Hmong in Select States and Urban Areas, 1990 and 2000

State/county	Foreign-born adult population		Percentage naturalized		Percentage with BA or higher[a]		Median household income[b]		Proportion below 100% of poverty[b]	
	1990	2000	1990	2000	1990	2000	1989	1999	1989	1999
California	18,443	25,121	7.7	36.1	2.6	5.4	$24,871	$29,000	54.3	53.3
Fresno County	7,927	8,650	7.4	41.8	3.1	7.4	$25,575	$25,700	54.1	59.7
Merced County	2,196	1,568	5.0	35.3	4.0	1.6	$20,414	$21,650	54.7	65.6
Sacramento County	2,098	6,904	4.6	33.0	2.6	4.7	$24,207	$36,000	55.1	45.2
Minnesota	7,254	17,195	8.2	35.7	2.6	7.0	$21,093	$41,000	55.2	42.1
Ramsey County	4,608	10,883	8.5	35.8	3.7	7.6	$20,450	$40,300	62.3	48.2
Hennepin County	1,969	4,887	3.0	31.0	0.9	3.9	$21,093	$40,000	50.2	36.7
Wisconsin	6,290	12,707	14.6	37.4	5.4	8.9	$19,319	$41,000	75.0	25.9
Milwaukee County	1,128	3,560	5.5	46.0	9.2	11.6	$21,950	$46,500	64.7	22.7
Marathon County	830	1,837	25.8	41.2	9.2	7.2	$33,573	$36,200	31.3	40
Sheboygan County	1,595	788	12.9	26.5	0.0	3.7	$15,053	$40,750	95.5	38.7

[a] Includes foreign-born, 25 years and over only.
[b] Includes foreign-born, 18 years and over only. Income figures have been adjusted for inflation (in 1999 dollars).
SOURCE: U.S. Census Bureau, Census 1990 5 percent PUMS and Census 2000 5 percent PUMS, weighted samples.

TABLE 1.5 Industry Distribution of Hmong Americans by Select States and Sex (Percentages), 1990

	California		Minnesota		Wisconsin	
	M	F	M	F	M	F
Agriculture, forestry, and fisheries	8.0	6.4	3.9	0.0	2.6	0.0
Mining	0.0	0.0	0.0	0.0	0.0	0.0
Construction	5.1	0.0	0.0	2.7	0.0	0.0
Manufacturing	21.9	15.6	52.0	51.6	37.1	39.4
Transportation, communications, and utilities	1.6	0.0	5.1	2.7	4.1	0.0
Wholesale trade	3.7	7.0	4.6	9.7	0.0	2.3
Retail trade	15.8	6.0	10.8	4.0	11.3	7.9
Finance, insurance, and real estate	1.0	1.7	6.5	0.0	3.7	0.0
Business and repair services	8.5	4.3	5.5	0.0	12.4	0.0
Personal services	0.0	9.2	4.4	7.6	0.0	0.0
Entertainment and recreation services	1.3	0.0	0.0	0.0	1.1	0.0
Professional and related services	27.5	31.8	5.6	21.8	27.6	48.0
Public administration	5.7	18.0	1.6	0.0	0.0	2.3

NOTE: Includes employed, foreign-born, 20- to 65-year-olds only. Columns do not add up to 100 due to rounding.
SOURCE: U.S. Census Bureau, Census 1990.

TABLE 1.6 Occupational Distribution of Hmong Americans by Select States and Sex (Percentages), 1990

	California		Minnesota		Wisconsin	
	M	F	M	F	M	F
Managerial and professional specialty occupations	19.3	10.2	19.2	12.4	19.7	26.8
Technical, sales, and administrative support occupations	26.5	29.4	13.1	18.3	6.3	7.9
Service occupations	9.8	33.2	14.5	15.1	41.5	7.9
Farming, forestry, and fishing occupations	7.3	0.0	3.9	0.0	2.6	0.0
Precision production, craft, and repair occupations	15.5	5.4	21.6	0.0	7.2	16.8
Operators, fabricators, and laborers	21.6	21.7	27.6	54.2	22.8	40.6
Total persons	2,035	900	1,400	671	926	429

NOTE: Includes employed, foreign-born, 20- to 65-year-olds only. Columns do not add up to 100 due to rounding.
SOURCE: U.S. Census Bureau, Census 1990.

STATE AND LOCAL POLITICAL CONTEXTS

Just as the places where Hmong Americans concentrate have distinct socioeconomic profiles, they also differ in terms of political behaviors and representation. Table 1.7 shows the voter turnout during the 2016 U.S. presidential election by political party among counties with at least one thousand Hmong American residents. In California, tens of thousands of Hmong Americans live in Democratic-majority or Democrat-leaning counties such as Fresno, Sacramento, Merced, and San Joaquin. But thousands of Hmong live in Republican-majority counties, such as Yuba and Butte. As we will see in chapter 3, Hmong Californians' movement for benefits restoration in the mid-1990s emerged in Northern California, specifically in the politically conservative counties of Butte and Yuba. Most of the Hmong leaders of this movement were residents of Butte County, and one of the initial Hmong community strategic planning meetings took place in the Hmong-led Christian Missionary Alliance church in Yuba City, which is only thirty miles from Butte County. Tellingly, during Hmong veterans' movement for naturalization accommodations throughout the 1990s (see chapter 4), even when several other Republican congressmembers throughout California had signed on as cosponsors of the Hmong Veterans' Naturalization Act (HVNA), the congressmembers from California's Third Congressional District, of which Yuba County is a part, and California's First Congressional District, of which Butte County is a part, were almost always absent from the list of cosponsors. The sole exception was U.S. representative Frank Riggs, a Republican and representative of California's First Congressional District, who in 1997 signed on as a cosponsor of HVNA.

In Minnesota, the vast majority of Hmong live in either Ramsey County or Hennepin County, both of which are Democratic-majority counties. The late U.S. representative Bruce Vento, who introduced HVNA and continued to reintroduce it each new congressional session until its passage in 2000 (see chapter 4), represented Minnesota's Fourth Congressional District. That district encompassed nearly all of Ramsey County and part of Washington County. In the early 1990s, congressmembers Martin Sabo, a Democrat representing Minnesota's Fifth Congressional District, Gerry Sikorski (D-MN-Sixth), and Bill Frenzel (R-MN-Third) were also state allies to Hmong veterans in their movement for naturalization accommodations, as indicated by their cosponsorship of HVNA. In the late 1990s, congressmembers David Minge (D-MN-Second), Jim Ramstad (R-MN-Third), and Bill Luther (D-MN-Sixth) were also state allies to Hmong veterans.

In Wisconsin, less than half of the counties in which Hmong Americans concentrate are Democratic majority or Democrat leaning (Milwaukee, Dane, La Crosse, Eau Claire, and Portage). Most Hmong Wisconsinites, however, live in

TABLE 1.7   Voter Turnout during the 2016 Presidential Election by Political
Party among Select States and Counties with At Least 1,000
Hmong American Residents

State	Percentage voted Democrat	Percentage voted Republican	Percentage voted other	Total votes cast
California	61.5	31.5	7.0	14,237,884
Los Angeles County	71.8	22.4	5.8	3,434,308
Sacramento County	58.0	33.8	8.3	562,285
San Diego County	56.3	36.6	7.1	1,306,400
San Joaquin County	53.4	39.2	7.5	227,002
Merced County	52.7	40.6	6.7	70,789
Orange County	50.9	42.4	6.7	1,197,521
Riverside County	49.7	44.4	5.9	751,391
Fresno County	49.2	43.2	7.6	287,062
Butte County	42.9	46.5	10.6	97,002
Tulare County	41.7	51.1	7.2	114,102
Yuba County	34.4	57.3	8.3	22,998
Minnesota	46.4	44.9	8.6	2,945,233
Ramsey County	65.1	26.0	9.0	273,143
Hennepin County	63.1	28.2	8.7	679,977
Wisconsin	46.5	47.2	6.3	2,976,150
Dane County	70.4	23.0	6.6	309,354
Milwaukee County	65.5	28.6	5.9	441,053
La Crosse County	50.9	41.4	7.7	63,674
Eau Claire County	49.7	42.4	7.9	55,025
Portage County	48.0	44.8	7.1	38,589
Winnebago County	42.5	49.9	7.6	87,135
Brown County	41.4	52.1	6.5	129,011
Outagamie County	40.5	53.1	6.4	93,933
Sheboygan County	38.5	54.4	7.1	59,766
Marathon County	38.1	56.2	5.8	69,518
Manitowoc County	35.6	57.0	7.4	40,786

SOURCE: Social Explorer, U.S. Presidential Elections 2016.

Republican-majority counties such as Brown, Sheboygan, Outagamie, and Marathon. Interestingly, as we will see in chapter 4, before HVNA became law, all but one of the congressmembers from Wisconsin who cosponsored this bill were members of the Democratic Party. Despite the fact that a majority of Hmong Wisconsinites live in Republican-dominant counties, most of their state allies have been Democrats who represent other places in Wisconsin.

In general, the voting patterns of the voters in most of the counties where substantial Hmong American populations reside have been fairly consistent since the 1992 U.S. presidential election (Bill Clinton vs. George H. W. Bush).

That is, with few exceptions, counties that have tended to vote for Democratic over Republican candidates have continued to do so; counties that have tended to vote for Republican over Democratic candidates have continued to do so.

Until recently, there has not been any nationally representative survey of Hmong Americans' voting patterns. My analysis of data from the 2016 Post-Election National Asian American Survey shows that across the United States, 74 percent of Hmong Americans reported they voted for Hillary Clinton, while 21 percent voted for Donald Trump. The available evidence also suggests that neither of the two major political parties made concerted efforts to reach Hmong in 2016 (Xiong 2020). Next, I describe Chico and Fresno, California, which are the primary sites of my fieldwork.

Chico, California

Chico, California, is predominantly White, with racial minorities composing about a quarter of its population. Hmong began resettling in Chico starting in the late 1970s and early 1980s (Moon 2003). By 1990, there were 1,600 Hmong in Chico, constituting 4 percent of the city population. By 2000, there were at least 2,887 Hmong (Pfeifer et al. 2012). In 2010, Chico was 74 percent non-Hispanic White, 15 percent Hispanic, 4 percent Asian, 2 percent Black, and 1 percent Native American. Between 2000 and 2010, the population of Asians in Chico grew by about 1,000 persons, even though their proportion stayed the same, at 4.2 percent.

In the early 1990s, Hmong professionals and clan leaders established the Chico Hmong Advisory Council to address social issues that affect the growing Hmong community there. In 1994, several Hmong students formed the Hmong Student Association at California State University, Chico, also known as Chico State. Whereas in the 1990s there were only a few Hmong students at Chico State, today the campus enrolls several hundred Hmong students. Since the mid-1990s, the Hmong of Chico have celebrated the Hmong American New Year as one of their largest public events.

Fresno, California

Between 1990 and 2010, Fresno County experienced significant demographic changes. As the data in table 1.8 show, whereas in 1990 non-Hispanic Whites made up 51 percent of the county's population, by 2000 they made up only 40 percent. By 2000, the population of Hispanics had surpassed that of non-Hispanic Whites; and in 2010, Hispanics became the numerical majority (50.3 percent), at almost half a million strong. According to the U.S. Bureau of the Census (2010), 91.5 percent of Hispanics in Fresno County are Mexicans, 2 percent are Central Americans, and 1.3 percent are Puerto Ricans. In contrast, both the Black (5 percent) and American Indian (less than 1 percent) populations remained relatively small and their proportion changed little since 1990.

TABLE 1.8   Population of Racial Categories and Asian Subgroups in Fresno County, California, 1990–2010

	Fresno County, California			
	1990		2000	
	Number	Percentage	Number	Percentage
White, non-Hispanic	338,595	50.7	317,522	39.7
Hispanic	236,634	35.5	351,636	44.0
Asian and Pacific Islander, non-Hispanic	54,110	8.1	63,711	8.0
Black, non-Hispanic	31,311	4.7	40,291	5.0
American Indian, non-Hispanic	5,070	0.8	6,223	0.8
Other race or multiple races	1,770	0.3	20,024	2.5
Total	667,490	100.0	799,407	100.0
Hmong	18,321	32.4	22,371	35.5
Laotian	8,174	14.5	6,373	10.1
Japanese	6,722	11.9	5,721	9.1
Asian Indian	5,216	9.2	7,963	12.6
Chinese	4,793	8.5	4,759	7.5
Filipino	4,312	7.6	5,629	8.9
Cambodian	3,812	6.7	4,168	6.6
Vietnamese	2,008	3.6	2,471	3.9
Korean	986	1.7	1,326	2.1
Thai	387	0.7	355	0.6
Other Asian	1,786	3.2	1,922	3.0
Total Asian, including Hispanic Asian	56,517	100.0	63,058	100.0

SOURCE: U.S. Census Bureau, Census 1990 and 2000.

On the other hand, during the past twenty years, the proportion of Asians increased from 8.1 percent to 9.4 percent. Compared to thirty years ago, this represents a significant increase considering that Asians composed only 3 percent of Fresno County's population in 1980.[5] Japanese (6,500) and Asian Indians (4,700) were the first and second largest Asian subgroups in Fresno County during the 1980 U.S. census (Reder et al. 1984, 2); however, by 1990, these positions were overtaken by Hmong (18,300) and Laotians (8,200). But whereas Hmong held their position, Laotians did not. Between 1990 and 2010, even as the populations of Asian Indians and Hmong steadily grew, both the Japanese and Laotian populations declined. By 2010, Asian Indians became, once again, the second largest Asian subgroup (U.S. Bureau of the Census 1990, 2010).

In the late 1970s, Hmong refugees were attracted to the Fresno and Merced regions because they perceived or heard that people in these areas could buy farmland to grow and sell produce as means to a better life (Reder et al. 1984, 3). However, Hmong did not actually move into Fresno in any significant number until after the secondary migrations of the early 1980s. As Reder et al. (1984, 3) point out, "A county-sponsored refugee study estimated that 80.5% of Fresno's refugees were secondary migrants: nearly one-third (30.3%) of the refugee residents were secondary migrants from other counties in California and over half (50.2%) from other states. . . . Nearly one-fourth (23%) of Fresno's refugees came from Oregon (vastly more than from any other state) and 16.4% came from Orange County (more than from any other California county)." According to Reder et al. (1984, 20), Fresno's "relatively low cost of living and the feasibility of farming" attracted Hmong from other areas of California. However, in the case of the Hmong from Orange County, individual accounts suggest that push factors—unprovoked physical violence and the threat of further violence—were probably more important than pull factors in explaining Hmong's migration to Fresno. As Spenser Sherman (1985) points out, "In Santa Ana, [California], the population dove from 6,000 or 7,000 to about 2,000 after 1981. Cheu Thao, a community leader there, says many left because of an unprovoked attack on an elder Hmong couple that left the man dead."

Despite Hmong's high hopes, commercial farming was not as easy as they anticipated, and only a fraction of them eventually became farmers (Reder et al. 1984). In fact, by 1990 among employed, foreign-born Hmong twenty to sixty-five years old within Fresno County, only 10.1 percent worked in the agricultural industry. About the same proportion of this category worked in manufacturing (10.6 percent). The first and second most popular industries were professional and related services (30.1 percent) and public administration (15.7 percent), respectively (U.S. Bureau of the Census 1995).

According to longtime Hmong residents, the earliest Hmong arrivals to Fresno County settled in Clovis, a city northeast of Fresno, specifically in the south Clovis neighborhoods east of Highway 168 and between Barstow and Bullard avenues. Most Hmong young people attended Sierra Vista Elementary School.[6] As the Hmong community in Clovis grew, it attracted more Hmong to Clovis, but especially to the downtown Fresno area. Whereas in June 1979, Fresno County's public assistance records showed no Hmong at all, by March 1981, 1,066 Hmong individuals appeared on caseloads (Reder et al. 1984, 21). By October 1982, about 6,500 Hmong, 1,500 Vietnamese, and over 300 Laotians and Cambodians were living in Fresno County. A year later, in June 1983, Fresno's Hmong population had increased to 10,000 (1984, 3). As shown in map 1.1, Hmong Americans are most concentrated in the downtown Fresno area. Indeed, this has been the case since the mid-1980s. Let us examine this in greater detail.

Of the 18,321 Hmong residents in Fresno County in 1990, about 57 percent lived in the area officially designated by the City Council as Fresno's inner city. This inner city is a trapezoidal area of twenty-three to twenty-eight census tracts that together compose most of Fresno's urban core.[7] This urban core includes the city's originally incorporated area, its main government facilities (City Hall, Superior Court and U.S. District Court, the Convention Center, etc.), and its

TABLE 1.9   Percentage Concentration in Fresno's Inner City by Social
             Category and Year

Categories	1990 Count	1990 Percentage in inner city	2000 Count	2000 Percentage in inner city
Asian	56,517	42.0	63,058	28.8
Southeast Asians	32,315	61.2	35,383	44.3
Cambodian	3,812	77.6	4,168	51.4
Laotian	8,174	67.5	6,373	52.9
Hmong	18,321	57.3	22,371	43.3
Vietnamese	2,008	41.1	2,471	18.4
All others	24,202	16.3	27,675	9.0
Asian Indian	5,216	24.7	7,963	6.6
Filipino	4,312	16.6	5,629	11.1
Thai	387	14.5	355	16.6
Chinese	4,793	13.4	4,759	7.6
Japanese	6,722	8.1	5,721	5.7
Korean	986	4.8	1,326	5.4
Other Asian	1,786	36.3	1,922	27.6
Non-Hispanic Black	31,311	34.1	40,291	26.5
Hispanic	231,853	24.4	351,636	23.4
Mexican	218,844	24.5	302,120	23.3
Puerto Rican	1,499	24.2	1,711	21.6
Cuban	202	15.3	441	21.8
Other Hispanic	11,308	23.0	47,364	24.4
Non-Hispanic American Indian	5,070	22.0	6,223	21.2
Non-Hispanic White	338,595	13.5	317,522	9.5
Fresno County total	667,490	20.8	799,407	18.3

NOTE: Columns do not add to county total because multiracial and Native Hawaiian / Pacific Islanders were omitted.
SOURCE: U.S. Census Bureau, Census 1990 and 2000.

central business district (the Chamber of Commerce, Fulton Mall, the *Fresno Bee* offices, etc.). But the inner city also includes the old, historically segregated Chinatown located west of the main railroad and low-income housing projects in the Lowell area north of Divisadero Street (Chacon 1986). The boundaries of the Fresno inner city are formed by East Shields Avenue to the north, East California Avenue to the south, Highway 99 through South West Avenue to the west, and South Chestnut Avenue to the east (City of Fresno 2008). At least fifty-nine public and private K–12 schools are found in the inner city.

As table 1.9 shows, a much larger proportion (61 percent) of Southeast Asians—Cambodians, Laotians, Hmong, and Vietnamese—are concentrated in the inner city compared to other Asians combined (16 percent). For comparison, only 14 percent of non-Hispanic Whites, 22 percent of American Indians, 24 percent of Hispanics, and 34 percent of non-Hispanic Blacks reside in the inner city. Well aware of their coethnic concentrations, during the 1990s Hmong Fresnans informally called the cluster of neighborhoods north of East Kings Canyon Road and west of South Peach Avenue, "Zos Vib Nais," after the name of the Ban Vinai refugee camp in north-central Thailand.[8] At one time, Ban Vinai camp held around forty-five thousand Hmong refugees inside an area of four hundred acres, just six-tenths of a square mile (Long 1993, 58).

Hmong young people and adults in Fresno are familiar with and sometimes use the term "ghetto" to describe certain poor and dilapidated areas of the city. But with or without the term, it is clear that neighborhoods of concentrated poverty exist and both actual crime and criminalized activities frequently occur in them. Pakou, thirty, who was born in Thailand but raised in Fresno most of her life, describes an inner-city neighborhood as follows: "Back in the days [since late 1980s], a lot of Hmong lived in the Summerset apartments. It's funny; Hmong elders called it *xab maws xej*. A lot of Hmong families lived next door to each other.... I don't remember when exactly, but it was during a Hmong New Year in the mid-nineties. There was a drive-by shooting at Summerset; I think it was Hmong gangs [shooting at] each other. Two guys were shot, one in the leg and the other in the groin."[9] Summerset Village, a low-income apartment complex, is located just three and a half miles north of old Chinatown. Ironically, Summerset is sandwiched between several east-to-west streets named after Ivy League schools: Yale, Cambridge, Harvard, Brown, Princeton, and others. Just two blocks to the east is a gated neighborhood. Finally, Summerset is surrounded by several ethnically diverse church establishments, including United Methodist, Greek Orthodox, Seventh-day Adventist, and Bahá'í congregations. Today, Summerset Village remains, but most Hmong families have moved out. In recent years, the block directly north of Summerset has been developed into condominiums "designed to facilitate the housing needs of moderate and middle-income families."[10]

Field Research Design

The following chapters examine the processes through which Hmong were able to engage with political systems and have their interests represented in public policy. To understand this process, I examine Hmong's struggles within particular communities by describing and analyzing the claims-making activities in which Hmong actors, including activists and participants, and their institutional or state allies engaged. The analyses in this book are based on the extensive fieldwork that I conducted between 2002 and 2017. Although my research design for each case study differed slightly, in each case I drew on a wide range of data to investigate the social processes under study. Altogether, my sources included sixty-two in-depth interviews; many extended participant observations; a hundred fifty to two hundred primary sources such as protest flyers, speeches, email correspondences, and forum postings; several dozen official documents such as congressional testimonies, declassified documents, bills, and acts; and several dozen secondary sources such as newspaper and scholarly accounts.

My case study of Hmong's mobilization for benefits restoration exemplifies my data collection and analysis approach. From 2008 to 2009, I conducted semi-structured interviews with thirty-four Hmong men and women who were directly familiar with Hmong's campaign for benefits restoration during welfare reforms of the mid-1990s. Beginning with people I knew as a former resident of the area, I first contacted activists and participants (collectively, informants) within Chico and Marysville, California—the cities were the Hmong grassroots movement emerged—and then through snowball sampling recruited additional participants from Marysville, Chico, and other cities to which the movement had spread. About two-thirds of my informants were from Chico, Marysville, and Sacramento, while one-third were from the Stockton, Merced, and Fresno areas. In 2011–2012, during the course of my follow-up interviews with some of the former participants, I learned about other individuals involved in Hmong campaigns for benefit restoration and conducted interviews with six additional informants. In total, I interviewed forty persons, twenty-four men and sixteen women, all married; all speak Hmong as their primary language. Most were born in Laos, a few in Thailand.

Most (eighteen) of the men were veterans, and three of the women were widows of veterans of the Secret War in Laos. About a third were working or attending college, while two-thirds were retired, disabled, or no longer in the labor force. Among the employed were a university staff member, four college students, a high school teacher, a mechanic, three retail sales workers, and two caretakers.

During interviews, I began by asking informants about their background, pre-migration experiences in Laos, and postmigration experiences in the United States regarding family, life, work, and citizenship opportunities. Then I asked them to describe how they first heard about the cuts to people's benefits and how they or their families were affected; about their participation in any meetings, hearings, or actions related to welfare reforms; how they saw themselves as U.S. residents and minorities; and how they saw the United States as a country and why. If an informant was an activist/leader of the Hmong movement for benefits restoration, I also asked them about why and how they became involved in the movement, what challenges the movement faced, how activists made decisions about what to do during the movement, and what consequences resulted from these decisions.

After transcribing the interviews into Hmong, English, or both as the case may have been and importing the transcripts and my field notes into Microsoft Word, I began the textual analysis by using broad codes to categorize sections of the transcript. I coded for topics such as respondents' premigration experiences, postmigration experiences, encounters with groups or institutions in the contexts of reception, participation in collective actions, and identity claims. After this initial reading, I performed a closer reading of the coded sections and, drawing on my field notes on each case, coded more specifically for things such as Hmong's construction of group identity and social problems (e.g., what welfare reform means to individuals, how they diagnosed the problem of welfare reforms, how they constructed Hmong as a unique victim and the U.S. government as a perpetrator, what they proposed ought to be done about the problems and about Hmong's situation), their perception of political threats and opportunities and what choices they made in response to these, and their interactions or lack of interactions with others during mobilization. Finally, I compared across cases, analyzing for emergent themes and critical trends related to group identity construction and other strategies of mobilization.

To complement my interview data, between 2008 and 2017 I also compiled and analyzed various written documents that provided relevant information about the views or actions of individuals, organizations, and state segments during Hmong's campaign for benefit restoration. These documents included correspondences that Hmong wrote to the state and federal governments, protest speeches and event flyers, testimonies, photographs, and other documents that some informants shared with me during or after my interviews with them. I also analyzed official documents such as U.S. congressional hearings on the 1997 Hmong Veterans' Naturalization Act (H.R. 371, 105th Congress) and the Conference Report to the Agricultural Research, Extension, and Education Reform Act of 1997 (H. Rept. 105–492). My procedure for analyzing written documents is similar to the procedure I used to analyze my interview transcripts. I first skimmed each document to identify meaningful and relevant passages of text and then did a deeper reading and indexing of specific passages to arrive at specific concepts for analysis. The written documents complemented my interview data as they informed my understanding of the perspectives of actors, organizations, and state agencies that I did not have direct access to.

I also drew on Victor Hwang's (2002) article, which analyzes his experience as a staff member of ALC who worked with the Hmong community in Northern California during their mobilization for benefit restoration. His article usefully describes the organizational choices that the ALC made as it interacted with Hmong and the state. My study goes beyond Hwang's article by analyzing how the Hmong actors made their own strategic choices. Finally, although I was not engaged in research at the time, I was a participant in the initial 1997 meeting between the ALC and the Hmong community of Northern California, in my own family's state hearing for benefits restoration, and in the March and May 1997 immigrant protests against welfare reforms at the California State Capitol. These firsthand experiences further inform my understanding of Hmong men and women's perceptions of their social and political dilemmas, perspectives, and strategic choices. During the course of my interviews with my Hmong informants, I openly revealed my participation in the 1997 immigrant protests against welfare reform and my participation in my family's state hearing. Given Hmong men and women's experiences with political marginalization and my position as a researcher, I believe my experiences as a participant in these events and other commonalities that my research informants and I shared, including ethnicity and language, helped to create greater trust between us than might have been otherwise possible.

Similarly, my case study of Hmong professionals' movement to incorporate Hmong history into California's public schools is based on participant observations, in-depth interviews, primary documents, and newspaper accounts. Between 2002 and 2003, I was an active participant and observer in a handful of private and public internet forums whose participants discussed and shared information about Assembly Bill 78 (AB 78) and, subsequently, engaged in the highly charged debates surrounding Hmong's ethnic labels (known to some as the Hmong vs. Mong controversy). Nearly all of the participants in these forums were Hmong in the United States who varied in their age, gender, and occupations. They included Hmong American community members, college students, high school and college staff members, community organizers, professionals, and public intellectuals. I reread and analyzed several dozen email correspondences, letters, and official documents that were shared in public forums between 2002 and 2006. Between 2009 and 2011, I interviewed twelve Hmong informants in the Central Valley who were involved in the campaign to pass AB 78 or who had participated in one way or another in the debates surrounding the bill and Hmong's ethnic label. I contacted informants directly or through people I knew. During my interviews, I asked informants questions about their personal and professional backgrounds, how they became involved in AB 78, what their views were regarding the teaching of Hmong language and history in schools, and the availability of resources in Hmong communities. Between 2009 and 2011, I used LexisNexis to compile and analyze newspaper accounts of teenage suicides, AB 78, and Hmong in California.

Finally, my analysis of Hmong veterans' movement for U.S. citizenship relies on official documents and personal interviews. For example, I closely read and did a textual analysis of the hearing on the Hmong Veterans' Naturalization Act of 1997 before the Subcommittee on Immigration and Claims in the House of Representatives. I also interviewed ten Hmong veterans about their pre- and postmigration experiences, including their experiences surviving the Secret War in Laos, participating in veteran organizations, learning English, going through the naturalization process, and becoming U.S. citizens. Through these interviews, I gained a deeper understanding of and appreciation for Hmong veterans' stories and perspectives about the Secret War, Hmong, the United States, and the world.

ORGANIZATION OF THE BOOK

Chapter 2 provides a concise historical background of Hmong and their experiences before and after 1960 that have conditioned their collective political narratives and repertoires of contention. I also discuss Hmong refugees' immigration to the United States, the adjustments to their legal status, and their initial racialization by both mass media and official agencies. I pay particular attention to Hmong's involvement in America's Secret War in Laos and discuss information that has, until now, been missing from history books but is crucial for understanding Hmong former refugees' political claims within the United States. Using declassified official documents, I examine four crucial reasons why the U.S. government decided it was politically expedient to recruit Hmong into a secret surrogate army, separate from the Royal Lao Army, to fight communist forces in Laos. I also document and discuss how the United States secretly planned to keep Hmong political refugees permanently in Thailand, without telling the Thai government. This crucial information gives us a more complete understanding of Hmong's historically asymmetric relationship with the U.S. government. It also helps us understand why Hmong made the political claims that they did as they engaged with and confronted the U.S. political system. I suggest that far from arriving as "blank slates" to the United States, Hmong refugees arrived with collective political narratives and knowledge of various means of protesting and claims making (in short, repertoires of contention). As we will see in the movements in the 1990s and 2000s (chapters 3, 4, and 5), Hmong social movement actors draw directly on Hmong's collective political narratives of the Secret War in Laos to make political claims on the political system. Hmong leaders, especially former military leaders, rely on their extant repertoires of contention, such as their experiences working with and persuading high-ranking government officials and monarchs, to approach and lobby various representatives and segments of the U.S. political system, from the U.S. Congress to the White House, from the Central Intelligence Agency (CIA) to the U.S. Department of State.

Chapter 3 draws on my SECA model of immigrant political incorporation to examine the Hmong grassroots movement to obtain benefits restoration. Along with other immigrants, Hmong noncitizens and their families confronted the loss of public benefits such as food stamps and SSI under the welfare reforms of the mid-1990s. Instead of passively accepting the consequences of welfare reform, ordinary Hmong men and women organized themselves and fought back vehemently. Besides engaging in public immigrant marches and rallies, filing appeals, lobbying, and filing lawsuits, Hmong women and men also protested the U.S.

government by committing suicide. I argue that in their interactions with the political system, Hmong made strategic choices such as mobilizing ethnic organizational networks and institutional and state allies and framing their struggle in a way that distinguished their group identity and claims from that of other immigrant groups. Although they received significant support from other immigrant groups, Hmong ultimately broke ranks with other immigrants to mobilize a group identity that elevated their political standing and facilitated their capacity to engage in sustained claims making. Specifically, Hmong used what I call the military service frame to distinguish themselves as a deserving group of immigrants. In the process, Hmong obtained tangible policy benefits. However, in granting these benefits, the state redefined Hmong as tribal aliens, undermining their political standing and perpetuating the marginalization of Hmong as foreigners in the U.S. racial structure.

Just as chapter 3 examines Hmong movement actors' strategic collective actions to get their interests represented in public policy, chapter 4 analyzes Hmong veterans' sustained social movement to obtain much-needed naturalization accommodations for themselves and their spouses. Using official documents, including congressional hearings and personal interviews, I analyze how Hmong veterans, veterans organizations, and their state allies worked together to sustain this movement between 1990 and 2000. Instead of giving up after years of mobilizing support for the Hmong Veterans' Naturalization Act, Hmong veterans persisted. I examine the actions of Hmong veterans, their allies, and politically connected ethnic actors and how these actions eventually led to the passage of the Hmong Veterans' Naturalization Act of 2000. I argue that Hmong veterans' lobbying efforts before and after welfare reforms created the crucial conditions for sustaining the social movement. Hmong's state allies strategically responded to opponents of the act by framing the issue of Hmong veterans' naturalization in terms of national honor and as consistent with U.S. military interests around the world. The convergence of U.S. interests with Hmong interests and the fact that Hmong veterans were not being granted official veteran status persuaded congressional members on both sides of the political aisle to grant Hmong naturalization accommodations. This case demonstrates, once again, Hmong's collective agency in getting their interests represented in public policy and how the racial state perpetuated Hmong as allied aliens.

Whereas chapters 3 and 4 examine Hmong's concerted efforts to get their interests represented in national policies, chapter 5 examines Hmong's movement, led by a group of mostly Hmong women professionals, to persuade the California State Legislature to include Hmong history in California's public school curriculum. This social movement emerged out of a different set of circumstances—Hmong teenage suicides in Fresno, California. I examine how government agencies such as the Office of Refugee Resettlement framed the teenage suicides as a mental health problem and how the regional media diagnosed it as stemming from an intergenerational "cultural clash." I argue that instead of accepting the dominant framings of the social problem, Hmong women professionals recognized the cultural opportunity opened up by dominant framings of teenage suicides and exerted agency in reframing the problem in terms of racism and marginalization against Hmong within the broader society. In doing so, they proposed a different solution to the problem: the teaching of Hmong history in California's public schools. Hmong women professionals approached and worked with a California state assemblywoman to introduce AB 78; and they mobilized the Hmong community and sought the support of other organizational allies. On July 10, 2003, AB 78 was signed into law by Governor Gray Davis, becoming Section 51221.4 of the California Education Code. However, the final bill signed into law was not exactly what Hmong activists had hoped for. The reason? Before enacting the bill, policy makers decided to remove all occurrences of "Hmong" in the bill and replace them with "Southeast Asians." I argue that rather than being the inevitable outcome of ethnic infighting or simply reflecting the state's interest in providing a public good to the greatest number of people, this state decision represents the state's racialization and marginalization of Hmong—a practice more pervasive than it seems.

Chapter 6 concludes the book with discussion of the implications of immigrant agency and state racialization on the ongoing, dynamic process of immigrant political incorporation. I also examine what has happened to immigrants and refugees and their rights in the contexts of a strong rhetoric around national security/defense, especially as we have seen it play out during the Trump era and throughout the ongoing global COVID-19 pandemic.

A NOTE ON LANGUAGE AND CONCEPTS

Recognizing, as other scholars have, the close social and political connection between and among immigrant generations (Wong 2013), I use the term "immigrants" to encompass foreign-born immigrants and their descendants. However, I recognize that there are important differences between immigrants and refugees in terms of legal status as well as social and economic experiences. The U.S. Immigration and Nationality Act defines an immigrant as "any alien in the United States, except one legally admitted under specific nonimmigrant categories" such as temporary visitors, students, or diplomats. An alien is "any person not a citizen or national of the United States." The same act defines a refugee as "any person who is outside any country of such person's nationality or, in the case of a person having no nationality, is outside any country in which such person last habitually resided, and who is unable or unwilling to return to, and is unable or unwilling to avail himself or herself of the protection of, that country because of persecution or a well-founded fear of persecution on account of race, religion, nationality, membership in a particular social group, or political opinion" (8 U.S.C. 1101(a), INA 101(a)).

Although most foreign-born Hmong in the United States are political refugees, not everyone came as political refugees. Some were admitted as parolees
(in 1975 and 1976), most were admitted as political refugees (1976 and thereafter), some were admitted as refugees for family reunification, and an increasing
number have arrived as immigrant (non-refugee) spouses or children of lawful
permanent residents or U.S. citizens. Being war-torn and displaced refugees sets
most foreign-born Hmong apart from other foreign-born immigrants who did
not experience war or forced displacement and from immigrants who arrived
with sufficient transferable resources and credentials with which to start life and
obtain employment in this society.

I further distinguish between an ethnic group and a national origin group. An
ethnic group refers to a group of people who identify as members of the same
ethnicity because of a belief in shared ancestry, cultural-religious customs, or
language. National origin refers to the country in which a person was born. This
is an important distinction because different ethnic groups from the same
national origin do not necessarily experience the same contexts of exit and
reception. Although I recognize the problem in reifying groups or treating collectivities of people—such as ethnicity or race—as if they were substantial entities with their own interests and agency, I realize that I cannot fully avoid using
the term "group" when talking about collectivities of people doing things
together, such as engaging in political mobilization. Nevertheless, I am as clear
as possible about who is doing what to whom in which circumstances. For
example, I speak about the interests and agency of particular social actors or of
particular interest "groups" of Hmong society, while trying my best to avoid
implying that the ethnic group or entire "clans" or "lineages" within the ethnic
group have their own interests or agency.

Throughout this book I use the terms "Hmong" and "Hmong Americans"
interchangeably to refer to this multigenerational ethnic "group" in the United
States. At the time of this writing, it is still common and not at all unusual to find
Hmong American households whose members include foreign-born parents
and/or grandparents, foreign-born adult children, foreign-born or American-
born children-in-law (especially daughters-in-law), and American-born children
and/or grandchildren. Indeed, in some cases we might even find within the same
roof persons who are former refugees but are now naturalized citizens, persons
who are American-born but bilingual, persons who are mono-English speakers
but identify as "Hmong," and persons who are too young to know the difference
between "White" and "Asian." This complexity complicates any simple definition
of "immigrants." When I speak about "immigrant agency" or "immigrant political
incorporation," I am not speaking only about the actions or prospects of foreign-
born persons in Hmong households or communities. Rather, I am also talking
about the agency and prospects of Hmong persons, both foreign-born and
U.S.-born, who often live, work, interact, and do things together. After all, most

Hmong American social movements involve and affect a wide range of participants and stakeholders, not just the class of foreign-born or U.S.-born Hmong.

Like other immigrant communities, Hmong American communities usually extend beyond a single place and can span multiple cities, states, and countries. This is because many Hmong Americans maintain ties with their relatives in Laos, Thailand, France, Canada, Australia, and elsewhere. When I refer to a Hmong community of a particular place or context, I make that clear. I am aware of the many kinds of within-group differences, beyond generational status differences, that exist within this "ethnic group."

I am aware of the debates between some individuals and among some segments of the Hmong American community regarding the anglicized terms Hmong and Mong. It was during Hmong's movement for inclusion/recognition (see chapter 5) that one of the most emotionally charged debates emerged—about whether one or both of these terms should be used as the ethnonym for the ethnic group. I chose to use the term "Hmong" throughout this book for three reasons. First, the anglicized term "Hmong" is a product of Laos-based Hmong's political struggles in the 1960s and 1970s against historical political marginalization and ethnic subordination. Laotian Hmong on both sides of the Secret War perceived the externally imposed label "Meo" to be derogatory, with historical roots in Han Chinese and French oppression. It was not until the late 1970s that Hmong were able to rid themselves of this derogatory label. Although some less informed or prejudiced writers, including some journalists and academics, continued to use the derogatory term "Meo" well into the 1980s, since the 1970s pioneer scholars of Hmong background, including Dao Yang (1993), Gary Yia Lee (2007), Chia Koua Vang and Gnia Yee Yang (Smalley, Vang, and Yang 1990), have pointed out the negative connotations of this term. In my view, Laotian Hmong's collective political struggle is worth remembering and their hard-won collective achievement worth honoring. Second, although a few other anglicized terms, such as "Mhong" and "HMong," have been proposed by some Hmong American writers, the term "Hmong" remains the most commonly used term among Hmong Americans in the United States. Third, most English-language academic papers and books since 1975, including works by scholars of Hmong ethnic background, have used "Hmong" to refer to this ethnic group. Hmong native speakers refer to themselves and each other as Hmoob or Moob, depending on whether they speak the Hmoob Dawb dialect or Moob Leeg dialect. Within the contexts of Hmong communication, the term Moob or Hmoob, besides being the name of the ethnic group and its language, can also mean "people" or "humans."

Now, imagine that you are about to embark on a journey back in time to the 1960s and into the remote jungles somewhere in Southeast Asia. This journey begins with Hmong's turbulent history of war, displacement, and statelessness. As the journey unfolds, we will be witnesses to Hmong's remarkable story of political courage and agency.

2 · HISTORY AND CONTEXTS OF EXIT

In the past two hundred years, government oppression, armed conflict, and international migration have been the most profound and constant social forces impacting Hmong society. Historical records show that beginning in the early 1800s, a segment of the Miao population within China—mostly Hmong—migrated in successive waves from the provinces of Sichuan, Guizhou, and Yunnan into modern-day Vietnam, Laos, and Thailand (Mottin 1980). Hmong migrated primarily in response to decades of oppression by and armed conflicts with the Qing state, especially its practices of tax extortion, forced labor, and forced assimilation (Diamond 1995; Jenks 1994; Mottin 1980; Ovesen 2004). Their migration into northern Vietnam peaked between 1800 and 1860 (Mottin 1980). After reaching northern Vietnam, many Hmong settled permanently there. Others, however, engaged in a southeastern migration into the northern parts of Laos and Thailand (Culas and Michaud 2004).

Hmong oral histories suggest that Hmong first arrived in Laos between 1810 and 1820 (Yang 1972, 6). Unfortunately, we do not have oral or written histories of how many Hmong or of which lineage or clan arrived in which regions of Laos at what time. The histories that we now have are still incomplete. By one account, sometime in the mid-1800s, Mr. Ly Nhia Vu and members of his lineage or clan arrived in what is now northeastern Laos from Tonkin (Lee 2005, 146–147). Ly and his group settled in Nong Het, a district within Tran Ninh (later known as Xieng Khouang), and lived under the authority of the Lao Phuan princes in that area. Ovesen (2004, 220) describes Hmong's initial reception in Laos as follows: "Although the lowlanders regarded the Hmong as primitive savages, the Phuan ruler acceded to their presence as long as they stayed in the mountains and paid taxes. The same kind of relationship obtained as some of the Hmong moved into Luang Prabang in the mid-nineteenth century." Pholsena (2006, 21) points out that although the Lao controlled the government, they "had little interest in assimilating the upland population during the pre-colonial period."

In retrospect, Hmong escaped from Qing state oppression only to find them-selves, in relatively short order, under French colonial exploitation. For during about the same time that Hmong began migrating from southern China to northern Vietnam, the French had just built their first colonial outposts in Tourane (Da Neng) and Saigon, in 1858 and 1859, respectively (Nguyen and Haines 1997, 38). Although we do not know how many Hmong were in Laos, by the time that the French had colonized Laos in 1893, "there were enough Hmong for the French to impose taxes and other obligations on them" (Lee 2004, 441). In Laos, these other obligations included twenty days of corvée labor (Lopez Jerez 2019). Much of this involved forcing Laotians to build the network of French colonial roads that connected Laos and Vietnam (Stuart-Fox 1995).

In response to French colonial exploitation and oppression by other ethnic rulers, segments of Hmong society led by Hmong leaders such as Xiong Tai, Xiong Mi Chang, and Vue Pa Chai engaged in a series of rebellions in the mid- to late 1800s, in the early 1910s, and between 1918 and 1921 (Gunn 1986; Lee 2015). Originating within Tonkin (northern Vietnam) and spilling over into northeast-ern Laos, these Hmong-led rebellions were targeted against the French colonial-ists, "feudal" Tai overloads, and Chinese/mandarins (Gunn 1986). Hmong, of course, were not the only ethnic minority group in Indochina to rebel against the French colonial state. Between 1901 and 1902, the Alak, Nha-heun, Loven, and Sedang of southern Laos—groups that historically were categorized under the pejorative term "Kha," meaning "slave"—rebelled against the French (Murdoch 1974). After the French brutally suppressed the Hmong-led rebellions, and in order to preempt future rebellions, the French ordered a census of the Hmong by tribe and location (Gunn 1986). They also appointed a few Hmong as *kaitongs* and assigned them the role of middleman tax collectors, giving these few men authority over the Hmong in places such as Xieng Khouang province (Dunnigan et al. 1996; Lee 1982; Yang 1975).

Before the various wars between empires and nation-states that caused decades of great destruction and mass displacement of Southeast Asian peoples, Hmong typically lived in the highest elevations of Laos' lush mountain rainfor-ests. Located away from the lowlands and centers of business and government, Hmong villages were spread out across several provinces of Laos. A typical Hmong village contained several to a dozen household units that constituted a handful of lineages. The lack of roads and transportation in most parts of Laos' mountainous terrain made contact between ordinary persons of different prov-inces rare.[1] The lack of transportation and communication technology made it so that Hmong individuals' day-to-day activities revolved around their families, extended families, and coethnics within the same village or cluster of villages. Like most Laotians, Hmong villagers sustained themselves through rice, fruit and vegetable farming, hunting, fishing, animal husbandry, and local trade with

Chinese merchants (Barney 1961). Hmong also grew and traded opium as their main cash crop;[2] those who could not afford to pay colonial taxes with Indo-chine Française piastres often submitted hand-harvested opium in lieu of coins.

During this earlier period, Hmong's relations with major Laotian groups (Lao, Tai, and Kmhmu) generally fit what Ronald Cohen (1978, 390) calls "frag-mented relations" between ethnic groups.[3] That is, there was little or no reason for Hmong and other ethnic groups to interact given the low population density of Laos, ethnic groups' self-sufficiency, and their relative topographical isolation from each other. In Laos, Hmong have always been an ethnic minority both in terms of their population size and their political standing.

According to French colonial records, in 1911 the population of Hmong and Iu Mien was 15,205, or 2 percent of the 618,500 Laotian population.[4] By 1942, this figure increased to 49,240, or 5 percent of the Laotian population (Pholsena 2002, 178). In 1954–1955, a few years before America's Secret War in Laos, the Laotian Ministry of Interior counted about 52,900 Hmong and Iu Mien in Laos. Of this population, about 71 percent reportedly lived in Xieng Khouang prov-ince, while the rest were scattered across four provinces: Nam Tha (5 percent), Luang Prabang (13 percent), Sayaboury (7 percent), and Vientiane (4 percent). Within Xieng Khouang province, Hmong and Iu Mien made up 40 percent of the ethnic population (Pholsena 2002, 179). Subsequent censuses showed that the Hmong population in Laos was 231,168 in 1985, 315,465 in 1995 (Lemoine 2005, 3), and 451,946 in 2005 (Government of Lao PDR 2006). Given the techni-cal and political problems that affect how people are found, categorized, and counted in most countries, however, these population figures, especially earlier figures, were probably undercounts of the true populations. Based on the latest census, as of 2015, Hmong constituted about 595,000 or 9 percent of the Laotian population of 6.5 million. This makes Hmong the third largest of forty-nine rec-ognized ethnic groups in the Lao PDR, after the Kmhmu (11 percent) and the majority Lao ethnic groups (53 percent) (Lao Statistics Bureau 2015).

What is clear is that Hmong had lived in Sam Nuea (now Hua Phanh) and Xieng Khouang provinces since migrating to Laos and significant numbers of them were concentrated there by the mid-1900s. It is no coincidence that throughout the early to mid-twentieth century, nearly all of the most well-known Laotian Hmong figures emerged in Xieng Khouang and Sam Nuea. These fig-ures include Lo Blia Yao, Ly (Xia) Foung, Touby Lyfoung, Fay Dang Lobliayao, and Vang Pao, all of whom were born in the Nong Het district of Xieng Khouang. Shong Lue Yang, the inventor of the Hmong Pahawh writing system, was born in 1929 in the Nong Het district. It is also not a coincidence that during the Secret War in Laos, the U.S. CIA placed its top-secret headquarters and airbase in Long Tieng, also known as Long Cheng, a flat valley of roughly five square miles sur-rounded by mountains in Xieng Khouang province.

THE AMERICANS CAME TO OUR COUNTRY

From the 1940s to the mid-1970s, the whole of Southeast Asia was a constant battleground for powerful nation-states and empires. These wars included the Franco-Thai War of 1940–1941, the First and Second French Indochina Campaigns from 1940 to 1945, the First Indochina War from 1946 to 1954, and the much longer war, the Second Indochina War, from 1955 to 1975. While Americans refer to the latter as the "Vietnam War," Vietnamese call it the "American War." In recognition of both labels, I refer to this conflict as the American-Vietnam War (1955–1975). Overlapping the American-Vietnam War was the Laotian civil war and America's secret involvement in that war.

Fractionalization was both a cause and a consequence of the Laotian civil war. At the government level, three factions vied for political power: the rightist faction led by the Royal Lao government, the neutralist faction led by Prince Souvanna Phouma, and the leftist faction led by Pathet Lao nationalists (Chan 1994). However, on the ground what was most immediately consequential to the lives of ordinary civilians was the struggle between anticommunists and communists. The civil war forced segments of the Laotian and Hmong populations into polarized factions.[5] As Culas and Michaud (2004, 84) point out, "Told to take sides or else suffer serious reprisals, Hmong mountain dwellers chose one side or the other according to the area where they resided at the time, the amount of pressure put on them, and their own estimation of what was best calculated to ensure their liberty in the long run." This circumstance or rather fate was confirmed to be fairly accurate by most of the Hmong men and women whom I interviewed over the course of my research who were firsthand witnesses to the Secret War in Laos. As Nhia Pao Xiong, a sixty-five-year-old veteran of the Secret War, recalled,

> In the north [Muang Xai, Laos], we [Hmong in their villages] first saw the [Hmong communist] recruiters in 1959. People greeted them as *ai nooj* [a Lao word meaning "brothers"], and they called others *ai nooj*. They talked to Hmong villagers about the rise of Hmong's messiah (*niam txiv vaj Hmoob*), about equality for men and women, and equality for ethnic peoples. At that time, we hadn't even heard of the word *xav tum*, which is a Lao word meaning "enemy," which we came to realize later on was being used by the communists to label those they called, the "arms and legs" of the Americans. The recruiters came to our villages and went back afterward, we didn't know where to. . . . Later, when the war was actively going on, both the *nyob laj* [a label used by the Hmong of the U.S. side to refer to the "enemy"] and the *xav tum* demanded that people choose a side. They threatened people who wanted to remain neutral with, "Yog hais npaum no los nej tsis yuav, seb nej yuav tuaj tog twg ces txawm tuaj laiv!" ("We have said

enough, if you don't agree with us, you better take a side!").... People understood that they weren't given choices in those situations.[6]

For some segments of Hmong society, their preexisting affiliation with different
Hmong leaders also shaped which side they ended up on. For instance, during
the Japanese occupation of Laos in the 1940s, Hmong led by Touby Lyfoung
worked for the French while Hmong led by Fay Dang Lo worked for the Japanese (Yang 2000). Later, during the civil war, Hmong led by Touby Lyfoung and
Vang Pao sided with the Royal Lao and U.S. governments, while those led by Fay
Dang Lo became members of the Pathet Lao.

Taking advantage of the bitter factional conflicts in Laos to further its Cold
War policy of containing communism in Southeast Asia by "not let[ting] Laos
fall to the Communists" (Greenstein and Immerman 1992, 578),[7] the U.S. executive branch approved a secret military plan to be carried out by its CIA on Laotian soil without appearing to violate the cessation of hostilities and neutrality of
Laos as stipulated in the Geneva Agreements of 1954 and 1962, respectively (Goldstein 1973, 171; Leary 1995). This secret plan was that the U.S. military would recruit,
train, and finance a secret irregular army composed of mostly Hmong with a much
smaller number of Lao, Kmhmu, Iu Mien, and Lahu to fight the Pathet Lao and
North Vietnamese military forces that were occupying or perceived to be occupying the most crucial region of Laos: the northeastern region directly bordering
North Vietnam. This region spanned Xieng Khoung and Sam Nuea provinces. The
United States saw this area as an especially crucial buffer zone—with the CIA
secret army serving as the actual buffer—between North Vietnam and the Mekong
Valley, in which lay Vientiane, the Laotian capitol, and which was the gateway into
threatened Thailand (Ahern 2006; Parker 1995).

THEY RECRUITED US

In late 1955, a U.S. military mission disguised as a humanitarian aid mission to
Laos called the Programs Evaluation Office was under way (Leeker 2010a). In
late 1960, James William (Bill) Lair, a U.S. CIA military specialist, drafted the
plan for recruiting and supplying the Vang Pao–led "Meo hilltribe irregular
army," as they were called. This plan received approval from Admiral Harry D.
Felt (then the commander in chief of the Pacific Fleet), the U.S. State Department, and President Eisenhower (Leary 1999).[8] As Leary (1995, 506–507) points
out, it was the U.S. president who "assigned the task [of creating the secret army]
to the CIA." Leary (1995, 506–507) elaborates,

> Although critics of U.S. policy later would portray the CIA as responsible for
> the "secret" war in Laos, they failed to take into account the circumstances
> surrounding the employment of the intelligence agency. Given the nature of the

Geneva Agreements, Under Secretary of State for Political Affairs U. Alexis Johnson once explained to a congressional committee, the CIA "is really the only other instrumentality that we have." G. McMurtrie Godley, U.S. ambassador to Laos, 1969–73, agreed. "These operations that the CIA are conducting in Laos," he testified in 1971, "were not initiated by them." The task, he emphasized, had been assigned by the President.

To create plausible deniability for the U.S. government, Vang Pao, who was Hmong and who in 1960 was technically a major in the Royal Lao Armed Forces, was put in command of this CIA secret army. However, as U.S. federal officials were well aware, the CIA secret army was only "technically" operating under the Royal Lao Armed Forces, the predecessor to the Royal Lao Army (U.S. Department of State 1998d, 1). In reality, throughout the war in Laos, the CIA's secret army was "organizationally separate" from the Royal Lao Army (Stuart-Fox 1997, 145). In fact, both armies were financed almost entirely by the United States (Anthony and Sexton 1993). According to Anthony and Sexton (1993, 12), in 1955 "the Eisenhower administration began supporting the RLA with a direct cash subsidy of $34 million . . . through the United States Operations Mission." To maintain plausible deniability throughout the war, U.S. officials, especially ambassador William Sullivan and his successor, G. McMurtrie Godley, created the impression and public narrative that there were never any U.S. troops in Laos and that the United States was merely providing "military assistance" as requested by the Royal Lao Government in its fight against communism. In a CBS television news segment, Godley, in response to the reporter's question about the reports of escalating U.S. military commitment in Laos, stated, "We have no commitment in Laos. Our military assistance in material is being supplied pursuant to the request of the Royal Lao Government and in consonance with the Geneva Agreement of 1962." When asked to comment on the "itemization of American military involvement," Godley replied, "Certainly, no comment."[9] Throughout much of the American-Vietnam War, the CIA's secret operation in Laos was kept unknown to the U.S. general public and to most in the U.S. Congress until the leakage of portions of the classified Pentagon Papers to the *New York Times* in June 1971. Commissioned in 1967, the Pentagon Papers, officially known as the Report of the Office of the Secretary of Defense Vietnam Task Force, is a U.S. Department of Defense historical report containing over eight thousand pages that describe the U.S. political and military involvement in Vietnam between 1945 and 1967. The complete report was released to the public only in 2011.[10]

Contrary to popular beliefs that Hmong were recruited by the United States because they were fierce "warriors" or that they had a history of animosity toward Vietnamese,[11] declassified U.S. documents reveal a different and more plausible set of reasons why the United States recruited Hmong into its secret army: the United States understood that (1) Hmong and the dominant Lao ethnic group did not necessarily get along, and thus U.S. promises of patronage would pique Hmong's interest in vying for political power within Laos; (2) most Hmong resided in Xieng Khouang province, which is hundreds of miles from Vientiane, the headquarters of Laotian power, political factions, and international press corps, making covert operations in Xieng Khoung and across Military Region 2 (MR 2) harder for prying eyes to detect; (3) Hmong were a substantial ethnic group, large enough to be made into an effective covert military force but small enough not to pose a political threat to U.S. control or transcend their command; and finally (4) the United States considered Hmong lives as cheap or extremely cheap. The first three reasons are found in a January 17, 1964, "Memorandum from the Deputy Director for Coordination, Bureau of Intelligence and Research (Scott) to the Special Group," in which Deputy Director Joseph Scott within the U.S. Department of State writes,

> The U.S. is engaged in overt and covert support to paramilitary forces in Laos but in large part the elements being aided are remote from the centers of power and unlikely to be involved in any future power struggle. . . . The genesis of this program stems from high level U.S. Government approval in late 1960 and early 1961 in response to a recommendation by the U.S. Ambassador in Laos that CIA enlist tribal support to fight communism. The main effort in this program has been development of the Meo [Hmong], the largest non-Lao ethnic group in Laos, as an effective guerrilla force and the provision of plausibly deniable U.S. air support for the program. Since the program's inception CIA has worked with the two key Meo leaders, Touby Lyfong and Vang Pao. (U.S. Department of State 1998d, 2–3)

The same memorandum continues,

> The danger of an attempt to gain power by the principal paramilitary group, the Meo, is more remote. The Meo, as all tribal groups in Laos, *are isolated from the country's political arena and are not integrated into Lao society.* They are located away from the main centers of the country, living in scattered villages at the higher elevations (the Yao and Kha tribal groups are even more isolated and too few in number to pose a threat). Moreover, the Meo are *subject to U.S. guidance and direction.* The development of the Meo as a rival center of armed power with political objectives in a national Lao context *does not* seem to be a realistic possibility. (U.S. Department of State 1998d, 5, emphasis added)

But besides these calculated reasons, declassified documents suggest that the United States recruited Hmong because their lives were considered to be cheap and much more expendable than American lives. Whereas U.S. army privates of the American-Vietnam War earned basic pay between $102 and $145 a month (in 1968 dollars),[12] depending on the number of years they had served in the army, Hmong army privates, if they were paid at all, received between $1.50 and $3.00 a month (Hwang 2002).[13] Hmong battalion commanders (majors) were paid about $60 to $75 a month, an amount nine to sixteen times less than what a U.S. major (O-4 salary range) made in a month ($536–$936 in 1968 dollars) during the height of the American-Vietnam War.[14] Whereas Hmong T-28 pilots were paid between $168 and $240 a month by the CIA according to Hmong pilots' own accounts (Vang 2019, 98–99), pilots of Air America's so-called commercial planes in Laos were paid between $3,000 and $5,000 per month (Schanche 1963). Throughout the Secret War, the U.S. government clearly was more concerned about getting the most "bang for its buck" than about sparing non-American lives. This view can be seen in the following declassified memorandum of conversation between the U.S. ambassador to Laos, the U.S. Secretary of State, and a staff member of the Far East of the National Security Council:

> One other point which Ambassador Godley wanted to raise in connection with the U.S. operations in Laos, as distinct from the Steel Tiger strikes, was that the total cost was less than $500 million per year, including AID, MASF, CAS, and the bombing. In all this, we were not losing a single American, and we were killing over 30 North Vietnamese a day. $500 million was what one U.S. division cost us in South Vietnam. In Laos, this same sum enabled us to tie down two North Vietnamese divisions, numerous Binh Tram, plus many trucks and antiaircraft artillery sites. We were getting a bigger bang for a buck in Laos than anywhere else. (U.S. Department of State 1998a, 8)[15]

The above reasons combined with Hmong's substantial concentration within MR 2 made the recruitment of Hmong into a surrogate army both strategic and convenient for the United States. In the 1960s, of an estimated 300,000 Laotian Hmong population, the majority lived in Xieng Khouang and Sam Nuea provinces, which directly bordered North Vietnam (Smalley, Vang, and Yang 1990, 4). In 1962, Xieng Khouang and Sam Nuea provinces were conjoined into MR 2, one of five military regions in Laos drawn at the time. Taking advantage of the MR 2's border with North Vietnam, the CIA built its most important radar site, code named Lima Site 85, atop Phou Pha Thi, a mountain in Sam Neua with cliffs so imposing that CIA forces thought, incorrectly, they would be impossible for the enemy to surmount (Castle 1999). From the 1960s through the early 1970s, top U.S. military and government officials considered MR 2 as the most crucial buffer region between North Vietnam and the rest of the Lao Mekong Delta and Thailand (U.S. Department of State 1998f, 693–700), so much so that U.S. officials completely ignored Gen. Vang Pao's request to relocate the Hmong of Xieng Khouang to Sayaburi province during the late 1960s; instead, U.S. officials suggested that displaced Hmong be resettled in the Plain of Jars plateau (U.S. Department of State 1998e, 930). In the late 1960s and early 1970s, the Plain of Jars plateau and the skyline ridge of Long Cheng—both located in MR 2—became infamous as the sites of the most bombarded, bloodiest battles of the Laotian war (Leary 1995; Zasloff 1973).

In January 1961, CIA paramilitary specialist James W. "Bill" Lair and his training officers armed and trained about a thousand Hmong (Leary 1999). When the Laotian civil war escalated, widespread conscription into the CIA-organized secret army occurred. As Nhia Pao Xiong, who was conscripted to join the secret army when he was only sixteen years old, succinctly describes it,

> Every male between 15 and 65 years of age was conscripted. There was no choice. They told us that all of us needed to join the army. . . . When I showed up and they realized my brothers and cousins were missing, they asked me where they were. I told them they were in the village and that I came by myself. The commanders said that if I was not happy with them staying behind, they would send soldiers to go round them up and bring them. At that time, there were only a few men left in our village to look after my father and other aging uncles and aunts. I told them I was fine with it, so they left them alone. To this day I still have not told them [his brothers and cousins] about it.[16]

Chong Lee Chue, another Hmong veteran, recalls, "They came into the village and they told me to provide five soldiers. I could only come up with four, so they said, 'OK, then you have to go.'"[17]

By the end of June 1961, Walter McConaughy, the assistant secretary of state for Far Eastern Affairs, reported to Chester Bowles, the undersecretary of state, "We have been providing arms, ammunition, and other support to about 7,700 Meo tribesmen in Laos who are members of the Auto-Defense Corps of the Lao Army. Most of these are situated in Northern Laos back of the enemy lines. Owing to the hostilities, a large number of Meo and their dependents have lost their usual means of livelihood. . . . Because of the destruction of their crops and their failure to plant, relief may be required over the next 18 months, at least, and may cost between $3 and $5 million" (U.S. Department of State 1998e, 263). By June 1963, the CIA secret army grew to nineteen thousand soldiers (U.S. Department of State 1998d, 1). It eventually grew to over thirty thousand Hmong, Lao, Kmhmu, Iu Mien, and Lahu soldiers, all placed under the command of Major General Vang Pao and his subcommanders. In addition to supplying the CIA secret army with weapons, ammunitions, and planes, the U.S. military also sent into Laos several hundred U.S. Air Force pilots and personnel disguised as civilians or trainers (Leary 1995; Leeker 2010b; Robbins 1987).

THEY MADE PROMISES TO US

Hmong's ongoing feelings of U.S. betrayal can be linked to several events in which the United States broke their promises to the Hmong. At the time of this writing, there are at least two documented promises that agents of the U.S. government made to Hmong. In a letter to his Hmong friends in the Namphong refugee camp, Thailand, on December 31, 1975, former CIA Paramilitary Operations Officer Jerry "Hog" Daniels wrote, "I hope you all believe me when I say that your welfare has always been, is now, and will continue to be of the highest priority interest for me and my fellow U.S.A. co-workers. I still remember that I and perhaps other Americans who are representatives of the United States government, have promised you, the Hmong People, that you fight for us, if we win, things will be fine. But if we lose, we will take care of you" (Miller, Kiatoukaysy, and Yang 1992, 18). Throughout the 1960s and 1970s, Jerry Daniels worked directly with General Vang Pao as his personal case officer (read military advisor) and was the CIA's chief of operations in Long Tieng from 1970 to 1973 (Morrison 2013).

In a 1979 *60 Minutes* report titled "Our Secret Army,"[18] the following conversation was recorded between CBS correspondent Mike Wallace and Edgar "Pop" Buell, a former CIA operative and USAID area coordinator.

BUELL: "They became refugees because we [were] encouraging them to fight for us. I promised them myself: Have no fear, we will take care of you. And 'taking care of you' is not in a refugee camp."

WALLACE: "We promised, the United States government—you as a representative of the United States government—promised the Hmong people, the Meos, 'We will take care of you. [Buell: "Absolutely."] You fight for us, we'll pay you. If we win, fine. If we lose, we'll take care of you'?"

BUELL: "Absolutely. And I think they still have that faith in us."

Buell was in charge of sustaining the tens of thousands of internally displaced Hmong refugees in MR 2 with food and supplies, often dropped by planes, so that Hmong could continue to fight the communists (Thompson 2010).

WE GAVE BLOOD AND TEARS

The Secret War in Laos—which remains the largest secret operation in CIA history—led to massive destruction of lives, livelihoods, and land. Although we will probably never know the full extent of this destruction, we do know that the United States dropped over two million tons of bombs in Laos, destroying countless human lives and obliterating land and crops, making Laos the most bombed country per capita in human history (Khamvongsa and Russell 2009). The United States also sprayed nearly twenty million gallons of powerful herbicide and defoliant chemicals, including Agent Pink, Agent Purple, Agent Blue, Agent White, and Agent Orange, on Laos, Vietnam, and Cambodia (Buckingham 1982). Much of Laos' valleys and rainforests, but especially those of northeastern and southeastern Laos, became dangerous wastelands. By the official end of the Secret War in 1975, about 350,000, or a tenth of the Laotian population, had perished (Herman and Chomsky 2002, 260). An estimated 30,000 to 40,000 Hmong soldiers had been killed and thousands more had been wounded (Lee and Tapp 2010, xvii; Vang 2016, 42). About 50,000 Hmong civilians were killed (Lee and Tapp 2010). About 700,000 to 800,000 Laotians, representing about a third of the Laotian population, became internally displaced.[19] However, for Hmong, the official end of the war was just the beginning of many more tragic events to come.

THEY ABANDONED US

Despite these acknowledged promises and perhaps other promises we have yet to discover, when Long Tieng was besieged by communist forces in April and May of 1975, the United States betrayed the Hmong by leaving tens of thousands of Hmong soldiers, civilians, and their families to fend for themselves. Out of an estimated 40,000 desperate Hmong soldiers and civilians who were in Long Tieng, only 3,000 to 3,500 individuals were airlifted to Nam Phong, Thailand, between May 13 and 14, 1975 (Rosenblatt 2015). Nam Phong was a Royal Thai Air Force base in Khon Kaen province that also housed some 3,000 U.S. Marines (Dunham and Quinlan 1990). Most of those airlifted to Nam Phong were Hmong military officers and their families, but thousands of Hmong civilians also rushed, most unsuccessfully, to get onto the CIA planes (Morrison 1999). Hmong soldiers and their families describe this abandonment as one of the most heart-wrenching events of their lives. Consequently, over 30,000 war-ravaged Hmong in Long Tieng and tens of thousands more Hmong elsewhere throughout northern, central, and western Laos were left stranded and largely defenseless. Nam Phong eventually became a temporary refuge to 1,406 Hmong families totaling 8,868 individuals, most of whom arrived there by foot.[20] Later, Hmong refugees in Nam Phong were transferred to the Ban Vinai refugee camp in Loei province, Thailand, where tens of thousands of other Hmong refugees were also staying.

Hmong on the losing side had few real options. Many understood they had lost the war, but the decision to leave or stay involved complex considerations. Many adult children were compelled to stay because of the need to care for their own parents who were too frail to make the arduous escape or too heartbroken and stubbornly against leaving behind everything they had owned, grown, raised, or cared for, such as their land, homes, crops, and livestock. Many wanted to leave but could not because a safe escape route was simply impossible. Nonetheless, for tens of thousands of Hmong, especially those who were soldiers or military officers, persecution or its threat was imminent. To escape political persecution and reprisal, Hmong soldiers, their families, and their extended families engaged in dangerous treks to try to reach Thailand. Between May 1975 and 1990, over a hundred thousand Hmong would eventually become political refugees in Thailand.

WE BECAME STATELESS REFUGEES

Most Hmong of central and northeastern Laos had to trek across one to two hundred miles of unfamiliar jungles while avoiding being captured or killed by the enemy or pirates. These journeys took weeks depending on the distance, the size of the group, and the type of dangers they encountered along the way. As Lee Lescaze, then a journalist in Nongkhai, Thailand, recounts, "For some of the refugees, particularly Lao from the capital, Vientiane, escape is not difficult. Patrols are lax. Boatmen can be paid to cross the Mekong. But for most Hmong, against whom the Communist government is carrying on a campaign, there is a long and difficult walk followed by a likely encounter with Communist troops on the riverbank."[21] The accounts of Hmong former refugees whom I spoke to reveal that chaos, misery, and death were common during their arduous journey to Thailand. Many people, young and old alike, died from injuries, exhaustion, starvation, and/or illnesses. Some infants and small children died from accidental poisoning with opium, which was sometimes used by parents in desperation to dampen children's cries in order to try to avoid the capture of entire groups by the enemy. Except for Hmong in the Sainyaburi province of Laos who were already on the western side of the Mekong River, most Hmong from other Laotian provinces had to cross the wide and turbulent waterway that separated Laos from Thailand. Thousands of Hmong drowned while trying to cross. Some were lucky enough to cross by chartered boat or canoes; these were sometimes prearranged, sometimes not. Stories of unsuspecting Hmong being forced overboard by those they hired were also common. Most crossed by either swimming or using makeshift floats such as bamboo or wooden rafts, poles, or logs.

Some have estimated that about fifteen thousand Hmong refugees lost their lives while trying to escape to Thailand (Wain 1981). We will probably never know the true number of persons and families who drowned in the Mekong or other rivers while trying to get to safety. However, most Hmong refugee families I know have a family member, cousin, relative, or friend who drowned in the Mekong in the aftermath of the war. Based on one news account, a group of Hmong villagers that started off with ninety-three persons made it to Thailand with only twenty-six still alive.[22]

Data from the UNHCR show that between 1975 and 1990, a total of 320,155 Laotian refugees arrived in Thailand. In 1975 alone, at least 54,854 Laotian refugees, including 10,195 "lowland Lao" and 44,659 "hilltribe" individuals, arrived in Thailand's refugee camps (Chantavanich et al. 1992). Subsumed under the externally imposed category, "hilltribe," were Hmong, Iu Mien, Lua, and Kmhmu.

Hmong refugees were the most numerous among them (Chantavanich et al. 1992; Thompson 2010, 231). This is not surprising given that the U.S. secret army was composed of mostly Hmong soldiers, and it was they and their civilian families and relatives who were most at risk of political persecution after 1975. Over three-quarters (250,000 out of 320,000) of all Laotian refugees who left Laos to seek safety in Thailand left between 1975 and 1980. Between 1975 and 1980, at least 102,555 Hmong, Iu Mien, Lua, and Kmhmu arrived in Thai refugee camps, composing 41 percent of all Laotian refugees (250,112) who had arrived in Thailand during that period. Between 1981 and 1990, the number of Hmong, Iu Mien, Lua, and Kmhmu refugee arrivals in Thailand declined to 18,888, or 27 percent of the total 70,043 refugees from Laos during that period (Chantavanich et al. 1992).

Those who were fortunate enough to escape to Thailand with their lives faced a new kind of political struggle and another U.S. act of betrayal. Because Thailand was not a signatory to the 1951 Geneva Convention on the Status of Refugees, the Thai government was not bound by the convention's principles on the protection of refugees. This meant that Thailand was not obligated to protect refugees against discrimination, penalization, or forced repatriation (also known as refoulement). Instead, the Thai government had "complete discretion" to determine the legal status of everyone within its borders, including escapees from Laos, Vietnam, and Cambodia (Chantavanich and Rabe 1990).

Hmong relatives whom I have talked to recall their traumatizing experiences during the initial months after they set foot on Thai soil. When a group of about eight thousand Hmong refugees (my parents were among them) crossed from Nam Pouy of southern Xayaboury, Laos, into Nam Tuang of eastern Nan, Thailand, in June 1975, they encountered a group of about five to seven hundred armed Thai soldiers within hours after they had crossed into Thai territory. To their surprise, this group of Thai soldiers did not stop them but instead went to secure the route at the border they had used to enter Thailand. However, because few refugee camps had been built by summer 1975, they had to survive without food or medicine in the jungles for two months. In desperation and facing starvation, several families returned to Laos. In August, when they tried to leave their makeshift camp to go to a recently built refugee camp, Nam Yao, thirty kilometers away, Thai soldiers were sent to stop them and keep them from going anywhere. Although they finally made contact with representatives of the United Nations and began receiving food and supplies later that August, it was not until November 1975 that they were finally permitted to move into the newly established Sob Tuang refugee camp.[23]

Ban Vinai was another major refugee camp near the Lao and Thai border.[24] Located in Loei province, Thailand, Ban Vinai was a refuge to 43,000 to 45,000 Hmong, Iu-Mien, and Lao refugees inside an area of four hundred acres, or six-tenths of a square mile (Long 1993, 62). Barred from going anywhere outside the camps without official permission, Hmong refugees depended entirely on the Thai government and the UNHCR for shelter, food, medicine, formal information, and protection. Violation of camp rules, such as the nightly curfew or going outside camp to collect firewood, often resulted in physical punishment or imprisonment by Thai security guards. Hmong refugees not only had no right to become Thai citizens but also were subject to whatever regulations Thai authorities imposed. At some camp sites, such as Ban Vinai, Thai authorities assigned Hmong refugees to live in areas designated as centers that sat on top of newly flattened cemeteries—the worst possible treatment of human beings who had barely escaped death or were still mourning the loss of loved ones left behind.[25] Subjugation and miserable camp conditions perpetuated Hmong refugees' condition as a stateless people. Thousands of Hmong in the refugee camps died from malnutrition, diseases, illnesses, and other unknown causes (Kundstadter 1985; Munger 1987).

ANOTHER U.S. SECRET PLAN, ANOTHER BETRAYAL

To make matters worse for Hmong refugees, in late 1975 the U.S. government had no desire or plan to admit them for resettlement in the United States. Declassified U.S. documents reveal that in September 1975 President Gerald Ford approved a secret U.S. State Department plan to resettle Hmong permanently in Thailand under the Meo Refugee Relief and Assistance Program (U.S. Department of State 1998c, 1–3). In an August 5, 1975, "Memorandum from the President's Assistant for National Security Affairs (Kissinger) to Secretary of Defense Schlesinger, Deputy Secretary of State Ingersoll, and Director of Central Intelligence Colby," Kissinger writes, in part,

> Spokesmen for the Royal Thai Government have indicated Thai willingness in principle to permit the Meo [Hmong] to remain in Thailand if adequate financial assistance is provided by the United States. It is requested that a working group comprising representatives of the addressees, and under the chairmanship of the representative of the Department of State, on a priority basis *develop a plan for the permanent resettlement of the Meo refugees in Thailand. Knowledge of this plan should be limited to a strictly need-to-know basis.* This plan should be forwarded for the President's review no later than August 15, 1975. (U.S. Department of State 1998b, 1, emphasis added)

Although we do not know the exact motive behind this plan, it is clear that the U.S. government, and more precisely the executive branch, having just lost the military and political wars in Vietnam and Laos, felt no obligation to its Hmong army in the aftermath of the war. The U.S. government's refusal to evacuate the vast majority of Hmong soldiers and families from Laos and its secret plan to keep Hmong refugees permanently in Thailand contradict any claim that the United States in 1975 saw itself as having the moral responsibility to rescue their "allied aliens" (Hein 1993, 24).

In retrospect, the U.S. plan to permanently resettle Hmong refugees in Thailand may have been done to further its own political interests and those of the Thai government, who was a U.S. ally throughout the Secret War in Laos. As I suggested above, throughout the Secret War, the U.S. government saw and used the Vang Pao–led Hmong army in MR 2 as a buffer against the advance of the North Vietnamese into the Mekong Delta, which joined southern Laos and northern Thailand. Following the war, the remnants of the CIA secret army were scattered across select places in Laos and Thailand. Taking orders from their immediate commanders as well as from exiled Laotian leaders in France and the United States, they were involved in an anticommunist resistance movement that lasted throughout the 1990s (Lee 2004). According to some Hmong veterans' accounts, although Thai soldiers were not overtly involved in the Laotian resistance movement, Thai officials accepted bribes and allowed members of the resistance to carry on their work such as crossing and reentering the Thailand-Laos border without penalty. By denying Hmong refugees the possibility of exit, other than exit to Laos, the United States compelled some refugees to return to Laos or to engage in the underground resistance movement, no matter how futile such movement was. For its part, the U.S. government generally turned a blind eye to the Laotian-Hmong resistance movement until the 1990s, when the U.S. market and political relations with Vietnam and Laos began to shift and improve largely in response to China's real and perceived increased influence in that region of the world.

If foreign policy interest was the most crucial factor in the U.S. desire to keep Hmong in Thailand, racism, xenophobia, and heartlessness played the most important role in keeping them out of the United States. In the 1970s, the United States used the prejudice of Hmong primitivism as an excuse to deny them entry. In response to a question from Congress regarding the prospects that Cambodian and Laotian refugees would be resettled outside of Thailand, ambassador Habib expressed the official Washington position as follows: "I think that, with time, that some of them will. I would say, offhand, that the hill tribesmen, for example, probably will not, and they are particularly suited for the area of Thailand, where they will remain. . . . But by and large, they are not as easily resettleable. What the UNHCR will probably be able to do all the time is to take a goodly number . . . a goodly number of the Cambodian may be resettleable, certainly some of the Meo—those who had achieved a level of education which would permit them to be absorbed in foreign cultures readily."[26] U.S. officials and news media reinforced this prejudice throughout the 1980s and 1990s. In 1987, Senator Alan Simpson (R-WY), who was the ranking minority member of the Senate Committee on Immigration and Refugee Affairs, went on a tirade in front of Congress in which he chided "pressure groups" for asking the United

States to take in more Southeast Asian refugees. Simpson singled out and deni-grated Hmong refugees as "the most indigestible group within our society."[27] In 1990, the *New York Times* openly characterized Hmong as "the most primitive refugee group in America."[28] The claim of Hmong's primitiveness, besides serv-ing as a convenient excuse for barring Hmong refugees from the United States, perpetuated the prejudices and nativist sentiments that some segments of the American public and some in the U.S. Congress held against Southeast Asian refugees and immigrants more generally (Hein 1993, 39–40).

In the 1970s and 1980s, the U.S. English-language media and official docu-ments frequently referred to Hmong in Laos or Hmong refugees as a "Laotian hill tribe" or "Hmong tribe."[29] One Associated Press article, for example, referred to a Hmong refugee family in Iowa as "members of the Hmong tribe, a relatively primitive group that roamed the hills of northern Laos."[30] As some scholars have pointed out, the term "tribe" is closely associated with the rise of European colo-nialism and its racist ideology (Lobban and Fluehr-Lobban 1976). Prior to the European colonial conquests of the 1800s, writers who wrote about African or Native American peoples used terms such as "nations," "kingdoms," and even "states" to refer to them. However, in the 1800s European colonizers and some anthropologists used the term "tribe" to refer to non-Western peoples who had been politically and militarily colonized, had been classified into "tribal" groups, and were expected to pay "tribute" to their conquerors. Moreover, the label "tribe" and the descriptor "tribal" often were imposed on subordinated African, Native American, and Asian peoples but seldom used to refer to European peoples. European colonialists often associated the people they tribalized with primitiveness, "tribalism," and savagery. Not coincidentally, racial classification systems that put Europeans at the apex of their schemes also emerged during this historical period (Lobban and Fluehr-Lobban 1976).

Throughout the 1980s, the English-language media as well as U.S. officials perpetuated the U.S. portrayal of Hmong as primitive and one of the least assim-ilated immigrant groups.[31] For example, Phillip Hawkes, who directed the U.S. Office of Refugee Resettlement from 1981 to 1986, referred to "Hmong, the Mien, the Lo Men, and others" as "agricultural, pre-literate, almost pre-technological people" (U.S. Congress 1983, 67). In the 1990s and 2000s, news media, books, and films continued to portray Hmong Americans negatively. In 1994, an article in the *Atlantic Monthly* depicted them as "nomadic Hmong mountain tribes of Laos" and repeatedly cast their immigration to Wausau, Wisconsin, as a relent-less, unstoppable flow.[32] The same article portrayed Hmong Americans as an economic threat to "native-born taxpayers," as "organized gangs," and as an unas-similated people who threatened the predominantly White community, their institutions, and their middle-class American Dream. Anne Fadiman's 1997 book, *The Spirit Catches You and You Fall Down*, reinforced this image of Hmong as exotic and unassimilable people (Chiu 2004–2005).

It was through the combined strategic efforts of a number of well-positioned U.S. institutional actors sympathetic to Hmong refugees' plight that the first substantial group of about eleven thousand Lao and Hmong refugees was able to immigrate to the United States in the spring of 1976 under the Expanded Parole Program. As Thompson (2010) describes in detail, Mac Thompson, John Tucker, Lionel Rosenblatt, and CIA officer Jerry Daniels worked with a dozen former Peace Corps volunteers in Udorn, Thailand, to screen thousands of Hmong refugees who would be potential parolees. Lionel Rosenblatt, a Vietnam veteran and Foreign Service Officer within the U.S. State Department, worked with his contacts within Washington, especially Julia Taft, who was head of the White House's Interagency Task Force for Indochinese Refugees, and Shepard Low in the State Department's Office of Refugee and Migration Affairs. The State Department, in turn, eventually convinced the House Judiciary Committee in Congress to give its approval to the U.S. attorney general to use his authority to admit the eleven thousand parolees (Thompson 2010, 100–112).

Nevertheless, by the mid- to late 1970s, sixty to eighty thousand displaced Hmong refugees were still stranded in Thai refugee camps. Most of these refugees eventually found their way to Western countries over the next thirty years. However, many Hmong families, out of fear and uncertainty or because of the mediated desire to return to Laos, chose not to apply for resettlement in the West (Hafner 1985). Hmong and other Laotian refugees who remained in Thailand were given no legal right or channel to apply for Thai citizenship. As they lingered in great uncertainty, many refugees also experienced forced repatriation.

Between 1989 and 1996, tens of thousands of Laotian refugees were repatriated under a multilateral policy known as the Comprehensive Plan of Action for Indochinese Refugees (CPA; Robinson 2004). Established in June 1989 with the blessing of the UNHCR and seventy governments, including the United States (Robinson 2004, 320), the CPA was essentially a refugee screening program plus a repatriation program designed to rid first-asylum countries such as Thailand of refugees by the end of 1995. According to the UNHCR (1996), between 1989 and 1996, "The CPA facilitated the recognition and subsequent resettlement of over 74,000 Vietnamese refugees, and supported the repatriation to their country of origin and subsequent reintegration of over 88,000 Vietnamese who did not fulfill internationally recognized refugee criteria. The CPA also facilitated the resettlement of some 51,000 Lao and supported the voluntary repatriation and reintegration in their country of origin of some 22,400 Lao, most of whom were recognized as prima facie refugees." In short, the CPA effectively prevented the immigration of at least 110,400 Vietnamese and Lao who fled their former countries but were denied refugee status and subsequently repatriated.

Reflective of the Royal Thai government's and the Lao PDR's improved relations, in 1989–1990 Thailand, the Lao PDR, and the UNHCR established a policy known as the Luang Prabang Tripartite Agreement to repatriate Laotian refugees from Thailand to the Lao PDR (Rhie 1994). Between 1990 and 1994, the U.S. government, under the Bush and Clinton administrations, contributed about $18 million to support the repatriation of Laotian refugees under this Tripartite Agreement (Quincy 2000, 469). In effect, the Tripartite Agreement and the CPA functioned to control Laotian refugees' movements and international migration. The Royal Thai government began closing refugee camps in the early 1990s and forced Hmong refugees to relocate from one camp to another (Tapp 2005, 107). Throughout the 1990s and 2000s, Thailand also repatriated thousands of Lao and Hmong individuals and families that it deemed "illegal immigrants" (Jacobs 1996; Médecins Sans Frontières 2009).[33] It placed Hmong refugees who were unwilling to return "voluntarily" into detention camps, such as the Sikiew detention center in Nakhon Ratchasima province and the Nong Saeng detention center in Nakhom Phanom province.[34] Hmong refugees in Thailand and their compatriots in the United States could do little to stop the forced repatriation because the repatriation program was jointly supported by the UNHCR, the United States, Thailand, and Lao PDR (Jacobs 1996).

IMMIGRATION TO THE UNITED STATES

Despite the various overt and covert political obstacles to their international migration, at least 1.75 million Cambodians, Laotians, and Vietnamese refugees managed to gain entry to other Eastern or Western countries between 1975 and 1989. More than three-fourths of the 1.75 million immigrated to the United States, Canada, Australia, and France. But China, Hong Kong, and Japan also took in 16 percent. The rest of Western Europe took in less than 5 percent (Hein 1993, 2).[35] In 1975 alone, about 125,000 Vietnamese, 4,600 Cambodian, and 800 Laotian refugees arrived in the United States. Over the next seventeen years, an average of 56,200 Southeast Asian refugees would arrive each year, such that between 1975 and 1992, over a million (1,085,612) Southeast Asian refugees, including Amerasians from Vietnam, had arrived in the United States. Of this, at least 148,000 were Cambodian, 223,000 were Laotian, and 585,000 were Vietnamese refugees (Nguyen 1995, 319–320). The arrival of Southeast Asian refugees made them the largest refugee population in the United States.

Hmong and other ethnic minority refugees from Laos immigrated to the United States at different times. Between late 1975 and May 1983, 63,100 Hmong, Iu Mien, Lua, and Kmhmu refugees resettled in the United States (Literacy and Language Program, Southeast Asian Refugee Studies Project and Lao Family Community 1985). Of this number, about 50,000 were Hmong refugees (Dunnigan et al. 1996, 197). In the following decade, between 1984 and 1994, 60,700 Hmong, Iu Mien, Lua, and Kmhmu refugees resettled in the United States. Altogether, 115,102 Hmong, Iu Mien, Lua, and Kmhmu refugees had arrived in the United States by 1994 (Dunnigan et al. 1996). Between 1996 and 2004, however, the United States admitted far fewer refugees from Laos than it had in previous decades. The most recent and perhaps final group of Hmong refugees to come to the United States arrived between 2004 and 2005. This group had been living in and around a Buddhist temple, Wat Thamkrabok, Thailand, since the closing of Thai refugee camps in the early 1990s. From 2004 to 2005, about 14,500 Hmong refugees arrived in the United States (Jefferys 2006).

ADJUSTMENT OF LEGAL STATUS

On October 28, 1977, the U.S. Congress passed the Adjustment of Status of Indochina Refugees Act (Public Law 95–145), which allowed refugees from Vietnam, Laos, or Cambodia who had been in the United States for at least two years and who met other criteria under that law to become lawful permanent residents. Table 2.1 presents data on the number of Southeast refugees and asylees who were granted lawful permanent resident status between 1971 and 1996. Most of the refugees from Cambodia (89 percent) and Laos (72 percent) and half of Vietnamese were granted permanent resident status during the 1981 to 1990 decade. Many children of Southeast Asian refugees were born in Thailand; however, we do not have accurate data on how many of these children were of Lao, Hmong, Cambodian, Vietnamese, or some other ethnic background. In any case, the data show that most (60 percent) refugees born in Thailand also become lawful permanent residents between 1981 and 1990. Provided that they do not commit any crimes that would subject them to deportation, those with permanent resident status have the right to live permanently in the United States. They also have the right to work in the United States and be protected by all U.S. laws. Lawful permanent residents are allowed to travel outside of the country and keep their status as long as they are not absent for longer than a year and may return to the United States as long as they have a proper reentry permit. They are, however, unable to vote—a right among others that is reserved for U.S. citizens.

TABLE 2.1   Number and Percentage of Refugees and Asylees Granted Lawful Permanent Status by Country of Birth and Decade

	1971–1980		1981–1990		1991–1996		1971–1996
	Number	Percentage	Number	Percentage	Number	Percentage	Total
Cambodia	7,739	6.1	114,064	89.2	6,088	4.8	127,891
Laos	21,690	10.9	142,964	72.1	33,701	17.0	198,355
Thailand	1,241	2.4	30,259	59.5	19,323	38.0	50,823
Vietnam	150,266	23.3	324,453	50.4	169,569	26.3	644,288

SOURCE: U.S. Department of Justice, 1996 Statistical Yearbook of the Immigration and Naturalization Service.

RACIALIZATION

Although obtaining legal status such as U.S. citizenship in theory gives all persons with this status the same rights and benefits, in practice how people are racialized matters a great deal for whether and how much they will actually be able to access the rights and benefits accorded to them by law (Feagin 2006). Indeed, throughout most of U.S. history, White racial status was a precondition for groups' access to citizenship in the United States (Masuoka and Junn 2013; Molina 2010; Ngai 2004). Especially in a racially unequal society like the United States, racialization remains one of the most powerful ways through which dominant groups and institutions structure immigrants' access to rights and resources and their capacity to make claims on the political system. How a particular immigrant group is racially defined can provide it with greater or lesser political legitimacy and privilege. Racialization can also affect whether a newcomer group is seen as a group that "belongs" "here"—that is, belongs to the "imagined political community" (Anderson 1983). Immigrants racialized as "White" are granted greater legitimacy and privileges. On the other hand, those racialized as other than White are not afforded the same legitimacy or privilege.

Since the 1970s, Hmong have adopted the anglicized term "Hmong" as their preferred ethnonym to the derogatory label "Meo," which had been imposed on them by the French and others since the late 1800s (Lemoine 2008). When Hmong refugees arrived in the United States in the mid-1970s and early 1980s, most identified themselves as Laotian by national origin and Hmong by ethnicity. Very few Hmong identified themselves as "Asian," in part because many had not yet become familiar with who Asians are or where Asians are positioned vis-à-vis other racialized categories within America's racial structure.

In the aftermath of the American-Vietnam War, the U.S. racial state labeled all refugees from Vietnam and Cambodia as "Indochinese" refugees, following French colonial convention. This is apparent, for example, in the title and language of the Indochina Migration and Refugee Assistance Act of 1975. When significant numbers of Hmong and Laotian refugees from Laos arrived in the late 1970s and early 1980s, they were lumped into the Indochinese category and racialized as a subtype of Asians. By the decennial census of 1980, the United States explicitly identified Vietnamese as a subgroup of the "Asian or Pacific Islander" "racial group" (U.S. Bureau of the Census 1983). By the 1990 census, Cambodians, Hmong, and Laotians were explicitly identified as subgroups within the Asian or Pacific Islander racial category (U.S. Bureau of the Census 1993a). Since then, the U.S. Census Bureau has continued to categorize Hmong as "Asians." Racialized as Asians, Hmong and other Southeast Asian refugees are vulnerable to the U.S. practice of "racial triangulation"—that is, positioning Asian Americans between Whites and Blacks on the racial hierarchy and casting them as foreigners relative to Whites and Blacks, who are often presumed to be "natives" (Kim

1999). This practice of treating Asians as perpetual foreigners is linked to the racial state's long history of exclusion and discrimination against Asian immigrants (Ngai 1998; Tuan 1998).

POLITICAL NARRATIVES AND REPERTOIRES OF CONTENTION

Far from arriving as "blank slates," Hmong refugees came with individual stories as well as collective political narratives—that is, the common stories that people within a group tell about people, events, and unanticipated crises or troubles. These common stories become discursive resources in social movements to the extent that social movement actors are able to use them to effectively construct collective action frames, such as the military service frame (see subsequent chapters). Hmong refugees also arrived with certain repertoires of contention or knowledge of various kinds of collective action, including protest, which they can adapt and use to oppose decisions or conditions that they consider unjust or threatening.

Hmong refugees are no strangers to social movements and armed conflicts. Nor are they strangers to using various means to make claims that bear on the interests of different individuals, groups, and governments. Most Hmong refugees from Laos had firsthand experience with war—specifically, the armed conflicts between the United States and Royal Lao governments on one hand, and the Pathet Lao nationalist faction and North Vietnamese government on the other. Many were direct, albeit seldom voluntary participants in these violent conflicts for years if not a decade or longer. After the Secret War officially ended, small segments within the displaced Hmong refugee population turned to resistance movements (Lee 2000). The circumstances and events of war and displacement exposed Hmong soldiers and former refugees to various routines and forms of political claims making. These include ways of constructing political identities, forming alliances, producing, distributing, and receiving political propaganda, holding meetings, recruiting and organizing people, rewarding loyalty and punishing disloyalty, mobilizing resources, collecting and intercepting intelligence data, interpreting complex sets of political opportunities and constraints, making demands, protesting, putting direct pressures on government officials, using criticism against governments, using violence against violence, taking power by force, adjusting to failures and unforeseen contingencies, and so on and so forth. Although some of these methods of contention are specific to Hmong's premigration contexts or the set of relationships in those contexts, some of them are not limited to these contexts and can be employable across many other contexts by a variety of actors against a variety of targets. Scholars have called these transferable repertoires of contention "modular" repertoires and recognize that all repertoires vary in their degrees of transferability across different contentious contexts (Tarrow 1993; Wada 2012).

Hmong's experiences with the Secret War in Laos exposed many of their leaders and followers to tactics of recruitment, resource mobilization, and collective action. Tactics of recruitment included the use of political propaganda, often communicated by word of mouth but also by public radio channels, to persuade people to choose and support one side of the war. But Hmong former military leaders are also familiar with the use of positive incentives as a way to recruit Hmong soldiers in villages and regions throughout northern Laos, such as using U.S. CIA money to air-drop rice for Hmong and to build schools in remote Hmong villages. When persuasion failed, some leaders used coercion and punishment to compel people to join political factions and to fight. Throughout the Secret War, Hmong military and civilian leaders were preoccupied with the mobilization of various kinds of resources, from money to weaponry and from ammunition to human labor, to try to sustain the CIA secret army's war efforts. Hmong former military leaders also relied on Hmong's preexisting social structure, which comprises clans, lineages, and families, as a way to more efficiently recruit Hmong soldiers into the CIA secret army. They took advantage of the reciprocal obligations of trust and collective responsibility commonly found among members of the same Hmong clan or lineage to try to control recruits and guard against disloyalty. All these experiences compose Hmong's repertoires of contention, providing them with knowledge of a wide range of collective actions that they can adapt and deploy to try to effect or stop social change.

Moreover, Hmong's shared experience of the Secret War, their losses in that war, and their subsequent displacement strengthened their sense of ethnic group identity. Hmong refugees' mistreatment by the Laotian and Thai governments and their betrayal by the U.S. government further solidified their sense of group identity. To be sure, Hmong had always had an unequal asymmetric relationship with the U.S. political system. Until their arrival as refugees in 1976, Hmong had interacted with the U.S. political system mostly indirectly, via the CIA or USAID. Nevertheless, Hmong's interactions with officials and agents of the CIA, USAID, and their subsidiaries exposed some of the multilingual and more politically connected segments of Hmong society to certain U.S. political thinking and actions, especially covert actions.

As we will analyze in later chapters, when Hmong interact with the U.S. political system, they often draw on their collective political narratives of the Secret War and the U.S. government's betrayal of them in that war. Like the few honest Americans who acknowledge that "the Hmong were tools of the United States in a war perceived to be against a monolithic, international communist conspiracy to take over the world" (Thompson 2010, 47), Hmong former refugees recognize U.S. hypocrisy and its tendency to selectively forget its own and other people's histories. Hmong former refugees and increasingly their children draw on their collective political narratives not simply as a social movement tactic but also as a way to challenge U.S. historical amnesia. As we will also see, along with their strategic framing of claims, Hmong also often construct themselves as Hmong, refugees, American allies, or a combination of these depending on the concrete political situation they face.

3 · CAMPAIGN FOR JUSTICE

Under the U.S. Refugee Act of 1980, refugees were eligible to apply for lawful permanent resident status after they had been in the United States for at least one year. By 1988, of the refugees who arrived between 1975 and 1977, 82 percent of Vietnamese (about 432,300), 80 percent of Laotians including Hmong (142,800), and 79 percent of Cambodians (111,400) had become permanent residents (Jasso and Rosenzweig 1990, 342). As lawful permanent residents, eligible Southeast Asian former refugees received time-limited cash and medical assistance, such as Aid to Families with Dependent Children (AFDC) and Medicaid. Many also received social services in the form of English-language training and employment services (Haines 1996, 19–21).

However, in August 1996 the U.S. Congress passed and President Clinton signed the Personal Responsibility and Work Opportunity Reconciliation Act (also known as the Welfare Reform Act). The Welfare Reform Act, among other things, replaced the AFDC program with a downgraded program called Temporary Assistance for Needy Families (TANF). Under welfare reform, recipients are required to participate in work or work-related activities as a condition of receiving aid, and their eligibility for aid is capped at five years over their lifetime (Singer 2004). Unless they were already U.S. citizens, most legal immigrants became ineligible to receive food stamps and SSI (Parrott, Kennedy, and Scott 1998; U.S. Department of Agriculture 2003). Only three categories of noncitizens were exempted from the cuts: (1) recent refugees and asylees within their first seven years in the United States, (2) immigrants who could show documentation of having worked forty quarters (about ten years) in the United States, and (3) immigrants who had served in the U.S. Armed Forces (Singer 2004). In 1997, at least 935,000 low-income legal immigrants in the United States lost their food stamps, representing 52 percent of the 1.8 million legal immigrants who received food stamps in 1995 (Cook 1998, 219). In December 1996 there were about 725,000 recipients of SSI who entered the program as noncitizens. Of these, approximately three-fourths were lawful permanent residents, while the rest were refugees and asylees who had not yet obtained lawful permanent residency. The Social Security Administration (SSA) estimated that only one-quarter of the lawful permanent residents, approximately 135,000, would meet one of the three eligibility criteria to continue receiving SSI benefits (Chesser 1997). This meant that over 400,000 noncitizens were expected to lose their only source of income.

In the early 1990s, about two-thirds of all Southeast Asian households received some form of public assistance, compared to 10 percent of Americans who received public assistance (Ong and Blumenberg 1994).[1] Hmong former refugees were especially vulnerable. In 1989, about 62 percent of Hmong families lived in poverty, and their per capita income, in 1989 dollars, was $2,692—the lowest income of any Asian American group (U.S. Bureau of the Census 1993b). In 1990, about 65 percent of Hmong were foreign-born, while 35 percent of them were U.S.-born. Among the Hmong foreign-born, 59 percent were noncitizens and only 6 percent were naturalized citizens (U.S. Bureau of the Census 1993a).

Along with other immigrants, Hmong refugees and their families confronted the loss of public benefits in the wake of welfare reform. In California alone, as many as twenty thousand Hmong were about to lose their food stamps.[2] Thousands of elderly and disabled Hmong throughout the United States were about to lose their only form of income, SSI. How did Hmong respond to this political threat? Why did Hmong social actors break ranks from the broader immigrant category to pursue their own settlement with the U.S. government? And how do their strategic choices and processes of group identity construction illuminate the more general processes of racialized immigrant political incorporation? To answer these questions, I draw on the Strategic Ethnic Collective Action (SECA) model of political incorporation, discussed in chapter 1, to examine the collective mobilization of Hmong as they fought to have their public benefits restored. Specifically, I examine how Hmong resisted racialization by strategically positioning themselves relative to other groups and how they constructed and deployed particular group identities as part of their political claims making. I also examine the responses of the state to Hmong's collective mobilization, including how the state racialized Hmong as it granted them limited policy concession.

I argue that during their interactions with the U.S. political system and in their attempt to influence public policy, Hmong made strategic choices such as mobilizing ethnic organizational networks, utilizing institutional and state allies, and framing their struggle in a way that distinguished their group identity and claims from those of other immigrant groups. Although they received significant support from other immigrant groups, Hmong ultimately broke ranks with other immigrants to mobilize a group identity that elevated their political standing and facilitated their capacity to engage in sustained claims making. In the process, Hmong obtained tangible policy benefits. However, in granting these benefits, the state redefined Hmong as tribal aliens, undermining their political standing and perpetuating the marginalization of Hmong as foreigners in the U.S. racial structure.

IMMIGRANT MOBILIZATION AND STRATEGIC CHOICES

Past research on immigrant political incorporation highlights the roles of resources and political opportunity structures in shaping political incorporation (Bloemraad 2006; Ireland 1994; Koopmans 2004). Browning, Marshall, and Tabb (1984) argue that a group's organization and resources affect its mobilization capacity and strategic choices (e.g., between protest and electoral strategies) and their actions generate political incorporation, which in turn affects policies. Hochschild and Mollenkopf (2009b, 16) build on this model but stress that states are not always receptive, that incorporation may fail, that states may engage in acts of exclusion of immigrants, and that the incorporation process involves feedbacks and contests over time.

In struggling for incorporation, individuals and groups make choices between sets of actions given the dilemmas and structural constraints they confront in concrete political circumstances (Jasper 2004). A growing literature examines the agency and strategic calculations of immigrant groups as they confront the U.S. political system and make choices about how to position themselves and whom to ally with during political struggles (Kim 2003; Reese 2011; Rogers 2006; Wong 2017). Immigrants strategically construct group identities, sometimes positioning themselves as members of larger racial categories and other times as unique ethnic groups. For example, Greer (2013) finds that Afro-Caribbean and African immigrants maintained their specific ethnic identities to differentiate themselves from the larger and more stigmatized "Black" racial category even as they adopted political strategies, collective action tactics, and policy positions similar to those of Blacks. Research also has found that immigrants' political choices, including their choices of group identity, are shaped by their premigration experiences and ongoing social ties to their former homelands (Rogers 2006; Torres 1999).

The present work adds two important considerations not acknowledged by prior authors. First, although scholars such as Hochschild et al. (2013, 16) recognize that individuals' and groups' capacity to make sustained claims on the political system is partly a function of their political standing in the polity, research has paid relatively less attention to how more recent immigrant groups, in response to perceived political threats or dilemmas, seek to alter their political standing within the political system. My study builds on the small but growing body of research that examines how some immigrants alter their political standing by strategically constructing group-specific identities and framing claims of deservingness (Fujiwara 2005; Patler 2018; Yukich 2013). Although Fujiwara (2005), Yukich (2013), and Patler (2018) offer important insights into how some economically or legally vulnerable immigrants were able to alter their political standing through strategic framing, their studies are limited in two ways. First, we know little about how other immigrant groups such as Hmong former refugees, who have a unique historical relationship with the U.S. government and experienced a unique set of conditions prior to their immigration, may be able to alter their political standing and make claims on the political system. Second, they pay little attention to the ways that the state can also make decisions to undermine groups' political standing even as it grants them policy concessions. In this study, I show how Hmong immigrants who were made ineligible for public benefits under welfare reforms worked to elevate their political standing by constructing particular group identities and using novel tactics of protest, which facilitated their ability to make sustained claims on the polity. I also show how the state, even as it granted Hmong tangible benefits, engaged in othering and subtle racialization practices that undermined Hmong's political standing. By taking account of both Hmong movement actors' agency and the state's agency in shaping political outcomes, my study contributes to a fuller understanding of the dynamic interactive process of immigrant political incorporation.

Second, although existing theories of political incorporation tend to take "groups" as already-defined and fixed, social movement research recognizes that collective identity formation occurs through struggles in historical and institutional contexts (Okamoto 2014; Oliver 2017; Polletta and Jasper 2001). The present study analyzes how Hmong activists strategically positioned themselves in order to get their interests represented in national policy. Hmong movement actors worked closely with a panethnic Asian American legal organization, and one might think that they would adopt an Asian American political identity. However, they did not. Hmong movement actors also participated in multiracial immigrant rights organizing and demonstrations but did not adopt an immigrant identity either. Instead, Hmong eventually lobbied for benefits eligibility as Hmong and specifically as a U.S. military ally. By showing how Hmong positioned themselves alongside other groups of actors and how they resisted racialization to construct particular nonracial political identities (e.g., military ally) to further their agenda, my study contributes to an understanding of how Hmong political actors negotiate racial and ethnic identities as they attempt to increase the effectiveness of their political lobbying.

HMONG'S MOBILIZATION FOR BENEFITS RESTORATION

In 1996–1997, Hmong in the United States mobilized to resist welfare cuts to legal immigrants. They worked in alliance with and received substantial support from pan-Asian and other ethnic organizations. But they also mobilized to be recognized as different from other immigrant and refugee groups based on their military service to the United States. In the process, they experienced both incorporation and disincorporation as they simultaneously gained benefits and ended up being racialized by the state as a "tribe" and a foreign other.

Ethnic Communities, Organizational Networks, and Political Alliance Mobilization

An effective strategy through which immigrant groups within local contexts can gain access into the upper echelons of the U.S. political system is to forge alliances with more established organizations that have the political experience to recognize and facilitate possible access points into the political system. This, in turn, depends on both the formation of an ethnic community that can support mobilization and proximity to established groups that can serve as allies. Hmong's access to a network of organizations was made possible by their institutionally developed ethnic communities and geographic proximity to well-established Asian American communities.

Recall that Hmong refugees began resettling in California's Central Valley starting in the spring of 1976 (see chapter 1). Although the U.S. government initially dispersed Southeast Asian refugees around the country, Hmong preferred to live near other Hmong and migrated toward two population concentrations, one in the Central Valley of California and the other in Minnesota and Wisconsin. By 1990, the city of Fresno was home to 19,400 Hmong residents—the largest Hmong concentration in the United States at that time. Between 1990 and 2000, Hmong communities grew rapidly in Fresno as well as other cities of the Central Valley, including Sacramento and Chico. Whereas in the 1980s the Hmong of Chico numbered 300 to 400, by 1990 their community had grown to about 1,600, or 4 percent of the city's population (Moon 2003, 152). The Hmong community continued to grow throughout the 1990s such that by 2000 there were at least 2,887 Hmong persons in Chico (Pfeifer et al. 2012).

The formation of Hmong communities both sustains Hmong's clan- and lineage-based social structure and gives rise to formal ethnic organizations such as the ones that participated in Hmong's movement for benefits restoration. The presence of significant Hmong in an area forms the basis for social movement recruitment and collective action. Especially because a majority of Hmong saw welfare reform as a threat to their immediate and long-term well-being, Hmong of various clans and lineages came together to work toward a common goal. Existing organizations within the ethnic community that had never previously worked together, such as the Chico Hmong Advisory Council and the Lao Veterans of America, consulted with one another about welfare reform issues and worked together to create an ad hoc social movement organization that mobilized Hmong in collective action.[3] In the absence of established ethnic communities, these interorganizational collaborations and the significant social movement constituency that emerged from it would have been extremely difficult to achieve.

In response to the real and perceived threats of welfare reforms, Hmong social actors mobilized a network of organizations through a stepwise process of

TABLE 3.1   Hmong's Network of Organizations during Welfare Reforms

Name	Type of organization	Headquarters
Asian Law Caucus (ALC)	Legal aid	San Francisco
Central California Legal Services (CCLS) Organization	Legal aid	Fresno, CA
Chico Hmong Advisory Council (CHAC)	Ethnic/immigrant	Chico, CA
Hmong Student Association (HSA)	College students	Chico, CA
Lao Family Community	Ethnic/immigrant	Sacramento, CA
Lao Hmong American Coalition	Veterans	Sacramento, CA
Lao Veterans of America (LVA)	Veterans	Fresno, CA
National Asian Pacific American Legal Consortium (NAPALC)	Advocacy	Washington, DC
Southeast Asian American Partnership of Butte County	Ethnic/immigrant	Chico, CA
Statewide Lao/Hmong Coalition (Lao/Hmong Coalition)	Social movement organization	Chico, CA

interorganizational and interethnic coalition building. These organizations included ethnic community organizations, student organizations, veteran organizations, and pan-Asian legal aid organizations, which are listed in table 3.1. Five organizations that played important roles demonstrate the range of organizational forms.

The Chico Hmong Advisory Council (CHAC) was formed in the early 1990s by Hmong professionals and clan leaders to address social issues that affect the growing Hmong community of Chico. Its board of directors was composed of delegates from each of the major Hmong clans in Chico. In 1994, several Hmong students formed the Hmong Student Association (HSA) at California State University, Chico, a diverse campus that enrolled several dozen Hmong students. CHAC and HSA were the first organizations within the Hmong American community to respond to the threat posed by welfare reform by sending a joint written critique of the act and a list of demands to California's governor Pete Wilson in November 1996.[4] Soon after the act was passed, members of HSA worked "a lot behind the scenes"[5] gathering and translating documents and helping non-English-speaking Hmong adults write letters protesting welfare reforms, while the CHAC mobilized the Hmong communities of Northern California to take part in several rallies against welfare reforms.

The Lao Veterans of America (LVA), founded in 1990 and still functioning, is the largest Laotian Hmong Veterans organization in the United States. Headquartered in Fresno, California, LVA has twenty-four state chapters throughout the United States as well as a Washington, DC, office. Despite its name, LVA's membership of about fifty-five thousand is mostly ethnic Hmong veterans rather than ethnic Lao veterans. LVA was experienced in rallying Hmong veterans, engaging with government officials, and representing Hmong veterans regarding their past military service to the United States. LVA lobbies the U.S. government on issues pertaining to veterans, domestic and nondomestic problems, and humanitarian crises.[6]

Members of CHAC, HSA, and LVA collaborated to form a new social movement organization called the California Statewide Lao/Hmong Coalition.[7] This social movement organization, in turn, not only helped to coordinate Hmong protests but also forged the crucial alliance with an established pan-Asian legal aid and civil rights organization, the Asian Law Caucus (ALC), to propel Hmong's campaign for benefit restoration.

The existence of well-established Asian American organizations in California and an interest convergence between some organizations' missions and Hmong's cause created the conditions that enabled Hmong social movement actors to form alliances with an established pan-Asian organization such as ALC. Based in San Francisco, ALC was founded in 1972 as a nonprofit legal aid and civil rights organization to serve Asian-Pacific Americans. ALC has a lobbying firm in Washington, DC,—the National Asian Pacific American Legal Consortium (NAPALC)—which it relied on to lobby the White House and Congress on Hmong's behalf. As a political law firm, ALC has a long history of both providing legal assistance to and serving as an educator and organizer for Asian-Pacific American communities in a number of areas including housing and civil rights (Hwang 2002). The passage of the Welfare Reform Act posed a grave threat to Asian-Pacific Americans' economic and social well-being. ALC recognized this threat and responded by prioritizing issues related to welfare and immigration law while suspending other issues such as hate crimes and affirmative action (Hwang 2002, 97).

When the Lao/Hmong Coalition reached out to ALC for information and advice on welfare reform, ALC agreed to a meeting in Marysville, California, between staff of its office and the Hmong community of Northern California. That initial meeting established a common interest between them: given Hmong's compelling story about their military service and given their show of willingness to engage in collective action, ALC saw an opportunity to help mobilize the Hmong as plaintiffs in a class-action litigation that could shape public opinion about the larger issue of immigrant contributions to America (Hwang 2002, 102). To further Hmong's campaign, ALC collaborated with an established nonprofit law firm, the Central California Legal Services Organization, to pursue litigation in federal court. When that did not work, ALC relied on its lobbying firm, NAPALC, to hire another well-respected law firm in Washington to issue a legal memorandum based on the sense of Congress in support of Hmong's cause.

At the same time, Hmong activists from California, Minnesota, and Wisconsin urged their congressional representatives, such as U.S. representatives Bruce Vento (D-MN) and Calvin Dooley (D-CA) and U.S. senators Paul Wellstone (D-MN) and Herb Kohl (D-WI), to fight for benefit restoration for Hmong veterans. It was through this stepwise process of collaborating with institutional and state allies that vulnerable immigrant groups such as the Hmong of California's Central Valley were able to have their voices heard within the U.S. Congress, the White House, and the U.S. Department of Agriculture.

Major Events and Interactions

Figure 3.1 shows the major events and interactions that took place during Hmong's mobilization for benefit restoration between 1996 and 1998. The top row identifies actions by the state, segments of the state, or state actors, while the bottom row represents strategic actions by Hmong social movement actors, social movement organizations, or their institutional allies. As alluded to above, the Welfare Reform Act was enacted into law on August 22, 1996. Although the law was not going to be implemented until about August 1997, notification letters from government agencies such as SSA started going out almost immediately to recipients of benefits and continued to be sent out throughout the rest of 1996 and 1997. It was through these official notices that most Hmong men and women first learned about the "redetermination" of their benefits, which, for noncitizens, meant the impending termination of their benefits, unless they could become U.S. citizens before the law was implemented. Given the welfare reform changes, this policy posed a serious threat to the basic survival of millions of immigrants and their families. For Hmong former refugees, this act was not just an economic threat but also a political threat. As a Hmong community member makes clear, "The Hmong feel a great sense of betrayal. They were recruited to fight by the CIA. They lost sons and famil[ies] in [the] war. When the Americans withdrew from Southeast Asia, they were left in the jungle to escape on their own. They blame the U.S. for leaving them behind. Here, they were just beginning to forget what happened. The cut in SSI is betraying them again."[8]

In February 1997, a delegation of mostly Hmong veterans from Fresno went to Washington to lobby the U.S. Congress. This lobbying effort was a continuation of Hmong's organized efforts—which began in the late 1980s and spanned multiple states—to try to get the U.S. government to grant language and testing accommodations to Hmong veterans seeking to become naturalized U.S. citizens (see chapter 4). But in 1997 it was also an effort aimed at finding a solution to Hmong's predicament under welfare reform. This concerted strategic effort led to the recognition of Hmong as a former ally of the U.S. military by the U.S. Congress and the Pentagon for the first time in May 1997. This public recognition, in turn, helped pave the way for the sense of Congress resolution on Hmong veterans in August 1997. This sense of Congress, in turn, created a window of opportunity for Hmong to engage in other claims-making activities.

In the following months (March and May 1997), Hmong of California's Central Valley participated in two massive immigrant rallies in protest of welfare reforms. Meanwhile, the Lao/Hmong Coalition reached out to ALC, and in the

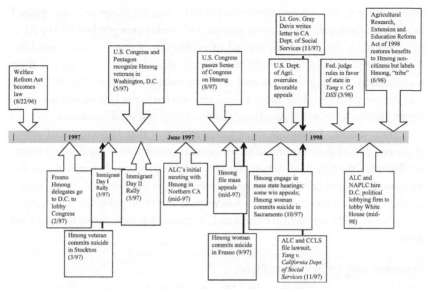

FIGURE 3.1. Timeline of Hmong's Ethnic Mobilization for Benefits Restoration, 1996–1998

summer of 1997 ALC began working with Hmong to file mass appeals for state hearings. Between March and October 1997, several Hmong older adults committed or attempted suicide after receiving notice that their SSI benefits were going to be cut. These suicides received prominent media coverage, and Hmong and their institutional allies capitalized on the visibility of Hmong suicides as part of their lobbying efforts. As a result of their sustained lobbying and mobilization, Hmong social movement actors and their state allies such as U.S. representative Bruce Vento were able to influence other members of the U.S. House of Representatives. These state allies, in turn, used the opportunity of the Agricultural Research, Extension, and Education Reform Act, which was introduced in the U.S. Senate, to carve out a compromise through a conference report (H. Rept. 105–492) that contained specific food stamp exceptions for Hmong and other select legal immigrants. Despite some opposition to the compromise, the act received majority bipartisan support, and its passage in June 1998 restored food stamps to Hmong veterans and other select groups.

ANALYSIS: ALTERNATING TACTICS, STRATEGIC POSITIONING, AND IDENTITY CONSTRUCTION

In 1996–1997, Hmong activists participated in immigrant protests and worked in alliance with and received substantial support from a pan-Asian organization as they mobilized ethnic organizations and ordinary individuals throughout the California Central Valley to resist welfare cuts to legal immigrants. But instead of emphasizing an Asian or immigrant identity, Hmong mobilized to be recognized as different from other immigrant groups. Although Hmong relied on the ALC as a "bridging" organization, instead of evoking an Asian American identity, Hmong emphasized their ethnic and military ally identities throughout their mobilization. Hmong activists and ordinary individuals drew directly on the narrative of the Secret War and their military service to the United States to construct Hmong as a former American ally deserving of special treatment.

In this section, I examine three kinds of tactics that Hmong social actors deployed during their mobilization for benefits restoration. Specifically, I examine Hmong's participation in two immigrant rights protests, their use of suicides as a nontraditional tactic, and Hmong veterans' lobbying of the U.S. Congress. As we will see, each of these tactics had varying effects on public policy owing to the different collective action frames and identities that were associated with the tactics.

Demonstrating for Immigrant Rights

On March 18, 1997, over a hundred Hmong men and women joined about two thousand other immigrants and activists at the California State Capitol to protest welfare reform by engaging in a demonstration, march and legislative visits.[9] Hmong protestors held signs that read "HMONG VETERAN DENIED FOOD STAMPS" and "I HELPED YOU IN THE VIETNAM WAR BUT NOW YOU WANT TO KILL ME" (Fujiwara 2008, 78). Besides the Northern California Coalition for Immigrant Rights, which organized the event and the CHAC, other organizations involved included Alternatives 4 Developing Change, California Federation of Labor, AFL-CIO, the Coalition for Ethnic Welfare Reform, Asian-Pacific Islanders California Action Network, California Latino Civil Rights Network, Center for Third World Organizing, the Chinese Progressive Association, and the Comite de Padres Unidos.[10] Two days after this Immigrant Day rally, California governor Pete Wilson extended food stamp benefits to legal immigrants through September 1997. This encouraged a second rally.

On May 28, 1997, the Lao/Hmong Coalition once again mobilized thousands of Hmong and Iu Mien in Northern California to participate in the Immigrant Day II rally at the California State Capitol. There they joined thousands of other immigrant protestors (Vietnamese, Chinese, Latinos, Bosnians, Russians, and Eastern Europeans) and representatives from about a hundred fifty other California organizations. The participating organizations included the Northern California Coalition for Immigrant Rights, which again organized the rally, the Network for Immigrant and Refugee Rights and Services of Santa Clara County, the California Statewide Lao/Hmong Coalition, religious groups, labor councils, and ethnic organizations.[11]

Despite the significant turnout at both immigrant rallies, the protests for legal immigrants' rights did not lead to any new policy. Although Hmong protestors held signs and Hmong activists at these rallies gave speeches that highlighted Hmong's role as American-Vietnam War veterans, the mainstream media paid little attention to Hmong's participation in the immigrant protests. It seemed that Hmong's voices were lost in the sea of cries for immigrant rights.

Suicide as a Novel Protest Option

Suicide has not historically been a common protest tactic in American society (Biggs 2013). However, suicide protest has historically been a part of Hmong's protest repertoire. A common and potent belief within traditional Hmong society has been that by killing oneself one is transmuted into a ghost that can then directly harm one's adversaries or indirectly harm them by summoning one's adversaries to attend trial and pay retribution in the Other World. Although suicide was rare compared to other protest tactics such as hunger strikes, Hmong adults were familiar with it and usually regarded it as a legitimate act of revenge and/or protest. Stories of Hmong women who committed suicide in protest of forced marriages, abusive husbands, and renegade boyfriends and who were "ultimately successful" are common. In the late 1970s and early 1980s, suicide was a common form of protest among young refugee Hmong couples who were prevented from marrying each other. Welfare reform led to a string of suicides and attempted suicides in the Hmong community of California's Central Valley and elsewhere in the United States.

Between March and October 1997, several Hmong women and men committed, attempted, or threatened to commit suicide in protest of the U.S. government and its welfare reform policy. In March 1997, Sai Chou Lor, a disabled veteran and Hmong refugee who arrived in Stockton, California, in 1995, attempted suicide after receiving notice that he would lose his SSI.[12] In September, Ye Vang, fifty-nine years old, hung herself in Fresno, California. Vang was a Hmong refugee who, in 1993, resettled in Fresno to be closer to her brother and his family. Prior to her death, Vang received SSI due to her disability. But since the passage of welfare reform, Vang had tried unsuccessfully to pass the U.S. citizenship exam, the only ticket to possibly keeping her SSI income. In October, Chia Yang, a fifty-four-year-old Hmong woman in Sacramento, California, hung herself inside her family's garage. According to news reports, Yang left cassette tapes that blamed the U.S. government for betraying Hmong and cutting her benefits.[13] She was the mother of two children and wife of Sua Chai Vue, a veteran of the Secret War in Laos. Prior to Yang's death, she received a notice from the state informing her that her SSI income of $640 a month would be cut because she was not a U.S. citizen. Earlier that year Yang had tried twice but failed to pass the English version of the U.S. citizenship test (Fujiwara 2008, 51–52). Chia Yang's last words, addressed to her family but also the world, were, "What if I lose my SSI? What if my husband and children lose their AFDC grant? If they stop my grant I'm going to die anyway. . . . I am very sorry I had to bring you to this country and leave you behind. It feels like I'm sitting in a pot of boiling water every day."[14] The anguish and anger that many Hmong elders felt toward the U.S. government are conveyed by Chong Her Lo, a sixty-seven-year-old veteran: "We thought Americans and Hmong were friends. We believed in the U.S. commitment to the Hmong, but the promise wasn't kept. Kill me instead of letting me suffer in society without help."[15] In April 1997, Chue Tou Vang, an eighty-three-year-old veteran and resident of Wisconsin, committed suicide after receiving notice that his SSI was going to be cut. According to his son, his father grew so upset that he could not talk, eat, or sleep: "He didn't tell me he wanted to kill himself. He didn't leave a note. He just was mad."[16]

The Hmong suicide protests in California and Wisconsin received prominent media coverage and public attention. For example, the New York Times, Associated Press, Los Angeles Times, Sacramento Bee, and Philadelphia Inquirer reported on Hmong suicides specifically.[17] This broad and generally sympathetic media attention helped to elicit compassion by highlighting welfare reform's tragic impact. However, despite the public attention and sympathy that the Hmong suicide protests garnered, this tactic did not immediately change the provisions of the Welfare Reform Act. They needed another kind of tactic.

Strategic Positioning and Group Identity Construction

As part of their efforts to obtain benefit restoration, Hmong constructed themselves as a former American ally. To understand why Hmong distinguished themselves from other immigrant groups, it is important to understand how Hmong defined themselves and how they perceived welfare reform as a policy. For many Hmong people, the question of who Hmong are is intricately tied to the question of why Hmong are in the United States. When asked about why he and his family immigrated to the United States, Za Chong Xiong, a sixty-two-year-old veteran who participated in both immigrant rallies, explains, "Had the Americans not come to [intervene in] our country [Laos], we would have remained in our country as our parents always have. But because the Americans came to our country and relied on us to fight [the Communists], we faced persecution and had to leave in order to survive."[18] Similarly, in a letter to California's governor Pete Wilson, Hmong representatives of Chico proclaim, "We came because we had no other way. The majority of Hmong refugees who came to the United States came not for economic reasons but for political refugee reasons. We came because of the secret war in Laos. We came to get away from war, death, and famine, which would have wiped out our people if we had remained in Laos."[19]

Throughout their mobilization for benefit restoration, Hmong drew directly on the narrative of the Secret War and their service to and sacrifice on behalf of the U.S. government to construct Hmong as a former American ally deserving of special treatment. A letter written by representatives of the Northern California Hmong community to Governor Pete Wilson just three months after the Welfare Reform Act was signed into law not only made clear Hmong's "adamant opposition" to welfare reform for "barring of SSI and food stamps to Legal Permanent Residents," but also urged the government to consider the "special circumstances inherent in the Hmong community . . . before a blanket policy is established." As the letter points out, "There are many complicated special circumstances that need to be considered with the Hmong community that may not apply to other ethnic groups." One passage clearly captures Hmong's use of the Secret War narrative to construct themselves as American allies, albeit unrecognized allies:

> We are deeply incensed at the government's blatant nonacceptance of the Lao-Hmong Special Guerrilla Units as an officially recognized arm of the United States Armed Forces. Fifteen long years of proud duty and allegiance to the United States in service during the Vietnam War has been shamefully ignored by the American people. It is as if 45,000 of our people's lives and countless numbers of casualties are seemingly invisible to American Leaders. We, too, now feel invisible, insignificant and dispensable with their official threats of cutting off vitally needed assistance—SSI, Medi-Cal, AFDC, Title XX Services and Foodstamps. Lao-Hmong Forces have not even been afforded the same privileges or federal benefits that U.S. American Veterans are given, yet, the Lao-Hmong forces bled the same as the American soldiers, died the same as the American soldiers, and equally suffered and sacrificed their fathers, mothers, brothers and sisters . . . the same as the American Soldiers. But yet many of our honorable, fine and gentle people have been unfairly induced into a poverty-stricken state because of America's unwillingness to recognize them as American Veterans and have been consequently reduced to having to accept SSI, AFDC, Food Stamps and Medi-Cal because we have no alternative in order to survive in America.[20]

Responding to the stereotype that immigrants in general are poor because they are dependent or unwilling to work, Hmong argue they were made poor by U.S. dependency on them and refusal to recognize their status as veterans.

Despite stressing their unique situation, Hmong activists were well aware of the stereotype of immigrants as "welfare freeloaders," and they protested this stereotype and defended the rights of documented immigrants. This position is clearly seen in an impassioned speech that Yee Xiong, an activist, delivered during the March 1997 immigrant protest:

> The distinction between citizen and non-citizen, refugee and other legal immigrant rights is arbitrary and unfair. Hmong refugees and all legal immigrants are subject to the same tax structure as are citizens, including payroll, sales, and property/real estate taxes. Should the draft be reinstated, our young men can be and have been drafted to defend the U.S. . . . . We deserve the same rights as

American born people because we have given just as much, if not more. . . . This country's Constitution talks about "we, the people . . ." not "we the citizens. . . ." We are here today because our people gave up our husbands, wives, and children's lives for over 200,000 American men, their families, and this country during the Vietnam War. We are not freeloaders here for a free ride on the welfare train. We take offense at the way the government of the U.S. has used us and then thrown us away, and now with the welfare reform, it is doing the same thing to us again.[21]

Besides breaking ranks from other immigrant groups, Hmong social movement activists, especially Hmong veterans, continued their lobbying efforts. Hmong veterans' sustained lobbying of the U.S. federal government was crucial in creating a political opportunity that, in turn, facilitated two sets of movement actions: first, it provided Hmong social movement actors and their institutional allies with a discursive resource with which to advance their claims for benefit restoration, and, second, it helped increase Hmong's state allies' ability to persuade the state to grant Hmong veterans specific policy concessions. Next, I discuss this lobbying effort, the political opportunity that it created, and how Hmong eventually gained food stamps restoration.

Prior to their participation in Hmong's organized protest against welfare reforms, many Hmong veterans were already experienced participants of protest and lobbying efforts. Since the mid-1980s and several years before LVA was founded, Hmong veterans had been engaged in public protests against human rights violations in the Lao PDR and lobbying the U.S. government to intervene in these problems.[22] By the early 1990s, Hmong veterans, many of whom were paying members of various chapters of the LVA, were actively lobbying their congressional representatives to introduce policies that would benefit Hmong veterans. This early effort persuaded U.S. representative Bruce Vento (D-MN) to introduce the Hmong Veterans' Naturalization Act of 1990, which was intended to provide certain language and test accommodations to Hmong veterans seeking to become naturalized U.S. citizens. When the Welfare Reform Act became law in 1996, Hmong veterans and the LVA accelerated their lobbying efforts by tackling two interrelated goals: (1) get the Hmong Veterans' Naturalization Act passed and (2) obtain benefits restoration for Hmong veterans. In both cases, they sought to get the U.S. government to recognize Hmong's military service.

In February 1997, four months before the Welfare Reform Act became effective, a delegation of Hmong veterans from Fresno traveled to Washington to lobby members of the U.S. Congress to create a benefit exception for Hmong noncitizens. There they "introduced" Congress to Hmong's history of military service and their plight in the United States.[23] This effort proved effective as it led to events between May and August 1997 that opened a crucial window of political opportunity for Hmong's movement for benefits restoration. On May 14, 1997, after months of organizing by LVA, its lobbying firm in DC (the

Center for Public Policy Analysis), and former CIA agents, about four thousand mostly Hmong veterans from California, Minnesota, Wisconsin, and elsewhere participated in a formal recognition ceremony at the Vietnam Veterans Memorial in Washington. Many of the Hmong men in attendance wore army uniforms, while the Hmong women wore traditional costumes. There, Hmong veterans were recognized for the first time by the U.S. Congress for their military service to the United States. On that day, U.S. Congress members, Pentagon officials, and former CIA officers presented 2,500 Hmong veterans with the "congressionally-authorized Vietnam Veterans National Medal."[24] A proclamation of support signed by twelve U.S. Congress members was also read.[25] The following day, May 15, a granite plaque with golden texts recognizing Hmong and Lao veterans was installed at the grounds of the Arlington National Cemetery. This positive reception by the U.S. Congress and Pentagon officials signaled the opening of a window of opportunity for Hmong and their state allies to push for greater recognition for Hmong veterans.

On August 5, 1997, at the urging of U.S. representative Bruce Vento (D-MN), the U.S. Congress passed a sense of Congress resolution whose most relevant parts read, "It is the sense of the Congress that Hmong and other Highland Lao veterans who fought on behalf of the Armed Forces of the United States during the Vietnam conflict and have lawfully been admitted to the United States for permanent residence *should be considered veterans for purposes of continuing certain welfare benefits* consistent with the exceptions provided other noncitizen veterans under the Personal Responsibility and Work Opportunity Reconciliation Act of 1996."[26] Although this sense of Congress statement did not mandate any specific concessions to Hmong veterans, it served as another political opportunity that Hmong social movement actors recognized and used to advance their mobilization efforts toward benefit restoration.

Recognizing the opportunity that the sense of Congress provided, ALC collaborated with the Central California Legal Services in Fresno to file a lawsuit against the state of California's Department of Social Services and the U.S. Department of Agriculture on behalf of a Hmong veteran, Chong Yia Yang, who had lost food stamp benefits for himself and his two foreign-born children.[27] They drew on the sense of Congress to argue that Yang's public benefits should be restored because he is a veteran. Unfortunately, the U.S. District Court ruled against Yang based on its judgment that the sense of Congress did not carry the weight of law. However, expressing sympathy for Hmong's cause, District Judge Robert E. Coyle stated, "The court must decry the inequitable treatment of a class of residents that sacrificed much to serve this nation. . . . It is the court's sincerest hopes that Congress will take steps to remedy this inequity as soon as possible" (Hwang 2002, 111–112).

The opportunity to create a remedy for Hmong came when a federal bill with strong Republican support was introduced and passed in the U.S. Senate. In

September 1997, U.S. senator Richard Lugar (R-IN) introduced the Agricultural Research, Extension, and Education Reform Act of 1997 (S. 1150), which, among other things, provided significant federal funding for agricultural research, education, and extension activities of the Agricultural Research Service within the U.S. Department of Agriculture. Originally this bill did not contain any food stamp provisions. The bill quickly passed in the Senate. However, before its passing vote, the U.S. House of Representative amended the bill (H. Rept. 105–492) to include a provision of food stamp restoration for certain disabled aliens, American Indians, elders, children, and Hmong and Highland Laotians (Title V, Sections 501–508). Because of the differences in the amended versions of the bill between the U.S. House and U.S. Senate, a committee meeting to resolve differences was ordered.

The committee meeting resulted in a Senate Conference Report (CR S. 4680) that, among other things, carved out a compromise by keeping the food stamp provisions for select legal immigrants but included new urgently needed crop insurance funding for U.S. farmers. A majority of Republicans favored the latter; it was the food stamp provision for legal immigrants that they were against. However, during open debates, several U.S. representatives and senators, including U.S. representative Cal Dooley (D-CA), U.S. senator Paul Wellstone (D-MN), and U.S. senator Herb Kohl (D-WI), who were three of Hmong's closest state allies at the time, spoke strongly in favor of the food stamp provision for legal immigrants. Several Congress members, including U.S. senator John McCain (R-AZ), made explicit references to Hmong and their military service and expressed support for the food stamp provision.[28] In the end, the compromise received overwhelming bipartisan support and the Agricultural Research, Extension, and Education Reform Act of 1998 was passed, restoring food stamps to Hmong veterans and other select legal immigrants.

In sum, Hmong operated on many levels of group identity and made strategic choices between racial and ethnic identity throughout their campaign for benefits restoration. They marched alongside other immigrant groups and utilized a pan-ethnic organization (ALC) as an institutional ally. They protested welfare reform's exclusion of all documented immigrants and the U.S. tendency to lump political refugees with economic immigrants. However, instead of positioning themselves as an immigrant or Asian group, Hmong constructed themselves as a former military ally of the United States, lobbied to obtain legitimacy for this identity, and eventually achieved legitimacy in the sense of Congress resolution. Through strategic positioning and identity construction, Hmong were able to elevate their political standing from that of an undeserving to a deserving group of immigrants.

ANALYSIS: THE DYNAMICS OF RACIALIZATION

As we have just seen, Hmong's sustained claims making for benefits restoration eventually led the U.S. Congress to approve an exemption for them under the

Agricultural Research, Extension, and Education Reform Act of 1998 (AREERA). Constructing themselves as a U.S. military ally was persuasive, in part, because this identity distinguished Hmong from other immigrant groups who were pursuing similar goals. However, just as social actors can construct and deploy particular political identities to meet the needs of their present circumstances, the state can undermine a group's political standing and curtail its political incorporation through othering and racialization practices.

AREERA restored food stamp benefits to Hmong noncitizens. Specifically, AREERA provided that any U.S. lawful permanent resident who "was a member of a Hmong or Highland Laotian tribe at the time that the tribe rendered assistance to United States personnel by taking part in a military or rescue operation during the Vietnam era beginning August 5, 1964 and ending May 7, 1975" as well as his or her spouse and unmarried children could be eligible for food stamps. As Hwang (2002, 113) points out, "This tortured language was apparently the result of intervention by the Department of Veterans Affairs, which threatened to oppose this amendment unless it could be drafted *without characterizing the Hmong as veterans.*"

By labelling Hmong as a "tribe" who merely "rendered assistance" to the United States during a very specific time frame, the racial state temporarily distinguished Hmong from other ethnic immigrant groups who, in the words of one Immigration and Naturalization Service official, "do not share the unique situation of the Hmong" (U.S. Congress 1997), but more importantly, denied to Hmong the right to be incorporated as formal veterans. This state action also reveals a subtle way by which the state can curtail a group's political incorporation: through racialization or the practice of constructing racial or racialized categories and placing subjects in these categories to delineate new group boundaries or maintain old boundaries.

As I discussed in the preceding chapter, the term "tribe" is closely associated with the rise of European colonialism and its racist ideology. This term also has a racist history in the United States. Historically, White settler colonialists applied the label "tribe" to Native Americans to convey Native Americans' purported primitiveness and savagery (Ablavsky 2018). Filipinos recruited into guerrilla units to serve the U.S. military were racialized by the U.S. empire as uncivilized "tribes" who had a suspect "tribal loyalty" (Jung 2011). In these ways, tribe as a category has been used by White Americans to create and maintain the boundary between dark-skinned subjects/others and light-skinned colonialists in much the same way that formal racial categories have been used to maintain the boundary between "non-White" and "White" categories of people. That the U.S. government used "tribe" to refer to Hmong in a federal policy without any discussion, let alone debate about the term, instead of some other more neutral term (e.g., "ethnic group," "people," "population") suggests that it still perceives Hmong as a peculiar, primitive, and potentially suspect group of people. Such stereotype undermines Hmong's political standing.

The state's othering of Hmong can also be seen in the language that it used to describe them in another federal policy that passed not too long after the AREERA became effective: the Hmong Veterans' Naturalization Act of 2000 (HVNA). Despite its title, HVNA did not automatically grant Hmong veterans citizenship. Indeed, it never recognized them as officially veterans. Instead, HVNA merely provided certain language accommodations, such as exemption from English proficiency testing, on the testing and interview portions of Hmong applicants' naturalization application process. Hmong are described in the HVNA title indirectly as "aliens who served with a special guerrilla unit operating from a base in Laos in support of the United States" and in the act's body as refugees from Laos who served in guerrilla or irregular forces in Laos in support of the United States. By explicitly referring to Hmong as "aliens" in HVNA, the state once again clearly marked them as others/foreigners in the United States.

The carefully crafted language of AREERA and HVNA was for the purpose of restricting access to the broad benefits that accrue to U.S. military veterans, that is, for carefully curtailing Hmong's political incorporation and limiting their future political claims. But embedded in some policies is also the subtle practices of othering and/or racialization that undermine Hmong's political standing. The Hmong movement actors who fought for benefit restoration or for citizenship accommodations had few, if any, choices in the final language used in these policies, and the choice of language appears primarily to have been responsive to concerns that they not be defined as U.S. veterans, a concern that may be linked to resisting similar claims from other groups, such as those who fought for the United States in the Army of the Philippines during World War II (Quisumbing King 2018).

SUMMARY AND IMPLICATIONS

As strategic actors, Hmong were moving on multiple fronts, engaging in organized protests as well as lobbying, forming alliances as well as pursuing recognition as a distinct claimant. Seeking special exemption for themselves proved to be effective in winning Hmong policy provisions; however, it also led to their racialization. My study provides important insights into the questions of how immigrant groups acquire the capacity to make sustained claims on the political system and how the state can undermine groups' political standing and curtail their political incorporation. Consistent with the expectations of the SECA model of immigrant political incorporation, my study demonstrates that immigrants' material and cultural resources, political opportunities, and group strategic choices all matter for their political incorporation. Here, I discuss two major processes that my SECA model suggests and my case study reveals: (1) the crucial role of strategic positioning and construction of group identity in immigrants' ability to elevate their political standing, and (2) the role of state othering and racialization practices in undermining immigrant groups' political standing.

My study suggests that an immigrant group's ability to elevate its political standing depends in part on how its members position themselves alongside other minority groups, how they distinguish themselves from others, and whether they are able to obtain legitimacy for their unique collective identity. As strategic actors, Hmong marched alongside and spoke in defense of other immigrant groups and allied with and utilized the ALC as an institutional resource. However, most crucially, Hmong mobilized their own set of collective actions to distinguished themselves as an ethnic group. In other words, Hmong recognized the need for and operated on many levels of race and ethnicity.

Recognizing the distinction that the government was making between deserving and undeserving groups of immigrants and aware of their existing multiple vulnerabilities in terms of nativity, racial, ethnic, social class, language, religion, veteran status, and so on, Hmong movement actors drew on the narratives of the Secret War to carve out an unusual axis of identity: military alliance with the United States. Sustained political lobbying by Hmong activists and veterans led to the formal recognition of Hmong as a U.S. ally. This legitimated identity elevated Hmong's political standing and facilitated their ability to engage in sustained claims making, which eventually led to the restoration of food stamps for Hmong. Consistent with previous research, strategic framing of identity matters for political standing (Fujiwara 2005). But my study shows that, for Hmong, racial and ethnic boundaries were more fluid than fixed as Hmong political actors were able to negotiate these boundaries, choosing between race or ethnicity to increase the effectiveness of their political lobbying.

Whereas past scholars, including Browning, Marshall, and Tabb (1984), conceptualize political incorporation as the extent to which a group's "interests" is represented in policy making, I contend that this process of contestation is not just about winning policies and resources but also about collective identity and, specifically, racialized collective identity, which affects political standing in the nation. For immigrant racial minorities, political incorporation is racialized to the extent that the state uses othering and racialization practices to position immigrants in an inferior status, limiting their ability to make future claims and perpetuating their political marginalization. Even as the U.S. Congress granted Hmong tangible policy concessions, it ensured that Hmong were not given veteran status, othered Hmong as "aliens," and racialized them as a "tribe." In doing so, Congress delimited Hmong's incorporation, reinforcing the stereotype of Hmong as foreigners and perpetuating their marginal inclusion.

The way that the U.S. Department of Veterans Affairs and Congress racialized Hmong and deliberately denied them official veteran status has strong parallels with how the U.S. government racialized Filipinos as aliens under most federal policies concerning Filipinos and, through passage of the 1946 Rescission Act, misrecognized the military service of Filipino veterans of World War II in order to deny them promised veterans' benefits (Quisumbing King 2018). Given how the state practices racialization as part of policy making, past research on immigrant political incorporation that looks only at the extent to which a group's material interest is represented in policy making overlooks the important questions of how othering and racialization operate alongside political incorporation to maintain social closure in the political system and how seemingly race-neutral policies produce racial consequences.

Recent research suggests that similar processes of strategic group identity construction, principles of alliances among groups, racialization, and so on apply to other groups, such as Latinos. For example, anti-immigrant policies such as H.R. 4437 have fostered pan-Latino solidarity between undocumented, naturalized, and U.S.-born Latinos and galvanized them in organized protests (Martinez 2008; Zepeda-Millán 2017). As they mobilized for incorporation, Latinos drew upon existing family and social networks to recruit movement participants (Getrich 2008), constructed alternative group identities to challenge the state's criminalization of "illegal immigrants" (Summers Sandoval 2008), interacted with other non-Latino minorities, and forged critical alliances with well-established networks of organizations and advocacy groups (Cordero-Guzmán et al. 2008). Latinos, too, negotiate racialization alongside the ongoing process of political incorporation (Massey and Sánchez 2010).

As they sought to incorporate themselves into the United States and obtain policies that would help sustain them, the Hmong negotiated their collective identity and defined themselves as similar to some groups and different from others, at times joining alliances for common cause and at others seeking to chart a distinctive course. In the process of negotiating for themselves a distinctive group definition and benefits, they were reracialized as alien tribal others.

Like all immigrant groups, the Hmong had a specific history, encountered a specific set of conditions, and charted a specific course of struggle for incorporation of themselves into the United States. Each immigrant group has had a distinctive trajectory, but the SECA model provides broader principles for understanding their trajectories. Immigrant groups have unique contexts of exit and experience distinctive contexts of reception that are intertwined with imposed and asserted racial-ethnic identities that shape their struggle for political incorporation into a racialized social order. Immigrant groups have individual and collective agency that (in interaction with external constraints) shape their choices about whether and how to form ethnic organizations that undergird ethnic collective action. Immigrant groups, state agents, and established residents all exert agency in the ongoing intertwined negotiations and struggles over political incorporation and racialization.

4 · BATTLE FOR
NATURALIZATION

> Today I signed H.R. 371, the Hmong Veterans' Naturalization Act of 2000.
> This legislation is a tribute to the service, courage, and sacrifice of the
> Hmong people who were our allies in Laos during the Vietnam war.... This
> law is a small step but an important one in honoring the immense sacrifices
> that the Hmong people made in supporting our efforts in Southeast Asia.
> —Excerpt from President Bill Clinton's remarks
> on his signing of this act into law

The secrecy of the Secret War has made it possible for the United States to deny knowledge of U.S. military involvement in Laos and responsibility for Hmong's deaths, forced displacements, and statelessness. Despite having recruited, used, and sacrificed tens of thousands of Hmong as a surrogate army for U.S. political interests during the American-Vietnam War, the U.S. government has never recognized Hmong veterans of the Secret War in Laos as U.S. veterans. Consequently, to this day Hmong veterans of the Secret War receive no veterans benefits of any kind.

In 1990, U.S. representative Bruce F. Vento first introduced the Hmong Veterans' Naturalization Act of 1990, which was intended to waive the English-language requirement for Hmong veterans who were applying for naturalization. However, it was not until 2000 that the Hmong Veterans' Naturalization Act (HVNA) became law. This act is significant as it granted, for a limited time, language and civic knowledge accommodations to Hmong veterans. What were the crucial factors that facilitated the passage of this law? What roles did Hmong American individuals, veteran organizations, and state allies play in this movement? In what ways did the success of this movement depend on the convergence of U.S. government and Hmong American interests? This chapter addresses these questions by examining the interactions between Hmong Americans and the state. I draw on the perspectives of Hmong social actors and official documents, including the debates during the congressional hearings on HVNA.

Social movement scholars recognize that collective action efforts need to be sustained, rather than sporadic, if they are to increase their chances of success. They also recognize the role that framing and political opportunities play in facilitating social movements. In particular, they stress that for frame alignment to occur, social actors need to engage in framing processes such as frame amplification—that is, the "idealization, embellishment, clarification, or invigoration of existing values or beliefs" (Benford and Snow 2000, 624). For political opportunities to matter, they have to be recognized (and acted on) by social actors during crucial windows (Jasper 2012). Although social movement actors' sustained collective actions and recognition of political opportunities matter to the outcomes of movements, decisions are sometimes shaped by the convergence of goal granters' interests with those of challengers (Bell 1980). Broader political contexts can shape social actors' and the state's interests.

I contend that HVNA became law primarily as a result of Hmong Americans' sustained collective actions between 1990 and 2000. However, the U.S. government's decision to grant Hmong veterans this accommodation cannot be understood without some consideration of the decision's value to the racial state especially as it is embedded in a broader international political context. For this decision had value not only to those who were concerned about the immorality in denying Hmong political membership despite their military contributions to the United States but also to policy makers who can see that a decision to grant a former surrogate army, symbolic incorporation—that is, accommodations without guarantees of actual membership—was important in at least two ways. First, by granting Hmong naturalization accommodations, the state could claim to have repaid its debt to Hmong, redeeming itself from its long history of using and betraying the Hmong (as described in chapter 1). Second, by creating the impression that it fulfilled its moral obligation to a former ally, the state could claim credit for itself as an honorable country (read trustworthy patron), indirectly justifying its past military actions and furthering its contemporary military interests around the world. As this chapter will show, in their movement for citizenship accommodations, Hmong American movement actors drew, once again, on their political narratives of the Secret War in Laos and the U.S. involvement in that war to construct a military service frame. Hmong Americans' state allies utilized this military service frame as well as amplified the notion of national honor in order to briefly remind federal policy makers about the United States' broader political-military interests in the world. The broader political context, comprising of the U.S. government's ongoing political developments and imminent military involvement in Middle Eastern Asia, persuaded it to take the task of managing national honor seriously by granting Hmong, its former military ally, limited citizenship accommodations.

LOBBYING FOR CITIZENSHIP

From some people's point of view, Hmong veterans' social movement to become naturalized U.S. citizens was directly or conveniently connected with their desire to restore public benefits cut off by welfare reform (discussed in the previous chapter). For instance, in reference to the Hmong Veterans' Naturalization Bill reintroduced in 1997 (H.R. 371), Mark Krikorian, the executive director for the conservative Center for Immigration Studies, states, "It's clear that H.R. 371 and other legislation intended to expedite the naturalization of various groups is prompted, at least in part, by the welfare reform law enacted last year, which barred most non-citizens from most federal welfare benefits. The Hmong have a high rate of welfare dependency and a low rate of naturalization" (U.S. Congress 1997, 32). In fact, however, Hmong veterans' movement to become naturalized citizens had begun in 1990, at least six years prior to the passage of welfare reform. Additionally, as we saw in the previous chapter, the U.S. Congress and President Bill Clinton had approved an exception to food stamp ineligibility under the Welfare Reform Act for Hmong veterans and their families in June 1998—almost two years prior to passing HVNA. As such, Hmong Americans' social movement to restore benefits and their movement to become naturalized U.S. citizens constituted two related but separate social movements.

Context of the Hmong Veterans' Naturalization Act

HVNA was originally introduced in the U.S. House of Representatives on April 4, 1990, as H.R. 4513 by U.S. representative Bruce Vento of Minnesota.[1] Congressman Vento, a member of the Democratic-Farmer-Labor (DFL) Party, had been representing Minnesota's Fourth Congressional District since 1977. Prior to becoming a congressman, Vento had served six years as a member of the Minnesota House of Representatives. Three years before he first introduced HVNA, Vento had cosponsored and helped to pass one of the first and, to date, only major comprehensive federal policies in response to homelessness, now known as the McKinney-Vento Homeless Assistance Act. Vento was an original author, with U.S. representative Stewart B. McKinney, of that landmark legislation.

On May 24, 1990, U.S. senator Rudolph "Rudy" Boschwitz, also of Minnesota, introduced S. 2687, the counterpart to HVNA, in the U.S. Senate. Despite getting some bipartisan support, both bills failed to pass.[2] HVNA would be reintroduced five times spanning six congressional sessions before it eventually passed into law: in 1991, 1994, 1995, 1997, and 1999. Representative Bruce Vento introduced all of the bills in the House of Representatives, while several different U.S. senators, including David Durenberger (R-MN), Rod Grams (R-MN), and Paul Wellstone (D-MN), introduced similar or identical bills in the Senate. It is significant that all of the leading sponsors of HVNA were elected from Minnesota.

Minnesota has been not only the state with the second largest population of Hmong Americans in the United States, but the first state to produce a Hmong elected official in the country. In 1991, Choua Lee, a 1.5-generation Hmong woman, was elected to the Saint Paul School Board. That same year, Hmong veterans established the Minnesota branch of LVA, a nonprofit organization composed of mostly ethnic Hmong staff and members despite its reference to "Lao" veterans. In 1979, Senator Boschwitz, a Jewish refugee from Germany and the only former refugee in Congress at the time, introduced a successful amendment to the Supplemental Appropriations Bill that enabled the United States to admit and resettle one thousand additional Southeast Asian refugees a month, which raised the allowable total to eight thousand.[3] In June 1988, Hmong residents of Minnesota sought the help of Senator Boschwitz, who worked with the State Department to bring two young Hmong siblings whose parents were killed while trying to seek refuge in Thailand, to Minnesota.[4] In the late 1980s, Hmong veterans, especially staff and members of LVA, reached out to Congressmen Vento about the idea of a Hmong veterans benefits act, which later turned into HVNA of 1990.[5]

Speaking in 2000, Philip Smith, the Washington, DC, director of LVA, recalled, "For us, the struggle for this legislation began some 10 years ago, when we [LVA] first began to work with Congressman Vento to develop this legislation."[6] By the mid-1990s, LVA represented "some 55,000 Laotian and Hmong American veterans, and [their] family members, across the United States."[7] By then, LVA had cultivated ties with a number of U.S. veteran organizations, including the American Legion and the Special Forces Association. These organizations would later become supporters of HVNA.

By the mid- to late 1990s, several important demographic and political developments had occurred within the Hmong American community in the United States and in Minnesota. Between 1990 and 2000, according to the U.S. Census Bureau, the Hmong American population grew from 94,493 to 186,310, representing a 97 percent increase. In the same decade, the Hmong population of Minnesota grew from 17,764 to 41,800, representing an increase of 135 percent. This meant that Minnesota experienced a much greater increase in its Hmong population than the two other states with substantial Hmong populations (e.g., California's Hmong population increased by 32 percent, Wisconsin's by 99 percent). Recognizing that the U.S. census figures were likely undercounts of the true Hmong population, Hmong American community leaders and organizations estimated that the total number of Hmong in Minnesota was probably closer to 70,000, while the U.S. Hmong population was probably closer to 283,239 (Pfeifer and Lee 2000).

In May 1999, Lee Pao Xiong, who is Hmong and a resident of Minnesota, was appointed by President Bill Clinton to the President's Advisory Commission on

Asian American and Pacific Islanders. Prior to that, Xiong was the executive director of the Council on Asian-Pacific Minnesotans. While he was serving as a governor-appointed councilmember of the Metropolitan Council, a regional planning agency in Minnesota, Xiong was also working in Washington as a staff intern for U.S. senator Carl Levin. As we will return to below, Xiong's experience working in the government sector made him attuned to the political process while his work obligations brought him into contact with a broad network of people and policy makers in both Minnesota and Washington. It was he who recognized a crucial window of opportunity when HVNA was being considered in Congress, and it was he who was in the position to advise President Clinton regarding this act. Although Xiong's actions and those of other Hmong government employees, such as Yia Xiong, who was working as a constituent advocate for the late U.S. senator Paul Wellstone's office, took place behind the scenes and, until now, largely unknown to the Hmong American public, they were crucial to the passage of HVNA.

Major Events and Interactions

Figure 4.1 provides a timeline of the major events and interactions between Hmong and the state that occurred during Hmong veterans' movement for naturalization accommodations between 1989 and 2000. The events above the timeline represent actions of state actors or state allies and the responses of the state or state segments to Hmong's mobilization. The events below the timeline represent actions of Hmong social actors, actions of their nonstate allies, and Hmong's

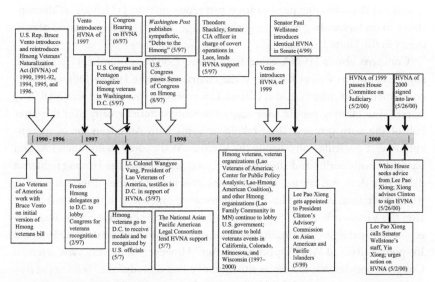

FIGURE 4.1. Timeline of Hmong Veterans' Movement for Naturalization Accommodations, 1989–2000

counterresponses to state actions. This movement began in the late 1980s when LVA reached out to and worked with U.S. representative Bruce Vento on the idea of a Hmong veterans bill. This effort led to the introduction of HVNA of 1990, as discussed above. Between 1990 and 2000, Vento reintroduced the bill five times over six congressional sessions. After years of lobbying by Hmong veterans and their allies, and shortly after Hmong veterans were recognized for their military service by the U.S. Congress and the Pentagon in May 1997, Congress held the first major hearing on HVNA in June 1997. As I return to shortly, it was during this congressional hearing that most of the claims and counterclaims around this bill, as well as the social actors behind those claims, became publicly known. However, it would take an additional two and a half years for HVNA to become law on May 2000. This chapter analyzes Hmong veterans' collective claims, how the state responded to them, and how this act became law.

Claims and Counterclaims

Before May 2000, the only congressional hearing on HVNA took place on June 26, 1997.[8] On that day, members of the House Judiciary Subcommittee on Immigration and Claims along with other members and nonmembers of Congress debated whether or not Hmong "veterans" ought to be provided with a waiver that exempts them from the English-language and residency requirements of the U.S. naturalization laws. Specifically, HVNA of 1997 would exempt legally admitted "persons" who "served with a special guerrilla unit operating from a base in Laos in support of the United States at any time during the period beginning February 28, 1961, and ending September 18, 1978" as well as the spouses of these Hmong persons from two requirements: (1) having to "demonstrate an understanding of the English language" and (2) having a period of residency in the United States.

Concerns about HVNA came from some Congress members. Expressing slight support as well as hesitancy, the chairman of the House Judiciary Subcommittee on Immigration and Claims, U.S. representative Lamar Smith (R-TX) states, "The Hmong people have unquestionably suffered greatly over the latter half of the 20th century. Their taking up arms with American forces in anticommunist guerrilla units during the Vietnam War caused them much loss and hardship, both during and after the war. America does owe the Hmong fighters a debt. This debt was repaid, thanks to the generosity of the American people, when more than 100,000 Hmong refugees were evacuated to the United States after the Vietnam War" (U.S. Congress 1997, 1). Representative Smith acknowledges the "anxiety in the Hmong community over the enactment of the Personal Responsibility and Work Opportunity Act." However, in Smith's view, even "if Congress decides that this is the situation needing remedy," the "[easing] of naturalization requirements" for "veterans of Hmong guerrilla units" would mean that "naturalization standards would be watered down" (U.S. Congress 1997, 2).

This last statement is consistent with Smith's view that the "debt" American owes to Hmong "was repaid" (presumably) with the "evacuation" of a hundred thousand Hmong refugees to the United States after the war. Such a position espouses views similar to those of President Jimmy Carter, who in 1977 claimed that because "the destruction was mutual" between Vietnam and the United States, "I don't feel that we owe a debt, nor that we should be forced to pay reparations at all."[9] Presumably, Hmong veterans, for their military service, for their enduring a decade of destruction and atrocities and decades longer of life in the total institutions of refugee camps, deserve only that much. From this standpoint, whatever devastation that Hmong (and other Vietnamese, Cambodians, and Laotians) had to bear in the decades before their resettlement and whatever happens to them after the point of entry do not merit the government's concern.

Others in the hearing recognized Smith's attempt to associate the HVNA with welfare reform and took immediate steps to reframe the social problem. Representative Melvin Watt (D-NC), the ranking member on the House Judiciary Subcommittee on Immigration and Claims and a cosponsor of HVNA, opens his statement by recognizing the "significant number of Hmong residents in Western North Carolina, which is my home state." He continues,

> But the more important part is that this is not and should not be characterized as simply a mechanism to ease the provision of welfare benefits. I think that's really secondary. The more important thing is what commitments have we, as a country, made to these people, either by implication or by precedent.
>
> A couple of weeks ago, we mocked up a bill and sent it on the floor, basically providing citizenship or waiving some of the naturalization requirements for an individual who saved some documents in Switzerland from being shredded. If we can pass a special bill for that individual, it certainly seems to me that we can honor some of the commitments that we ought to be making to people who fought alongside our troops in Southeast Asia.
>
> And so I'm hopeful that we can not just look on this bill as a mechanism to debate welfare reform again, or immigration reform again, but look on it as an opportunity to provide equity to a category of people who certainly deserve it. (U.S. Congress 1997, 9)

More direct opposition to HVNA came from a private organization. Introducing his Center for Immigration Studies as a "research organization" that "does not recommend . . . lawmakers [to] vote for or against any specific piece of legislation," Mark Krikorian begins by informing the audience that "I, too, laud the bravery of the Hmong in defense of their homes and of freedom. . . . My own grand parents . . . survived the first genocide of this bloody century." However, in statements that reinforce Representative Smith's view, Krikorian states, "Providing our former allies with safe haven in the face of an enemy extermination campaign would thus seem to have been the right thing to do. The bill under consideration, however, carries this responsibility further. It would eliminate two of the requirements, a minimum period of residency and a knowledge of the English language, which are intended to ensure that new citizens are sufficiently rooted and invested in the United States to be entrusted with a permanent role in our future" (U.S. Congress 1997, 31–32). Furthermore, Krikorian claims that "the process of minting new Americans" would be "further compromised" by "H.R. 371 and other measures like it," which, in his view, "[promotes] the further cheapening of United States citizenship" and "would also corrupt the immigration law with yet another special interest gimmick" (U.S. Congress 1997, 32). Moreover, Krikorian reinforces his nativist sentiments with a claim against what he calls "affirmative action citizenship." He claims, "National origins quotas were rightly eliminated from the Immigration law in 1965. The principle of a racially and ethnically neutral immigration policy in the national interest, however, cannot be upheld if the immigration law is shaped by the special pleading of the myriad ethnic groups that make up our population" (U.S. Congress 1997, 32). Finally, Krikorian tries to defend his "color-blind" position by projecting inter-ethnic conflicts and speaking on behalf of imagined others. According to Krikorian, "The inequity of such legislation [referring to HVNA] could inflame ethnic grievances and conflict. Mexicans, after all, are the largest national origin group seeking naturalization, and they are expected to meet all the normal requirements, while other groups ... would be admitted without meeting many requirements" (U.S. Congress 1997, 32). Besides opposing HVNA, in his oral and written testimony to Congress, Krikorian calls Hmong, "Hmong tribesmen" (U.S. Congress 1997, 31–33).

Krikorian, however, was not the only one to make claims about the "dilution of standards" and the "assaults on the integrity of the entire immigration and naturalization process" (U.S. Congress 1997, 33). Others who did not explicitly oppose providing an exemption to Hmong were concerned about the imagined future benefits that the passing of HVNA could have on imagined benefactors. According to Louis Crocetti, the associate commissioner for examinations with the Immigration and Naturalization Service, "The inclusion of H.R. 371 could set a precedent for other groups attempting to gain waiver categories who do not share the unique situation of the Hmong" (U.S. Congress 1997, 23).

Framing Hmong's Military Service

How were Hmong Americans and their state allies, especially U.S. representative Bruce Vento and his colleagues in the U.S. House and Senate, able to secure bipartisan support for the Hmong naturalization bill, against opponents who claimed that "freely handing out citizenship" would "[debase] the meaning of Americanism"?[10] I contend that Hmong veterans advanced key claims of the Hmong military service frame while their state allies amplified discourses about the honor of the country. This set of claims-making activities helped to create the moral sentiments and interest convergence that were needed to motivate action from policy makers on HVNA.

In a letter to U.S. representative Henry Hyde, the chairman of the House Judiciary Committee that was overseeing the hearing on HVNA, Wangyee Vang, a former lieutenant colonel and president of LVA, writes, "Mr. Chairman and Honorable Committee members, the Hmong soldiers did not come to America as economic migrants; they came to America as political refugees because they were veterans of the U.S. Special Guerrilla Units and other special units in the United States' Secret Army in Laos. The United States has a special obligation to them."[11] The same letter highlights U.S. historical amnesia and reminds the United States about its promise:

> Mr. Chairman and Honorable Committee Members, just last month, on May 14–15, after over two decades of silence since the end of the Vietnam War, the Hmong and Lao veterans who served in the U.S. Secret Army were honored for the first time nationally at the Vietnam War Memorial and Arlington National Cemetery. The national news media recorded this historic occasion—"The Lao Veterans of America National Recognition Day." . . .
>
> Edgar Buell, for U.S. AID/CIA official working with the U.S. Secret Army in Laos during the war years, said on [CBS] 60 Minutes, on March 4, 1979: "Everyone of them that died (Hmong), that was an American back home that didn't die, or one that was injured [who] wasn't injured. Somebody in nearly every Hmong family was either fighting or died from fighting. . . . They became refugees because we (United States Government) . . . encouraged them to fight for us. I promised them myself: 'Have no fear, we will take care of you.'"

Pointing out the U.S. betrayal of Hmong, Vang describes how the vast majority of Hmong were left behind while only a few thousand were airlifted to safety: "About April 1975, the United States withdrew its troops from Indochina. From May 12–14, 1975, the CIA evacuated about 2,500 Hmong officers and their families from the secret base at Long Cheng in Laos to the U.S. air base Namphong, Khonekene, Thailand. The rest of the Special Guerrilla Units (SGUs) and other special units who were left behind began to walk to the Mekong River and crossed to Thailand. Thousands of these soldiers and their families were killed by the Communists [sic] forces." Finally, Vang ends by describing the cost to Hmong lives and the difficulties that Hmong refugees have had in obtaining U.S. citizenship:

> Hmong of all ages—men, women and children fought and died alongside U.S. clandestine and military personnel in units recruited, organized, trained, funded, and paid by the United States CIA, U.S. Air Force and other agencies. It is estimated

that during the United States' involvement in the Vietnam conflict, 35,000 to 40,000 Hmong veterans and their families were killed in combat; 50,000 to 58,000 were wounded; and 2,500 to 3,000 were missing. When the United States withdrew from Southeast Asia, genocide followed the Hmong—thousands of Hmong were murdered by the Communists or fled to neighboring Thailand.....

Currently, the majority of these former soldiers and their refugee family members who are now in America cannot become U.S. citizens, because they lack sufficient English language skills to pass the naturalization test. The intense and protracted clandestine war in Laos and the exodus of the Hmong and Lao veterans into squalid refugee camps, or internment in reeducation camps, did not permit the veterans the opportunity to go to school. Once in America, they have led a difficult life—often in poverty-stricken inner-city conditions, raising large families, not permitting them sufficient opportunity to formally study English.[12]

In these ways, Vang articulated the major claims of Hmong's military service frame.

From the standpoint of many Hmong adults, veterans and nonveterans,[13] the military service frame includes the following set of interrelated claims: First, Hmong's presence in the United States is a product of specific historical events, namely the U.S. military's involvement in Vietnam and Laos. During the American-Vietnam War, Laotian Hmong soldiers under General Vang Pao fought for the United States and died in the tens of thousands protecting U.S. interests in Laos. Second, when the United States lost the (undeclared) war with North Vietnam and pulled out, countless Hmong families and soldiers were left behind to be persecuted or killed by the communists. The more fortunate ones escaped to Thailand and became prolonged political refugees in Thailand with very limited legal protection. Third, the abandonment was an act of great betrayal by the U.S. government because the United States had promised Hmong that they would be taken cared of should they lose the war. Fourth, because of Hmong soldiers' and their families' great sacrifice to the United States, Hmong refugees deserve legal protection, especially refuge from the United States, and they and their U.S. children deserve to receive the full benefits that its citizenry receive.

Framing and Amplifying the Honor of the Country

Responding to oppositions and concerns, Hmong's allies in Congress amplified existing notions about national honor. In response to claims about the "cheapening of citizenship," for instance, Representative Sonny Bono (R-CA) emphasized mutual obligations and fair social exchanges—components of the notion of honor.

I feel . . . that, you know, if it takes a little extra effort and you're talking about people that we had die for us and then the question of us graciously giving them a pittance—I'm not going to use a word like cheapen because I think we need a counter point to that. That's giving them a pittance for dying for us or getting blown up for us or getting killed for us.

It's out of the question. It's not fair in exchange. When this—I think humanity survives on exchange. If you buy something, you get something. If you ask some-body to do something for you, you pay them. . . . So I think it is absolutely our ethical obligation to make sure that we pay people back when they do especially things of this nature for us, so I think Mr. Watt's suggestion is very reasonable. It makes total sense. Work out the details. (U.S. Congress 1997, 37–38)

Reinforcing Bono's claims, Representative Zoe Lofgren (D-CA) emphasized the country's obligation to fulfill its promise to a loyal ally in order to remain an "honorable country":

The more important question is the policy question of what do we owe, if any-thing, to this brave group of people? When the CIA—I mean, it's one of the most important stories from the Vietnam War and the most inspiring stories, is the bravery of this group of people who stood by us, under unbelievable circum-stances, showing tremendous bravery and saving American soldiers and weigh-ing in on us, never wavering from our side, and do we owe these people any kind of thanks? Do we owe them performance on the promises made to them at that time, and my answer, as Mr. Bono has said, is yes, we do. We do if we are an hon-orable country. We should live up to the promises that we made back in those days. (U.S. Congress 1997, 38)

While pointing to the bravery and loyalty of Hmong, these statements framed the matter as involving the honor of the country.

In spite of the title of the act, throughout the congressional hearing, besides former colonel Wangyee Vang, only a few other persons used the word "veter-ans" to refer to Hmong soldiers who fought in the war.[14] Susan Haigh, chair of the Ramsey County Board of Commissioners in Minnesota, was one of the exceptions: "We should be able to understand from this the high incidence of post-traumatic stress disorder and the depression that haunts so many of the Hmong veterans and makes it even more difficult for them to learn the English language so that they can become citizens." In her prepared statement to Congress, U.S. representative Patsy Mink, a Democrat from Hawaii, used the term "Hmong veterans," compared them to Filipino veterans of World War II, and also referred to them as "Hmong patriots" (U.S. Congress 1997, 14). U.S. representative Calvin Dooley mentions "Hmong veterans" at least three times throughout his written testimony, including the following: "We must offer the Hmong veterans an oppor-tunity to obtain U.S. citizenship. They have sacrificed greatly for our country and we must be willing as a matter of simple decency to provide assistance to them.

Therefore, I strongly recommend that this committee pass H.R. 371" (U.S. Congress 1997, 15). On the other hand, U.S. representative Smith, who chaired the hearing, used the awkward phrase "veterans of Hmong guerrilla units." During the hearing, Smith and other opponents of HVNA refer to Hmong veterans as "Hmong guerrillas." Bruce Vento used almost exclusively the term "Hmong patriots," and makes it a point to tell his colleagues, "I keep referring to these as the Hmong patriots; we don't want to confuse it. At some particular point that may be an issue that's addressed beyond that" (U.S. Congress 1997, 12). The omission of "Hmong veterans" in most people's statements can be interpreted only as a deliberate attempt on the part of supporters to minimize opposition to the bill and/or opponents' deliberate attempt to exclude Hmong veterans from the definition of "veterans."

It was also Chairwoman Haigh who emphasized the academic success of the younger generations of Hmong in Saint Paul and their role in restoring economic vitality to an "abandoned . . . commercial strip" in Saint Paul. But, most of all, Haigh emphasized the sacrifices and "lasting and vital contribution" that the Hmong older generation made to America during the war "against the expansion of the Vietnamese communist in Laos." Haigh points out that "the vast majority of the Hmong generation who grew up fighting in this war for American never became literate in their own language, let alone in the English language. And illiteracy is a daunting barrier for the older Hmong who want to become citizens" (U.S. Congress 1997, 25). Putting "a human face [to] this story," Haigh tells the stories of who Hmong persons—Pao Yang who was "recruited to fight on behalf of the United States when he was 13 years old" and Pia Thao who "is a widow of a Hmong soldier who was killed in the war" who, in the course of trying to escape, witnessed her five-year-old son "shot as he was running to her arms" (U.S. Congress 1997, 25).

The significance of these claims cannot be understated. They helped achieve what Snow and Benford (1988, 199–202) call the three "core framing tasks" (diagnostic framing, prognostic framing, and motivational framing), which are needed to achieve collective consensus and motivate collective action on the problem. Not only did these claims do the crucial work of diagnosing key aspects of the social problem (i.e., Hmong's sacrifice during the war; their plight in the aftermath of the war; and their ongoing struggles, especially with English literacy after resettlement), but they also provided a clear prognosis for who and what is to be done to alleviate the social problem (i.e., the United States should grant naturalization accommodations as a way to alleviate the conditions Hmong veterans face). In these claims, we can also observe the emergence of a motivational frame—that is, claims that elaborate the "rationale for action" in order to urge or motivate action (Snow and Benford 1988, 202). In this case, this rationale for action is framed in terms of national honor—honor that can be had by making accommodations to a former ally seeking U.S. citizenship. But beyond these claims, two other kinds of claims were most crucial in mobilizing consensus and motivating collective action within Congress—action that eventually led to the passage of HVNA of 2000.

On one front are the claims of U.S. representative Bruce Vento that allude to U.S. militarization and the militarism of its foreign policy.[15] These claims appeared as allusions in Vento's discussion of why it would be "entirely appropriate" to remain committed to "Hmong patriots" that the U.S. government, through its CIA, covertly relied on during times of war and global uncertainty:

> This legislation [H.R. 371], of course, makes attainment of citizenship possible for these men, women and children. They were in these special guerrilla units. And it follows in line with the fact that for those that dutifully had served in uniform for the U.S., they are, you know, even though not a citizen, are given naturalization for their service. We have reached beyond that to the Filipino scouts and other groups.
>
> This does raise a question of whether or not there is some precedent for what we're doing here. Well, I would just suggest to you that in the context in which the United States projects its military activity and the context in which we project and act today, it is entirely appropriate, I might say, especially given the circumstances surrounding this.
>
> The CIA, in fact, went out and hired these individuals, engaged them, encouraged them, made commitments to them, and we kept those commitments. We've kept those commitments. We really have. I mean—and so I think that one more gesture here—this doesn't deal, incidentally, with veterans' benefits. I keep referring these as the Hmong patriots. We don't want to confuse it. At some particular point, that may be an issue that's addressed beyond that. (U.S. Congress 1997, 12)

The main thrust of Vento's claims is that a compelling reason (i.e., compelling government interest) to grant a public good (accommodations to citizenship) restricted to Hmong is to maximize the government's ability to count on current and future groups, whoever these may be, during military conflicts. After all, history has made clear that "non-American" allies, whether they are sovereign governments or colonized and exploited "tribal groups," have been crucial in America's wars. Furthermore, the years between 1990 and 1998 were turbulent times during which the U.S. military and their allies were engaged in military conflicts in the Middle East, namely in Kuwait and Iraq.[16] Moreover, Vento reminds Congress that it is merely granting a "gesture" of support and not actually "veterans' benefits" to Hmong. In other words, Vento suggests as an incentive to Congress that the symbolic recognition of particular allies during particular periods would promote the U.S. national (read military) interest without compelling the government to promote substantive immigrant political incorporation.[17] That Vento's claim was accepted by policy makers can be inferred from the fact that there was no objection from any member of Congress at the time Vento made this claim or during any later congressional hearing on the HVNA. That this topic of U.S. military projections around the world was never brought up again in public hearings is another indication that policy makers understood the broader implications of granting a former military "ally" national accommodation.

But the relevant claims are not limited to those that appealed to extant or perceived military processes and ideology. Representative Bruce Vento also drew on extant ideologies about national duty and honor to create moral sentiments (sympathy, merit, and virtue) within Congress. The attempt to create moral sentiments is found in the following passages, in which Vento emphasized Hmong's suffering along with their "outstanding contributions":

> But this is really, I think, a matter of honor. It's a matter of—and as you [referring to Mr. Chairman] suggested, if we alleviate the welfare problem on this end and alleviate the language test because of other reasons, then I think it's a question of what can we do as a nation to recognize the contributions, the outstanding contributions, of the Hmong, for this period of history in terms of being an ally of the United States. After all, we had had tens of thousands of Hmong that actually fought side by side. Twenty thousand of them lost their lives. We had men, women and children. There are films, U.S. films, on news reports which showed 10 and 12-year-old children carrying around guns and rifles in Laos at that time that were on the evening news during the '60s and '70s.
>
> So I think that at the end of the course, the end of the Vietnam War, we lost that conflict. They fled to Thailand. They fled to the United States. A 100,000 Hmong left Laos for fear of persecution, for fear of genocide. It wasn't apparent, I suppose, then, in the aftermath of that Vietnam War, but their contribution, plus our role there, has led to the new global order and the role of self-determination and democracy around the globe.
>
> . . . But I think that you're right. They haven't passed an English language test or a civics test or they haven't done various things, but they probably have passed the most important test, Mr. Chairman, and that is risking their lives for the values and beliefs that we revere as Americans in saving American lives. (U.S. Congress 1997, 11–12)

These moral sentiments, I contend, were instrumental in motivating others within Congress to act on HVNA. For three years later, during the May 2 and May 18, 2000, congressional hearings, several Congress members reiterated Representative Vento's argument that Hmong have "passed a more important test" and, as such, deserve accommodations in the naturalization process.[18]

A Crucial Window of Opportunity

Although the congressional hearing on HVNA of 1997 was an important one, the 105th congressional session ended before the bill could gain further traction.

In January 1999, Congressman Bruce Vento reintroduced HVNA of 1999, and in April 1999, Senator Paul Wellstone introduced an identical bill in the Senate. However, the bill never received a vote, probably because a committee hearing was never called. Unfortunately, in February 2000, Vento was diagnosed with cancer.[19] Despite this, Vento, working through his office staff, doubled his efforts to move HVNA along. In March 2000, the House Committee on the Judiciary voted to issue a report to the full chamber of the House that the bill be considered further. After minor amendment by the Committee on Judiciary, it was sent to the House for a vote; it passed in the House of Representatives on May 2, 2000.

Recognizing the May 2 decision by the House as a critical window of opportunity, Lee Pao Xiong, who at the time was the president and CEO of the Urban Coalition and a member of the President's Advisory Commission on Asian American and Pacific Islanders, telephoned Yia Xiong, who is Hmong and was working as a constituent advocate for Senator Paul Wellstone's office. Lee Pao Xiong inquired about the bill's counterpart in the Senate, especially to ensure that a committee hearing was called this time around. Lee Pao Xiong informed Yia Xiong that the bill had passed the House and that what was needed was for Senator Wellstone to call for a committee hearing on the bill in the Senate. Yia Xiong consulted with Wellstone's office. According to Lee Pao Xiong, "She got back to me that Wellstone's office had checked the bill and since the bill had no or little history of controversy, they could fast-track it," meaning that it would not have to go through all of the usual tedious processes.[20] On May 18, the Senate passed the bill by unanimous consent with minor changes and sent it back to the House to approve the changes. On May 23, 2000, both the U.S. House and Senate passed HVNA of 2000.

On the morning of May 26, Lee Pao Xiong received a call from Laura Efurd, who was the deputy assistant to the U.S. president and deputy director of Public Liaison. As deputy assistant to the president, Efurd "advised the President and Senior White House staff on policy and political matters of concern to the Asian American and Pacific Islander community."[21] As Lee Pao Xiong recalled,

> It was 11:00 in the morning, and I received a call from Laura Efurd. She informed me that the bill was on the President's desk, and asked me, "What should the President do with it?" I gave her three reasons why the President should sign the bill: 1) The bill would honor Representative Bruce Vento's longstanding efforts in lobbying for the bill in Congress (by then Vento had been diagnosed with cancer); 2) the bill does not have any negative fiscal impact; and 3) it does not guarantee citizenship. I wanted to give all the right reasons to him [the President] so that he would be more confident in signing the legislation.[22]

Finally, in the afternoon of May 26, President Clinton signed HVNA of 2000 into law.[23] President Clinton, in his statement on signing the act, states in part,

Today I signed H.R. 371, the Hmong Veterans' Naturalization Act of 2000. This legislation is a tribute to the service, courage, and sacrifice of the Hmong people who were our allies in Laos during the Vietnam war. . . . They work, pay taxes, and have raised families and made America their home. However, some Hmongs [sic] seeking to become American citizens have faced great difficulty meeting the requirements for naturalization for reasons associated with the unique circumstances of the Hmong culture. Until recently, the Hmong people had no written language. Without this experience, learning English, a requirement of naturalization, has been much more difficult for some Hmongs. This requirement has prevented many Hmongs from becoming full participants in American society.[24]

In the final analysis, Hmong culture and specifically the presumption that Hmong historically lacked a written language—a presumption that Duffy (2007) has shown to be false—became the stated cause of Hmong's political marginalization. That past U.S. policies and actions during and after the Secret War, U.S. refusal to recognize Hmong veterans as veterans, and pervasive class inequality and racism have prevented Hmong from becoming "full participants in American society" was never mentioned.

In the House of Representatives alone, the final bill (H.R. 371) had 108 cosponsors in addition to Representative Bruce Vento. Of these 109 sponsors, 65 (60 percent) were affiliated with the Democratic Party, 44 (40 percent) with the Republican Party. Of the 109 sponsors, 48 were elected from California, Minnesota, Wisconsin, North Carolina, and Michigan—the top five states with the largest concentrations of Hmong Americans. In the Senate, there were 17 cosponsors of S. 890 (the counterpart to H.R. 371) in addition to U.S. Senator Paul Wellstone, who introduced the bill. Of the 18 sponsors, 14 were Democrats and 4 were Republicans. Of the 18 sponsors, 6 were elected from the top four Hmong states (California, Minnesota, Wisconsin, North Carolina). In some cases, both senators from the same state were cosponsors: Barbara Boxer and Dianne Feinstein of California, Daniel Akaka and Daniel Inouye of Hawaii, Robert Kerry and Charles Hagel of Nebraska, and Russell Feingold and Herbert Kohl of Wisconsin.

DISCUSSION AND CONCLUSION

As we have seen, Hmong veterans and veteran organizations, by framing Hmong's military service, lobbying the government, and cultivating state allies, played a crucial role in sustaining the movement. At the same time, a few politically connected Hmong Americans in Washington recognized and took actions during crucial windows of opportunity that facilitated the passage of HVNA. By framing and amplifying the honor of the country, state allies were able to create interest convergence between policy makers and Hmong American movement actors and motivate collective action from the former. In the process, Hmong veterans won accommodations that enabled them to obtain U.S. citizenship. However, in the final analysis, the state granted Hmong symbolic recognition as allied aliens rather than formal incorporation as veterans.

Hmong Americans' movement for citizenship accommodations represents, to date, the longest sustained domestic-oriented social movement in their history. In the early 1990s, Hmong veterans formed LVA and established branches in states where there were substantial Hmong populations, including Minnesota and Wisconsin. LVA, in turn, raised funds through paid membership and organized Hmong veterans as participants in not only public ceremonies but also social movements. LVA also cultivated relations with state allies of the two major political parties, especially those who were familiar with and sympathetic to Hmong's premigration experiences. In the mid-1990s, when welfare reform caused cuts to noncitizens' public benefits, Hmong Americans and Hmong veterans in particular redoubled their efforts to lobby the U.S. government for public recognition of Hmong's military service. They achieved federal recognition for the first time in the May 1997 ceremony at the Vietnam Veterans Memorial.[25] After winning benefits restoration, Hmong veterans intensified their efforts in lobbying for HVNA. Fortunately, by the late 1990s, a few Hmong Americans were working in Washington. For example, Yia Xiong worked as a constituent advocate for Senator Paul Wellstone, and Lee Pao Xiong was an appointed member of the President's Advisory Commission on Asian American and Pacific Islanders. These few Hmong Americans recognized crucial windows of opportunities and utilized their political know-how to activate policy makers who were in the position to request hearings on bills, influence other policy makers in Congress, or sign the final bill into law. In the absence of these few Hmong American public servants who were familiar with the political process, were sympathetic to Hmong's cause, and provided advice to policy makers, it is doubtful that HVNA could have become law in the way that it did.

Notwithstanding the significance of Hmong Americans' collective agency, this movement cannot be understood without considering the convergence of the state's interest with that of Hmong. The government, through its temporary valorization of Hmong's military service, chose to frame its action in terms of national "honor." To be sure, Hmong veterans were granted only an English-language waiver, not automatic citizenship. But the message that the government expressed was that a waiver of the English-language requirement to an unassimilated, preliterate people was an exceptional gesture of support and inclusion into the nation. This symbolic incorporation served the nation as much as if not more than it served Hmong. The government had a compelling interest to grant its former "alien" "allies" some limited accommodations. Doing so promoted its national interests, which during that period included imminent U.S. military involvement in Middle East Asia (as the 2003 Second Gulf War later demonstrated) and, to a lesser extent, the effort to improve market and political relations in Southeast Asia. U.S. representative Bruce Vento needed to remind Congress only once about this compelling government interest. Paralleling the covert practices of war, in 2000 the government granted naturalization accommodations to an ally (Hmong) without making war and its supposed correlates—democracy, nation-state sovereignty, and national allegiance (which formal citizenship represents)—the focus of attention. By granting Hmong symbolic incorporation, the United States could claim credibility for itself as an "honorable" nation or, more precisely in the case of Hmong's unequal relationship with the United States, an "honorable" military instigator, commander, and patron.

That the racial state is much more interested in managing its own impression domestically and internationally than incorporating Hmong former refugees into its political system is demonstrated by its persistent refusal to recognize Hmong veterans as veterans. In the eyes of the U.S. government and as labeled in HVNA, Hmong veterans remain nothing more than "special guerrilla units" or "irregular forces" who served "in support of the U.S. military." In January 2011, when former major general Vang Pao died following his 2009 acquittal in the alleged plot to overthrow the government of Laos, Hmong Americans, especially veterans and their allies, petitioned the U.S. government to allow the general to be buried in Arlington National Cemetery. The Pentagon denied their request.[26]

In recent years, Hmong veterans have been turning to state governments, such as Wisconsin and Minnesota, to ask for veterans benefits. For example, a 2019 bill was introduced in the Wisconsin State Legislature to expand the definition of veterans to include Hmong soldiers who served in Laos and to grant them access to veterans benefits. Although this was not the first time that Hmong Americans were pursuing state-level benefits, it was the first time that they were seeking veterans benefits from state governments. It remains to be seen how state policy makers and public institutions will treat the few thousands of Hmong veterans who are still alive. While it is possible that state governments may follow the same disappointing pattern of federal behaviors toward Hmong veterans, it is also possible that the handful of Hmong American elected officials in legislatures such as the Minnesota State Legislature may make a difference as state allies if there is sustained collective action for such an effort by Hmong American activists and participants.

5 · MOVEMENT FOR INCLUSION

On July 10, 2003, California Assembly Bill 78 (AB 78) was signed into law by Governor Gray Davis, becoming Section 51221.4 of the California Education Code. This was an important historical moment for Hmong Americans because AB 78 was and remains one of the few public legislations to have ever resulted from the mobilization of Hmong social actors since Hmong refugees' arrival to the United States in the mid-1970s. AB 78 expresses the California State Legislature's encouragement that its public schools and, specifically, its social science curriculum in grades 7 to 12 teach about the Vietnam War, including the Secret War in Laos and the role of Southeast Asians in that war. The legislature also encourages that this instruction include oral or video histories that "shall exemplify the personal sacrifice and courage of the wide range of ordinary citizens who were called upon to participate and provide intelligence for the United States."[1] How were Hmong Americans in California's Central Valley able to, in a short period of time, mobilize public support for and successfully lobby the California State Legislature to pass AB 78? What role did Hmong American women professionals play in this movement? How did local framing interact with broader discursive opportunity to facilitate this movement? How did the state perpetuate Hmong's ethnic invisibility and marginalization in this movement?

I argue specifically that Hmong's mobilization to incorporate their history in California's public schools was effective because of several crucial factors. First, a condition (teenage suicides), once it became defined and legitimated as an ethnic "cultural crisis," created the crucial discursive opportunity for a segment within the Hmong American community to mobilize collective consensus and action around the social problem. Specifically, local and state health agencies and federal refugee service institutions along with the media were involved in diagnosing, prognosing, and encouraging action on the social problem. In the process, these institutions legitimated the social problem and offered a dominant discourse about "cultural collision" upon which social movement actors could eventually stake resonant claims. Second, a highly educated and well-integrated segment of the Hmong community—Hmong women and men professionals—recognized the discursive opportunity created by the legitimated social problem.

They took advantage of the opportunity by partly appropriating the media frame and partly rejecting it. As evidence of their creative agency, Hmong social actors reframed teenage suicide as a different problem (lack of curricular representation in schools) and then used a completely new frame—military service—to mobilize ethnic solidarity, activate institutional and state allies, and motivate state action on that new social problem. In the end, they won passage of the bill. However, before enacting the bill, state legislatures decided to remove all occurrences of "Hmong" from the bill and replace them with "Southeast Asians." This state racialization perpetuates the racial lumping and ethnic invisibility that Hmong social movement actors fought to change in the first place.

Most social movement scholars are in general agreement that the political opportunity structure or political context in which collective action takes place matters for social movements because it can constrain or facilitate movement actors' actions as well as impact movement outcomes (Kriesi et al. 1995a; McAdam 1982; Meyer 2004b; Tarrow 1994). Students of social movements also recognize the significance of framing as a dynamic interactive process that shapes movement outcomes (Benford 1997; Snow and Benford 1988). For example, past research has shown how social actors use framing to mobilize collective action among constituents and motivate action from those capable of granting goals (Snow and Benford 1992). Framing takes place during interactions in particular political and cultural contexts or discursive fields (McCammon et al. 2007; Steinberg 1998). However, what needs clarification but remains understudied in the framing literature is, as Steinberg (1998) has suggested, how social movement actors actively sort through, develop, and use discursive repertoires (or collective action frames) from within a discursive field to pursue their own political agendas. Second, although we know more about how racial majority groups pursue their own political agendas and how the state often treats White interests as public or national interests (Oliver 2017), we know much less about the conditions under which non-White immigrant actors may be able to select, develop, and use frames from within culturally dominant media discourses to pursue policy agendas and how the state might respond to them.

My study helps to illuminate these questions by analyzing the case of Hmong Americans' campaign to pass an education bill (AB 78) intended to recognize Hmong's contributions to the United States and encourage the teaching of Hmong history in California's public schools. Specifically, I analyze the agency of Hmong American actors who, in response to perceived discursive opportunities, rejected the frames that the mass media used and strategically recrafted new frames in order to advance their policy agenda. By clarifying the process in which Hmong American actors were able to appropriate dominant discourse and deploy their own collective action frames to pursue policy agendas and by showing how the state, through racialization, perpetuated Hmong's political marginalization, my study contributes to the research on political communication by social movement actors and the research on Asian American collective action and political incorporation (Lai 2011; Ong 2003; Wong 2017).

Although we know that perceived political opportunities and framing often influence social movements, we know less about how political opportunities interact with or shape framing strategies. Koopmans and Olzak (2004) propose the concept of discursive opportunities as a way of "bridging" political opportunities and framing processes. They define discursive opportunities as "the aspects of the public discourse that determine a message's chances of diffusion in the public sphere" (Koopmans and Olzak 2004, 202). The public sphere, they suggest, "mediates" between political opportunity structures and framing in that people's limited knowledge of politics or political developments is informed by the mass media. In their study of radical right violence, Koopmans and Olzak (2004) show that it is the media who make information (i.e., create discourse) about the political system as well as information about the public's reactions to violence publicly visible. In doing so, the media create discursive opportunities that, if recognized by social movement actors, can inform social actors about the kinds of mobilization strategies to adopt next. Koopmans and Olzak's (2004) insight that the media play a crucial role in creating public discourses and that these public discourses can serve as discursive opportunities or constraints for social actors' framing strategies is especially important as an insight into how social movement actors could interact with the media and how the former could select and use frames effectively within particular discursive fields.

However, social movement actors, in their interactions with their targets and/or the state, do not simply rely on discourses created by the media or let their collective strategies be bounded by culturally dominant media discourses. As Steinberg (1998, 858) points out, "Media, powerholders, and social movement organizations play an active role in demarcating the discourses within a field, but they cannot solely determine how actors combine discourses nor how they create meanings through them." In some cases, social actors may recognize the discursive opportunities opened up by culturally dominant discourses and take advantage of these opportunities in ways that will advance their goals. For example, instead of accepting the frames that the media create around a social problem, social actors may exert agency by rejecting the media's framing of that problem and reframing it in a different way to propel their own agendas. At the same time, social actors may appropriate and combine certain elements of media-legitimated discourses in order to meet the needs of the present. For example, in their study of women's jury movements to change public policies, McCammon et al. (2007) suggest that both the content of frames and the cultural contexts under which framing takes place matter for movement outcomes. According to McCammon et al. (2007, 726), to increase the chance that goal granters will grant goals, a frame must incorporate or respond to "critical elements in the broader cultural environment." Conversely, if activists frame their grievances "without regard to dynamics in the broader cultural context, their messages are far less likely to be politically effective" (McCammon et al. 2007, 726). This is the case largely because, as Ferree (2003) points out, "all discursive opportunity structures are inherently selective."

CULTURAL CONTEXTS OF THE HMONG IN CALIFORNIA

Dominant discourses in the United States have historically subordinated Hmong and other Southeast Asian refugees as culturally primitive and racially foreign (Ong 2003). As we learned in chapter 2, in 1975 the U.S. government secretly planned to keep Hmong political refugees permanently in Thailand without telling the Thai government. Despite having used tens of thousands of Hmong to fight its Secret War in Laos, some U.S. officials regarded Hmong as too primitive to adapt to U.S. society. The claim of Hmong's primitiveness, besides serving as a convenient excuse for barring Hmong refugees from the United States, was consistent with the negative opinions and nativist sentiments that segments of the American public and some in the U.S. Congress held against Southeast Asian refugees and immigrants more generally (Hein 1993).

When the first major group of Hmong political refugees arrived in the United States in the spring of 1976, U.S. policies formally racialized them as Indochinese refugees. At the same time, the American public often mistook them for Asian immigrants or foreigners or, worst, Vietnamese communists.[2] Since the 1980s, the English-language media have perpetuated the U.S. portrayal of Hmong as one of the least assimilated immigrant groups.[3] The image of Hmong as a static, culturally different, unassimilated, or ill-assimilated immigrant group has been perpetuated by books such as Anne Fadiman's (1997) *The Spirit Catches You and You Fall Down* and movies such as *Gran Torino* (2008). As we will see, the media play an important role in heightening culturally dominant discourses from time to time, especially when they diagnose "crises" that involve non-White immigrants.

Since the spring of 1976, most of California's Hmong population have lived in the Central Valley, which stretches from Bakersfield to Redding. By the 1990s, Fresno had become home to the largest concentration of Hmong in the United States. In a city of nearly 428,000, Hmong numbered about 22,500, or 5.3 percent of the general population and 41.4 percent of all Asians in Fresno, according to the 2000 U.S. census.[4] By 2010, Hmong residents in the Fresno metropolitan area numbered at least 31,771 (Pfeifer et al. 2012).

It was not until 2002 that Fresno elected its first public official of Hmong descent. On November 5, 2002, Tony Vang was elected as a trustee of the Fresno Unified School Board, becoming the first Hmong ever elected into public office in California. A month later California AB 78 was introduced. How AB 78 came into being, however, requires understanding how another social problem emerged. Specifically, it requires understanding how refugee institutions and the mass media played a role in legitimizing a social problem and, in doing so, creating a discursive opportunity for Hmong social actors.

FROM A CULTURAL CRISIS TO A
DISCURSIVE OPPORTUNITY

Between September 1998 and 2002, eight Hmong American teens in Fresno committed suicide—some with guns, some by hanging, drowning, or poisoning themselves. During this four-year period, at least three Hmong teens unsuccessfully committed suicide and over twenty Hmong students were referred by teachers and counselors to the Fresno Unified School District's ad hoc suicide prevention program.[5] Some of the young people who killed themselves were born in Thailand refugee camps but immigrated with their parents at a young age and grew up in the United States. The ages of the eight deceased individuals ranged from fifteen to seventeen, and most were enrolled in high school at the time of their death. Though the Hmong population represented just 3 percent of the county's population, Hmong teen suicides made up about half of the teen suicides (individuals age thirteen to seventeen) in Fresno County during that period.

Following these tragic events, Fresno school officials, people in the Hmong American community, and local and federal health department officials responded by defining the teenage suicides as a cultural crisis. Regarding this cultural crisis as a serious social problem, officials sought intervention through schools and mental health departments. The U.S. Office of Refugee Resettlement (ORR) within the U.S. Department of Health and Human Services, for instance, took notice of the Hmong teenage suicides and decided to take action. In an official letter, ORR wrote,

> To prevent further tragedies and to develop a plan of action for suicide prevention, a team composed of staff from the ORR funded Refugee Mental Health Program (RMHP), staff from Substance Abuse and Health Services Administration's Youth Violence and Suicide Prevention Programs, and a Hmong mental health professional from California State University in Sacramento, conducted a limited assessment of the current status and needs of the Hmong teen population. In October 2002 the team spent two days meeting with members of the Hmong refugee community (leaders and youth), Hmong service provider agencies, and school district personnel to learn more about the mental health needs of the Hmong youth and to learn more about the type of suicide prevention efforts that were in place in the community.[6]

As a result of this meeting, the team made a number of recommendations to the Fresno community about how to "help reduce suicide risk factors and enhance protective factors, as well as to promote the emotional well-being of members of the Hmong community." Three of the recommendations specified that the

Fresno community ought to "leverage resources and funding to support training programs in the area of intergenerational and family management and conflict resolution," "support creative approaches to celebrating Hmong cultural traditions, and using comedy and entertainment to bring understanding to the intergenerational conflicts and other problems of Hmong youth," and "develop programs for out-of-school youth . . . [and that] school gang prevention and intervention programs should be considered for 'vulnerable' youth."[7] A fourth recommendation was to "fund at least a part time position for a Hmong Suicide Prevention Task Force coordinator." This Hmong Suicide Prevention Task Force was formed by a group of "alumni and faculty of a master's degree program in social work . . . to provide preventative counseling services for Hmong adolescents" (Hardina et al. 2003).

This organized intervention effort was tied in many ways to local officials' diagnosis of the underlying causes of this social problem (teenage suicides) and their prognosis of the actions to be taken to alleviate the problem. Local officials and agencies working with the Hmong community in Fresno as well as the mainstream news media had similar understandings or assumptions about the putative conditions that produced this social problem. As Jesilow and Xiong (2007, 1) point out, officials and the media constructed the teenage suicides in Fresno "as an outgrowth of problems brought about by the Hmong immigration to the United States. The clash between Hmong and American cultures was fingered by those favoring change as the cause of the suicides. [However], other explanations were ignored." Instead, the "suicides were depicted in newspaper accounts and elsewhere as a problem that needed addressing and identified the school district and mental health facilities as the appropriate institutions to deal with the problem" (Jesilow and Xiong 2007, 1–2). However, in their attempts to deal with the problem, the news media associated suicides with Hmong's status as immigrants "in order to convince the Hmong that they needed to acculturate, in particular to accept and utilize mental health facilities" (Jesilow and Xiong 2007, 2).

A series of news articles by the *Fresno Bee* suggests the media's and public authorities' presumption for why accepting and using mental health facilities was the appropriate intervention. In their set of articles titled "Lost in America," *Fresno Bee* writer Anne Ellis and photographer Diana Baldrica poignantly retell the circumstances that preceded and followed the suicides of the eight Hmong teenagers.[8] This series contained thirteen articles, all written by Ellis. Of these articles, eight provided snapshots of the suicide victims and the reactions of their family members, one covered the "teen challenges" of a Hmong young woman who was not one of the suicide victims, while the rest covered the Fresno Unified School District's intervention in the "Crisis," "How to Get Help," and "Breaking the Silence."[9]

The journalist, however, was not simply writing to describe the lives of the suicide victims. Ellis's tone and remarks suggest that she was critical of a number of things: (1) the slow response of the "bureaucratic" county health department to the suicides; (2) the lack of "grants" to support mental health intervention work; but, most critically, (3) the Hmong American community itself and their leaders who presumably "offer[red] no contributions" to help. This is demonstrated by the following paragraphs, in which Ellis compares the "wisdom" of Hmong Americans in Fresno to that of Hmong in Saint Paul, Minnesota:

> St. Paul, Minn., has responded more logically and aggressively to Hmong mental-health issues. The area has the nation's largest Hmong population. Long ago, the Hmong leadership recognized the need for good mental-health care, and Hmong leaders assembled a department with four mental health professionals, five drug-and-alcohol counselors and more clients than it can handle. They are funded by grants and private health insurance. Unfortunately, the wisdom from Minnesota has not travelled to the Hmong community here. Even now, some Hmong community leaders are openly criticizing people who are helping, yet offer no contributions of their own.[10]

According to the media then, teenage suicides was not the only social problem that needed mental health intervention. The very organization and cultural values (or perceived lack of values) of the Hmong community and the actions or perceived inactions of their leaders were also presumed social problems in and of themselves that needed outside intervention. These negative assumptions and attitudes about "the Hmong community" (referred to by the news as if it were a monolithic entity) are further demonstrated in the text by the same *Fresno Bee* writer:

> There are underlying causes for the suicides that also can be mitigated by the community. English, gender, equity, conflict resolution, communication are all skills and values that can be learned, making homes more harmonious and healthy for children. The Hmong parents have great hopes for their children, and many have values that serve the community well. . . . Other traditions such as arranged marriage, parental control, religion, create a monumental cultural collision for young people raised in the United States, which values personal freedom above all. Whatever the underlying cause, we know that eight young people were crushed by the pull of two cultures.[11]

Even though the media appear to concede that there could be some other "underlying cause" of teenage suicide, they resolutely assert that "a monumental cultural collision" harmed the teenagers who eventually took their lives.

The mass media as an institution played an important role in framing and legitimizing the social problem. Through their relatively detailed coverage, the mass media framed the teenage suicides in terms of a "cultural clash." The media motivated collective action in two ways. First, the media attributed the cultural crisis to the lack of government funding and called for more funding and intervention. Second, the public discourse that the media created gave peculiar legitimacy to and encouraged government intervention in the social problem. The media specifically blamed the Hmong community of Fresno for having, presumably, failed to take "more [logical] and [aggressive] [steps] to Hmong mental-health issues." Underlying the media's message was the claim that "Hmong culture" not only remains static and backward but is in need of government intervention. Such diagnostic framing supports rather than threatens the dominant discourse about and public sentiments toward immigrants, their cultures, and their purported lack of assimilation. Relying on the legitimated social problem that they and the media helped to create, local institutions such as Fresno Unified School District were able to secure funding from federal government institutions to provide assistance in the form of mental health services to Hmong Americans (Jesilow and Xiong 2007). What local institutions and the media probably did not foresee was that mobilizers in the Hmong community would recognize the legitimated social problem as a discursive opportunity and use it to make other kinds of claims upon the state.

Thus far, I have described the cultural contexts leading up to Hmong professionals' movement for curriculum inclusion. Figure 5.1 provides a timeline of the major events that preceded the *Fresno Bee*'s "Lost in America" series and highlights the major interactions that emerged between Hmong professionals, their allies, their opponents, the California State Legislature, and state actors.

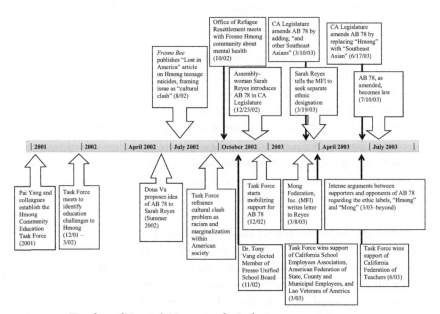

FIGURE 5.1. Timeline of Hmong's Movement for Inclusion, 2001–2003

ETHNIC MOBILIZATION FOR INCLUSION

Taking advantage of the discursive opportunity opened up by the mass media, a group of Hmong professionals initiated the idea of a statewide policy to have public schools include instruction specifically on the role that Hmong played in the Vietnam War and the contributions that they had made to the United States. Although there are many facets of Hmong's social movement for inclusion, in this section I focus on two processes to illustrate Hmong social actors' collective agency in effectively mobilizing a policy-oriented social movement: (1) Hmong social actors' mobilization of collective consensus through reliance on existing community infrastructures and (2) Hmong social actors' rejection and strategic reframing of the media frame around teenage suicides. I analyze each of these processes before turning attention to how the state racialized Hmong in this movement.

Mobilizing Consensus through Community Infrastructure

To mobilize support for AB 78, Hmong American activists relied on the existing networks of social relations, community organizations, and channels of communication within the Hmong American communities in the Central Valley. In Fresno, Hmong American activists, many of whom are women who are well-educated professionals and know each other, were able to activate a sympathetic state ally, Assemblywoman Sarah Reyes, to sponsor, introduce, and help mobilize support for AB 78.

Unlike previous social movements within Hmong American communities, such as their movements for benefits restoration (chapter 3) and naturalization accommodations (chapter 4), where Hmong men were lead organizers and Hmong women were their allies, supporters, and participants, in the AB 78 movement Hmong women professionals played crucial roles as movement leaders and organizers from beginning to end. One of the main leaders of the AB 78 movement was Pai Yang, who was working as director for the Refugee Resettlement Program at Catholic Charities. Yang founded the Hmong Community Education Task Force in 2001, which became the ad hoc social movement organization behind AB 78. However, years before the Task Force was created and well before the idea of AB 78 came into being, Yang had represented Hmong parents to successfully advocate for change in a public school in Fresno that served large numbers of Hmong students but lacked Hmong-speaking teachers and community liaisons. Also, through her volunteer work as a citizenship instructor within a major Hmong church, Catholic Charities, and an elementary school that served a large number of Hmong students, Yang had already established a network of social ties within the Fresno Hmong community. To give an idea of her extraordinary public service, she had personally helped close to twenty thousand Hmong individuals complete their naturalization applications.[12] Yang's network of relationships later turned out to be very useful when she and her colleagues needed to mobilize community support for AB 78.

The other key leader was Doua Vu, who was a resource specialist with the State and Federal Programs Title III Office of the Fresno Unified School District. According to the school district, Vu "saw a need for Southeast Asian students to understand their history and the reason they are living in the United States. She determined that low self-esteem stemming from a lack of a sense of belonging may have contributed to a problem with teen suicide in the Southeast Asian Community."[13] Vu had knowledge of education policies and practices, and it was Vu who, in mid-2002, proposed the idea of the AB 78 bill to Reyes. By the time AB 78 was first introduced in late 2002, Doua Vu and Pai Yang had lived with their families and been active participants in the Hmong community in Fresno for over two decades. Kao-ly Yang, PhD, an anthropologist, was the main coordinator to organize community support for AB 78. Educated in France and trilingual in French, Hmong, and English, Yang had immigrated to the United States three years prior to the introduction of AB 78. As we will see, she also became an active participant during the intense public debates between AB 78 supporters and opponents regarding the proper ethnic label that ought to be adopted in the language of AB 78.

Several Hmong men professionals were also on the Task Force. Peter Vang was appointed chairman. Vang had served in a number of public organizations throughout Fresno, including the Affirmative Action and Equal Opportunities Committee within the County of Fresno, the Laotian Chamber of Commerce, and the Police Chief Advisory group within the Fresno Police Department. Peter Vang lost his teenage son to suicide in 2000. Dr. Tony Vang was, at the time of AB 78, an associate professor of education at California State University, Fresno. He was also the founder and active executive director of the Fresno Center for New Americans (now the Fresno Center). In 2002, Tony Vang was also campaigning for public office within the Fresno Unified School District as a trustee—the first such campaign by any Hmong in Fresno. Vong Mouanoutoua moved from Southern California to Clovis, a neighboring town of Fresno, in 1996 and by the time of AB 78 had just graduated from law school and was working at a law firm.

Between December 2001 and March 2002, the Task Force met regularly to identify the educational challenges facing Hmong students. One of the issues the Task Force initially identified was the lack of outreach to prospective Hmong college students, which was attributed to the tendency of colleges and universities to lump Hmong into the "Asian" category while ignoring Hmong's unique challenges. Other issues included the discrimination of Hmong students and parents within the Fresno Unified School District, including the stereotype of Hmong school children at one public school as unclean.[14] In the summer of 2002, Doua Vu proposed the idea of a bill to Reyes, who was representing District 31, which includes Fresno, Selma, and surrounding areas. The bill sought to "improve the lives of Hmong children" by helping them know more about Hmong's courage and experiences during the Secret War in Laos, their history, and their heritage. In consultation with Vu and her colleagues in the Task Force, Reyes drafted and introduced AB 78 in the State Assembly on December 23, 2002.[15] During the six-month life course of AB 78, a few other state legislators also signed on to cosponsor it. These included Lou Correa of the 69th District of the California State Assembly, who represented cities within Orange County; Ken Maddox of the 68th District, which included cities within Orange County; and Steven Samuelian of the 29th District, which included cities within Fresno and Madera counties.[16]

The main content of AB 78, as originally introduced by Reyes on December 23, 2002, read as follows:

> The Legislature encourages instruction in the area of social sciences, as required pursuant to subdivision (b) of Section 51220, which may include instruction on the Vietnam War and the role of the Hmong people in that war. The Legislature encourages that this instruction include, but not be limited to, a component drawn from personal testimony, especially in the form of oral or video history of Hmong people who were involved in the Vietnam War and those men and women who contributed to the war effort on the homefront. The oral histories used as a part of the instruction regarding the role of the Hmong people in the Vietnam War shall exemplify the personal sacrifice and courage of the wide range of ordinary citizens who were called upon to participate and provide intelligence for the United States. The oral histories shall contain the views and comments of their subjects regarding the reasons for Hmong participation in the war. These oral histories shall also solicit comments from their subjects regarding the aftermath of the war and the immigration of the Hmong people to the United States.[17]

This initial version was focused specifically on Hmong and their involvement in the Vietnam War. Initially, organizers of AB 78 were unaware of any community opposition to the bill or its specific reference to Hmong.[18] Although AB 78 did not mandate instruction, it was unique and significant legislation in at least two respects. First, besides the federal legislation, HVNA of 2000,[19] California's AB 78 was, at the time of its introduction, the only state-sponsored bill in the United States that would have recognized the role of Hmong veterans in the Secret War of Laos. Both bills invoked the factual claim of Hmong's military service to the United States and requested that the American government recognize this historic relationship. Second, just as HVNA provided tangible opportunities for Hmong and Laotian veterans and widowed spouses of veterans to obtain U.S. citizenship, AB 78 represented an important step toward including Hmong American experiences within California's public schools. As such, both bills represented Hmong Americans' efforts to become more politically incorporated into U.S. society.

The effort to mobilize support for AB 78 occurred early on. About a week after introducing AB 78, Reyes held a public news conference about the bill at the Fresno Fairgrounds, where the Hmong International New Year celebration was also taking place.[20] Between late December and early January of each year, the Fresno-based Hmong International New Year celebration draws attendees from all over the United States. On typical days of the weeklong event, crowds usually number between ten and twenty thousand. Although hundreds of business booths and nonprofit organizations compete for attention at the festival, the event still serves as a popular place to attract public support. For instance, Hmong candidates running for public office have made use of the festival to campaign and to fund-raise. While at the public news conference mobilizing support for AB 78, Reyes was quoted as saying, "Many teachers would be willing to do this, especially in this area and other areas where there are so many Southeast Asians. . . . They're going to teach about Vietnam, so they might as well teach the entire aspect of the Vietnam War." According to Reyes, "The idea came from discussions with Hmong adults who were concerned that students don't understand the role the Hmong played in helping the United States during the Vietnam War."[21]

Sustained mobilization, however, was coordinated by Hmong women and men professionals of the Task Force and supported by ad hoc and formal organizations, Hmong churches, ordinary community members, and college students. Between late December 2002 and July 2003, Doua Vu, Pai Yang, Peter Vang, Kao-ly Yang, and others organized a number of community meetings, discussions, petition signing campaigns, and rallies at the State Capitol in support of AB 78.[22] Drawing on their existing ethnic relationships, the Task Force mobilized hundreds of supporters. For instance, Pai Yang drew on her network of Hmong church pastors, resettled refugees, and former citizenship students. The mobilization of Hmong American church leaders to engage in political action was quite novel. As Pai Yang pointed out, "*Lub sijhawm ntawv peb cov pastors lawv tsis kam* involve in anything political" (At that time, our pastors were not willing to get involved in anything political). To convince them to get involved, Yang told them about the history of Black pastors who organized their churches to address social injustices instead of choosing to ignore social problems or to see any political action as inappropriate or "sinful." She emphasized that church leaders are "responsible for being a voice for other people." "I had to instill the idea in some pastors."[23] Many pastors rallied behind Yang and the Task Force for AB 78.

The Fresno Center for New Americans provided facilities for some community meetings. At these community meetings, members of the Task Force discussed the goals of AB 78 and interacted with community members, encouraging participation from Hmong community leaders, educators, students, and parents in letter-writing campaigns and rallies in Sacramento.[24] Kao-ly Yang, a community organizer and supporter of AB 78, described the effort as follows: "For the support of this Bill, there was a mobilization [of the] Hmong community through radio talk shows, petitions, TV shows, public meetings and lobby[ing]. This organization with numerous supporters and volunteers, well-known leaders and committed students, have strongly organized the support: lobby[ing] at the State Capitol in Sacramento, dialog with Veterans, [and] private fundraising for transportation."[25]

Mobilizers made use of existing community infrastructure, especially Hmong kinship networks and Hmong-language radio stations, to "get the word out." By using the Fresno and Sacramento-based Hmong-language radio stations, the Task Force was able to reach Hmong American audiences well beyond the Fresno area, such as those in Chico, Oroville, Marysville, Sacramento, Stockton, and Merced.[26] As Christopher Vang describes,

Hmong leaders, educators, parents, college students and community organizations worked hard to gather public support for the bill throughout California. Hmong radio programs on KBIF 900 AM featured guests from the Hmong Community Education Taskforce discussing the nature of the bill. Hmong-Americans in the Central Valley held community meetings to recruit and organize manpower for political action at the capitol. Hmong-Americans are gathering signatures and letters of support to be sent to the state Legislature, asking lawmakers to vote in favor of the bill. Hmong college students are holding meetings on the University of California and California State University campuses to organize efforts to lobby for the bill. And most importantly, Hmong leaders and veterans are coordinating joint efforts to visit the capitol to meet with state lawmakers. Many are also prepared to give testimony or personal depositions.[27]

Several other formal organizations went on the official record of the Assembly and Senate Committees on Education as supporters of AB 78. For instance, on March 19, 2003, the Assembly Committee on Education record showed that the California School Employees Association, the American Federation of State, County, and Municipal Employees, and LVA registered support for AB 78.[28] On June 11, 2003, the California Federation of Teachers appeared on the Senate Committee on Education record as an additional supporter of the bill.[29] Of these organizations, LVA was the most recently established (in 1998). Nevertheless, the endorsement of the LVA, which represented thousands of Hmong veterans, was especially important because, as I return to below, mobilizers relied largely on a particular collective action frame—the military service frame—to convince the state to pass AB 78.

Moreover, just as Hmong college students had been important actors in Hmong's movement for benefits restoration, Hmong students and organizations at several campuses were also important supporters of AB 78. One such organization was the Hmong Students Inter-Collegiate Coalition (HSIC). Formed in

2001 by Hmong American college students, HSIC was an organization comprising representatives from about twenty-five Hmong student associations of college and university campuses throughout California. Its members were mostly Hmong American college students, but its advisory board was made up of community members and professionals. Through email messages and word of mouth, members of HSIC kept college students informed about and updated on the meetings on AB 78 that were taking place in the California Assembly and Senate. Letter templates were created and petitions distributed to members.

Hmong American college students also wrote personal letters and made phone calls to state legislators, especially members of the Assembly Education Committee. Many of them also attended the AB 78 hearings held at the State Capitol.[30] Besides mobilizing individual and organizational support for AB 78, Hmong American activists needed to also persuade the state to pass AB 78.

Frame Appropriation, Frame Rejection, and Reframing

Above, I described the mass media's framing of teenage suicides in terms of a cultural clash. This cultural collision frame drew upon a dominant American narrative that emphasizes the unchanging and backward nature of immigrant cultures and the need for immigrants to shed their cultural ideas and practices in order to assimilate into a putative "mainstream culture." This media frame of the Hmong teenage suicides posed no threat to the state or its institutions, for it blamed the family institution and, along with it, "Hmong culture" for causing the teenage suicides. Ethnic mobilizers in the AB 78 case appropriated certain aspects of this cultural collision frame by emphasizing the intergenerational gap in knowledge between Hmong children and their parents. This can be seen in a petition that was distributed electronically in support of AB 78: "For many of the younger and newer Hmong generations, AB 78 will further help us grasp a glimpse of a past so foreign to us, yet very much alive in the pictures and memories of our relatives. By signing this petition, we, as students, parents, and active community members, acknowledge that we want to learn more about the role of the Hmong and other Southeast Asians who risked their lives, their families, and their homes during the Vietnam War, especially during the 'Secret War' in Laos."[31] Hmong social actors appropriated the cultural collision frame by implicitly conceding that an intergenerational gap may have contributed to the teenage suicides. However, at the same time they rejected the cultural collision frame's semiexplicit suggestion that the difference between "Hmong culture" and "American culture" was an underlying cause of the suicides.

Instead of attributing the cause of suicides to Hmong cultural difference, constituents and adherents of the AB 78 social movement diagnosed the problem by linking it to racism and discrimination within American society. That Hmong social actors did this can be inferred from the direct observations of Kaoly Yang, who actively organized community support for AB 78:

When I collected signatures at various markets, many Hmong spontaneously offered to sign the petition, which was surprising to me. Because of my experience as a researcher working within minority communities, I know that it used to be difficult to involve people. This discovery made me suppose that the bill AB78 is important for Hmong people. It answers to Hmong people's expectations from American politicians and leaders. The reasons why they supported the bill were: AB78 will decrease gaps between Hmong parents and children; AB78 will decrease racism and cultural misunderstanding at school; AB78 will increase self-esteem of Hmong students towards teachers and outsiders, and participation of parents towards schools so that children will feel confident to succeed; AB78 will increase better understanding of each other's culture for better respecting each other; AB78 will increase the awareness of sharing the same values of peace and of mutual support because of knowing each other's contribution to this American Nation. AB78 is important for children to remember the past so that they will know better how to build the future by not repeating the same mistakes.[32]

Indeed, other Hmong individuals whom I interviewed appeared quite concerned about their shared experiences with "discrimination"—a practice that they link, explicitly or implicitly, to U.S. selective historical amnesia.[33] Many of my interviewees shared about having encountered racial prejudice in public places and institutions: for instance, being unfairly judged by outsiders who do not know them personally or who do not know about Hmong's history and how they ended up as refugees in the United States. These shared grievances helped to galvanize solidarity among supporters of AB 78.

However, Hmong social actors did more than merely present a different diagnosis of teenage suicides. They transformed the agenda around this social problem by constructing an entirely new social problem. That new social problem was that Hmong as a group are often misunderstood and their contributions to the nation as a people have gone unrecognized within the larger society because their history has been left out of the public school curriculum. Accordingly, the logical prognosis for this newly framed social problem was for the California State Legislature to encourage public schools to include instruction about Hmong history especially the contributions that Hmong soldiers have made to the United States during the Secret War in Laos. It was through this work of appropriating cultural discourses, rejecting media frames, and reframing a new social problem that AB 78 was born. But one of the most creative aspects of Hmong's mobilization was in their deployment of a particular collective action frame that both mobilized consensus among supporters and motivated action among goal granters.

In order to maximize the chances that the state legislature would grant their goal (i.e., pass AB 78), Hmong social actors constructed and mobilized around a specific collective action frame. It is Hmong's framing and use of this collective action frame, which I am calling the military service frame, that played the most important role in morally persuading representatives of the state to offer symbolic recognition and support to Hmong. Hmong American actors understood that their trajectory as an ethnic group in the United States has been circumscribed by Hmong's unique historical relationship with the U.S. government. As part of their claims making, Hmong social actors explicitly identified this relationship, framed Hmong's collective identity as a "U.S. ally," and emphasized Hmong's military sacrifices and contributions. Specifically, Hmong movement actors framed their claims as follows:

> During the Vietnam War the Hmong and other Southeast Asians were U.S. allies; many Hmong and other Southeast Asians served as guerrilla forces during the "Secret War" in Laos (part of the Vietnam War), rescuing downed U. S. pilots, gathering information, and defending frontiers against the enemy. According to the Lao Veterans of America, Inc. 35,000 to 40,000 Hmong and other Southeast Asians were killed in the war. . . .
>
> Although many Hmong and other Southeast Asians have become successful citizens in the U.S., many face discrimination. According to the author, including in social sciences classes the sacrifices the Hmong and other Southeast Asians made for the U.S. military may help American pupils understand these people, lessen this discrimination, and help others recognize them as contributing members of society.[34]

Hmong's collective reframing helped to both mobilize collective consensus among supporters and motivate action from the target. First, by making salient a new social problem (Hmong's exclusion from the public school curriculum), ethnic mobilizers were able to mobilize collective consensus by appealing to the ethnic community's sense of shared identity, history of war and migration, and struggles with racial marginalization in the United States. Second, by deploying the military service frame, movement actors helped to maximize the influence of Hmong's state allies in the state legislature by arming them with a set of compelling narratives and moral claims. Hmong's military service frame was compelling because it appropriated dominant cultural discourses—specifically, discourses about the honor of the country and national military duty/sacrifice, as discussed in the previous chapter.

AN UNEXPECTED TURN OF EVENTS

Unfortunately, the bill that actually passed into law was not what supporters of AB 78 or their opponents had originally wanted. Before AB 78 became law on July 10, 2003, it underwent several amendments that, from the Hmong community's point of view, were quite disappointing. In the version that finally became law, all references to "Hmong" and "Hmong history" were erased and replaced with "Southeast Asians" and "Southeast Asian history." Although representatives of the state claim or strongly suggest that this change resulted from their decision not to meddle in the intraethnic conflict surrounding the ethnic group label, I argue that this state action of racializing Hmong as Southeast Asians is consistent with its history of ignoring or repressing non-White minority groups seeking equal rights, resources, or representation within the state. Instead of acknowledging its role in creating unequal opportunities and outcomes within various minority communities, the state, through the practice of racialization or treating minority communities as the same in terms of identity, interests, and needs, excuses itself from the responsibility of ensuring that ethnic groups become politically incorporated.

In March 2003, four months prior to AB 78's passage, members of the Mong Federation, Inc. (MFI) publicly opposed AB 78 on the basis that its usage of the ethnic label "Hmong" excluded at least half of the ethnic population. The MFI argued that the ethnic term "Hmong," rather than being all-inclusive, has always referred to only Hmong Der speakers at the exclusion of Mong Leng speakers. Members of MFI prefer to call themselves and other Mong Leng speakers by the term "Mong." They argue that "Mong" and "Hmong" make up two "linguistically and culturally distinct groups" that have coexisted since "time immemorial."[35] According to the MFI, objective social and linguistic inequities exist within the ethnic group between Mong and Hmong speakers, these conditions negatively affect Mong, and corrective action ought to be taken to change these conditions:

> The misrepresentation of the Mong is evidenced by the already huge disparity between the educational programs, material development, informational materials, and services in the various public and private entities, local school districts, and colleges and universities in the United States between the Mong and the Hmong. *As a consequence, resources and funding have not been allocated to address the needs of the Mong.* When data are collected for funding purposes, the Mong are included with the Hmong; however, when funds are received, they are usually used to benefit the Hmong. Through the use of state and federal funds, curricula, informational materials, tests, and literature have been developed and have been translated into the Hmong language to serve the Hmong-speaking population. None of the materials have been translated into the Mong language to serve the Mong-speaking population. For these reasons, the term "Hmong" does not include the Mong. (Thao 2008, 47, emphasis added)

As such, the MFI demanded specifically that Assemblywoman Sarah Reyes include the term "Mong" "side by side" with the term "Hmong" everywhere in the text of AB 78.

In an article published in the *Mong Journal*, Paoze Thao (2004, 17), president of MFI, describes the initial actions that the organization took toward the state regarding AB 78. Thao (2004, 17) writes, "First, the Mong Federation, Inc. and the Mong Americans wrote letters to Assemblywoman Sarah Reyes on March 8, 2003 (Mong Federation, 2003, Mar 8). Secondly, since AB 78 was scheduled at the State Assembly Education Committee for consent agenda only for March 19, 2003, representatives of the Mong Federation, Inc. went to the State Capitol to request the State Assembly Committee on Education to add and amend the term 'Mong' side by side to the term 'Hmong' in the bill, but it was denied, ignored and rejected."

Based on the available evidence, the state's initial response to MFI's actions between March 8 and March 19 was to suggest that MFI "seek a separate ethnic designation through federal channels."[36] Representatives of MFI confirmed that this state response occurred, and the *Los Angeles Times* further corroborated this when it reported direct quotes from Reyes.[37] As Thao recalls, "Assemblywoman Sarah Reyes explained to the representatives of the Mong Federation, Inc. that, 'all Hmong are classified under that term' and directed the representatives of the Mong Federation, Inc. 'to seek a separate ethnic designation through federal channels' (Reyes, 2003, March 19). Assemblywoman Sarah Reyes also confirmed this statement to the *Los Angeles Times* staff writer Lee Romney as well" (Thao 2004, 17).[38] The *Los Angeles Times* reported the same state response but provided a more revealing quote from Reyes. On May 24, 2003, Lee Romney of the *Los Angeles Times* wrote,

> Reyes said she explained to the group that all Hmong in the United States are classified under that term and directed the Mong to seek a separate ethnic designation through federal channels. The bill neither favors one dialect over another nor mandates the creation of curricular materials, she said. "If I put Mong in there, are the Black Hmong going to come to me? Are the Red Hmong going to come to me?" the assemblywoman asked. "We as a Legislature decided not to get into this fight." Still, Reyes—who has seen Latinos bicker similarly over self-identifying terms—is sympathetic. "It's the struggle of a new community," she said.

In addition to referring them to "federal channels," the state framed the conflict between MFI and sponsors of AB 78 as "the struggle of a new community." But the manner in which the state did this was dramatic. First, the state manufactured resource scarcity. It did this in two ways: (1) by speculating about the effects or benefits of AB 78 and (2) by engaging in a purely hypothetical scenario in which other imagined categories of Hmong might make unwarranted AB 78-like claims upon the state. Through the manufacturing of resource scarcity, the state could "rationally" justify its decision "not to get into this fight." In essence, the state refused to hear the "MFI case" beyond the testimonies given at the Senate Committee on Education hearing. Moreover, by defining the social problem as "the struggle of a new community," the state showed indifference to the MFI's concerns about linguistic inequality and implicitly located the cause of linguistic inequality in the ethnic community rather than in state institutional practices. Finally, by redirecting the MFI to seek corrective action at "federal channels," the state conveniently relieved itself of responsibility as a source of structural inequalities.

However, attending to only Reyes's direct response to MFI presents an incomplete picture of the state's indirect but mediated involvement in this conflict. It begs the question, why did the state, instead of directly addressing MFI's concerns with respect to AB 78, choose to "refer" the MFI case to "federal channels"? Put differently, why did the state decide to define the disagreement between the MFI and their opponents as an ethnic problem instead of a state problem? The answer requires us to identify the broader political contexts in which state representatives were embedded. By identifying this political context (existing state policies and sentiments), perhaps we can better understand why the state took the action that it did toward the MFI in particular and Hmong Californians more generally.

Why did the state define the Mong versus Hmong issue as an ethnic problem but refuse to fulfill MFI's demand to add "Mong" to AB 78? The state may have been influenced to do so because of three factors: (1) the existing political context encouraged it to do so; (2) the state has an interest in providing public goods, but usually only to groups that it regards as powerful or legitimate political brokers; and (3) the state recognized the logic behind various groups' pursuit of ethnic claims upon the nation-state and refused to officiate the Mong as an ethnic or national origins group in order to prevent them from making future claims on the state. I discuss each of these factors in turn.

First, California's political context has been shaped, most recently, by a set of mutually reinforcing laws. This set of laws reflects the anti-immigrant, anti–affirmative action, and anti–bilingual education sentiments and positions of policy makers as well as those of the state's majority voters. These sentiments are found, respectively, in California's Proposition 187 (which passed in 1994),[39] Proposition 209 (1996),[40] and Proposition 227 (1998).[41] Each of these highly controversial propositions passed by a majority vote. According to California Secretary of State records, Proposition 187, Proposition 209, and Proposition 227 won 58.9 percent, 54.6 percent, and 60.9 percent of votes, respectively (Jones 1994, 1996, 1998).[42] The state and the majority of the general population constitute and operate under this political context. Under this context, the most plausible action of the state would be to define any issue that challenges these policies and sentiments as deviant or to refuse to hear the issue altogether by defining it as a nonstate issue. On the other hand, if an issue serves or upholds the status quo, it probably would most be considered a "compelling government interest." MFI's request to be recognized as a separate ethnolinguistic group in an education bill would probably be read by the rest of the state as an attempt to promote bilingual education.

But the state does, under certain circumstances, choose to hear or listen to particular groups who raise certain issues that go against the status quo. The state is interested, at least in theory, in providing a "public good"—that is, in providing a valued resource that serves the "greatest good." However, in practice most of the time the state caters to or provides rewards and goods to powerful groups whose programs or interests uphold the state's "compelling government interests." The compelling government interests in a given circumstance or period, in turn, are determined interactively by the influential representatives of the legislative, judicial, and executive branches of the government and by the representatives of powerful interest groups, such as corporations and other administrative governmental agencies. As the work of legal scholars shows, these government branches rely on, reinforce, validate, and influence one another more often than is usually acknowledged (Abourezk 1977; Crain and Tollison 1979; Kang 2004). Given the limited direct access that less powerful groups have to these branches of the government, they encounter difficulties when the state chooses not to define their issue as one that warrants state attention or state action.

I suggest that there is an even more compelling reason for the state to refuse to meet MFI's demand to include "Mong" in a state law—the state's unstated desire *not* to set any legal precedent that could allow Mong to make future claims upon the state as an *ethnic* or *national origins* group. For under state and federal law, ethnic/national origins groups are entitled to certain legal protections against discrimination in various public institutions. The state probably refused to add "Mong" alongside "Hmong" in a state bill as a way to avoid officiating the Mong as an ethnic or national origins group. In essence, the state's response to MFI was an attempt to prevent them from carrying out ethnic- or linguistic-based social movements in the future. The state's refusal to take responsibility for the social problem or to help correct it severely curtailed the MFI movement's impact on state practices; yet both the state and federally funded government agencies are largely responsible for maintaining Hmong Der as the predominant dialect in most government publications.

SUMMARY

My findings demonstrate the collective agency of Hmong American actors, especially Hmong American women professionals, as they recognized cultural opportunities, appropriated dominant discourses, constructed collective action frames, and used them to mobilize consensus and motivate action on social problems that they defined. As opposed to past movements, the movement for

AB 78 was led by Hmong American women professionals. These women were educated, experienced in community organizing, and bilingual or multilingual. Importantly, years before the AB 78 movement began, Hmong American women professionals like Pai Yang had already established a network of professional and personal ties within the ethnic community through their work as refugee program directors and citizenship teachers. Their sustained presence and extensive work within the Hmong community and their willingness to represent Hmong parents in their fight for changes in public schools made them credible activists within the ethnic community. Reflecting their political savvy, Hmong American women professionals founded groups such as the Hmong Community Education Task Force but invited other well-known and noncontroversial Hmong American men professionals to work with them, even appointing their male colleague as chair of the Task Force. That the AB 78 movement was focused on the inclusion of Hmong history in the public school curriculum also distinguished it from other movements, such as movements for women's rights or veterans' rights that could have been perceived by some as the province of women or men, respectively. Given these conditions and given that neither the Task Force nor its leading Hmong American women activists posed a threat to male leadership structures within or outside the ethnic community, this movement encountered little, if any, pushback for reasons related to gender. From the beginning and throughout the AB 78 movement, Hmong American women professionals were able to mobilize support from a broad range of ethnic individuals and leaders, including Hmong pastors and leaders of veterans organizations. Their collective efforts were crucial to the relative success of this movement.

State agencies and the mass media do create and maintain dominant discourses, which often limit social actors' discursive options, but social movement actors can draw upon dominant discourses to produce their own discursive repertoires in pursuit of their own agendas (Steinberg 1999). However, it does appear that collective action frames need to incorporate or engage in dialogue with certain aspects of the broader cultural contexts in order to appeal to a target audience and have a better chance of motivating them to take action on a social problem (Taylor and Van Dyke 2004). My case study shows that the California government was responsive to Hmong American concerns—as indicated by their decision to pass AB 78—so long as Hmong and their supporters framed disparate social problems in terms of the military service frame. By appropriating discourses about national honor while emphasizing Hmong's unique contributions to the United States, the military service repertoire created an opportunity for the convergence of the state's and challengers' interests.

The success of Hmong's campaign, however, had as much to do with Hmong actors' framing strategies as with the capacity of their community infrastructure to facilitate communication and support resource mobilization. As we have seen, existing organizations such as Hmong radio stations, Hmong churches, and college student organizations within the Central Valley facilitated the communication between social movement constituents and potential supporters, helping constituents to organize a network of supporters across the state. What is novel in the AB 78 movement is that some Hmong pastors, after some persuasion, were willing to mobilize their church members to engage in civic or political actions in support of the movement. Although it remains to be seen whether Hmong American–led churches will participate in more political actions, the churches and their extensive networks of social ties represent a potential source of politically relevant resources. Existing ethnic infrastructures matter because they can serve as mobilizing structures, providing communication channels, resources, and recruits. The strategic framing of claims backed up by a well-organized network of activists and supporters can help to sustain a movement, which, in turn, can lead to a positive outcome.

Once more, we see how the state deploys racialization as part of its policy of symbolic inclusion. Instead of granting Hmong social movement actors what they were asking for, which was specific recognition of Hmong's military contributions to the United States, the state decided to replace "Hmong" with "Southeast Asians." Such a decision perpetuated the state's selective forgetting of the U.S. military involvement in Laos and Hmong's sacrifice and military service to the United States. The vagueness of the term "Southeast Asian" makes invisible the unique experiences and contributions of *all* the ethnic groups subsumed under this label. While, on its surface, attention to Southeast Asians' role in the Vietnam War might seem inclusive, this vague phrase is quite problematic. For one thing, it does not do anything to clarify who makes up this quasi-racial category. Second, it makes no distinction between refugees and immigrants from Southeast Asia. Third, it makes no distinction between people whom the United States secretly used to fight communism, people whom the United States openly used to fight communism, people whom the United States killed for being alleged communist, people whom the United States evacuated from Southeast Asia, people whom the United States left behind in Southeast Asia, and so on. Given this, at best, we have some kind of symbolic inclusion of a vague category of people the state has decided to label "Southeast Asians"; at worst, it has nothing to do with the inclusion of groups at all. Rather, the state is more interested in reinforcing racial categories for the purpose of curtailing ethnic groups' future claims on the political system. Instead of addressing long-standing social disparities within ethnic communities—problems for which the state and its various bureaucratic agencies are responsible for creating and maintaining—the state government chose to label certain problems "ethnic problems" in order to shift responsibility to the federal government.

6 · RACIALIZED POLITICAL INCORPORATION AND IMMIGRANT RIGHTS

Although political incorporation is often seen as something that states do, in the contemporary U.S. political context, immigrant groups sometimes incorporate themselves through collective action. By examining the conditions, mechanisms, and outcomes of Hmong Americans' movements for public benefits, citizenship, and representation, I have highlighted ethnic collective action as a crucial mechanism by which Hmong Americans opened the U.S. political system to have their interests represented in public policies. While underscoring the significance of immigrant collective agency, I also revealed how the racial state plays a powerful role in shaping and delimiting immigrants' political incorporation. Whereas past research takes political incorporation to be a process in which groups interact with the political system to have their interests represented in public policies or to obtain resource distribution, I demonstrated that, for immigrant groups racialized as non-Whites, political incorporation entails more than just obtaining resources or public goods. For non-White immigrant groups, political incorporation is also about obtaining political standing in a racially and economically stratified political system. Having political standing, as opposed to merely having formal membership, matters for immigrant groups' capacity to influence the political system. As such, immigrant political incorporation should be understood as an ongoing, dynamic, multipronged process involving minimally both the immigrant group's concerted efforts to influence public policy, especially in getting their self-interests represented in public policy and obtaining legitimate political standing within the political system and the state's efforts at disincorporating them.

Thus I have argued here that during the past three decades Hmong former refugees and their descendants have sought to incorporate themselves politically into the U.S. political system by engaging in strategic ethnic collective actions. Hmong movement actors, in response to perceived political threats and/or opportunities, engaged in collective framing, especially the framing of self-incorporated political identities, and mobilized a network of ethnic organizations and institutional and state allies to influence the political system. In response to threats such as the welfare reforms of the mid-1990s, Hmong American movement actors drew on their collective political narratives to construct themselves as a former U.S. military ally—a political identity that they deployed in this and subsequent movements to call out the state's selective historical amnesia, challenge its hypocrisy, and demand state accountability. They utilized existing Hmong civic organizations and newly created ad hoc organizations as structures through which to both mobilize ethnic members and connect the Hmong community to potential institutional and state allies, from whom they received sympathy and substantial support. Nonetheless, these Hmong men and women, veterans and professionals, were the instigators of these social movements. They did the labor-intensive work of mobilizing resources and organizing people, they were proactive in forming alliances, and led the efforts to strategize and implement plans of action. They organized their communities to write letters, march, demonstrate, and show up for these efforts, at times in full soldier uniforms, to voice their grievances and demands before government officials. Through these sustained, strategic ethnic collective actions, Hmong Americans were able to push the political system to grant them tangible benefits, rights, and symbolic representation.

However, even as Hmong Americans obtained policy concessions by positioning themselves in strategic ways, they were positioned by the racial state in ways that undermined their political standing. I have shown that the state defined Hmong veterans as anything but veterans, othered Hmong as aliens, and racialized them as a "tribe" or as "Southeast Asians." In defining Hmong in these ways, the state perpetuated the image of Hmong as foreigners to the nation, weakening their political standing and curtailing their capacity to make future political claims, such as those for veterans' benefits. While underscoring the significance of immigrants' collective agency in incorporating themselves, clearly the evidence shows that state racialization continues to powerfully shape immigrants' political standing and delimit their political incorporation.

The SECA model of immigrant political incorporation that I have developed throughout this book conceives of immigrant political incorporation as an ongoing, dynamic, multi-pronged process involving immigrant groups' concerted efforts to both influence public policy, especially to have their self-interests represented in policy, and obtain legitimate political standing within the political system and the state's efforts at disincorporating them. The interaction between immigrant groups and the state is mediated by a number of factors and takes place within nested cultural and political contexts that can facilitate or constrain either side's opportunities for taking action. This framework contributes to a more complete understanding of the process of political incorporation by taking account of how immigrant groups' contexts of exit and reception shape their col-lective actions, especially group identity formation during political struggles, and how the state, through othering and racialization practices, can perpetuate the political marginalization of immigrant groups.

During the past three decades, Hmong Americans' strategic ethnic collective actions have entailed the following: (1) the actions of "ordinary" Hmong men and women who, motivated by grievances and the sense of shared history and fate, chose to participate in various forms of individual and collective action, such as rallies, demonstrations, hearings, litigation, suicide, and so on and who provided the oral and written narratives upon which ethnic leaders and insti-tutional and state allies often drew to construct political identities and frame collective action frames; (2) the actions of Hmong American men and women professionals who recognized political opportunities and threats and actively organized, formed, and led groups in political claims making in response to these opportunities or threats, or did not lead organized groups but nonetheless recognized political opportunities and engaged in claims making that per-suaded policy makers to follow through on policies that benefit Hmong; and (3) the actions of a network of existing Hmong-led organizations that served as (a) mobilizing structures transforming ethnic bystanders into movement par-ticipants, (b) bridging organizations connecting Hmong interest groups and communities to other minority organizations (potential institutional allies) and representatives of the government (potential state allies), and/or (c) social movement organizations directly engaged in lobbying their intended targets.

Next, I discuss the implications of my findings for our understanding of immigrant political incorporation. I focus on three sets of interrelated processes within political incorporation: immigrant groups' ability to enter into the politi-cal system, their capacity to influence public policies, and the impact of state racialization on immigrant groups' political standing and incorporation.

INFLUENCING THE POLITICAL SYSTEM

My research suggests that immigrant groups' ability to participate in and influ-ence the political system is contingent on at least two interrelated processes: (1) the creation of meaningful access points into the political system and (2) the capacity of immigrant movement actors and groups to engage in and sustain col-lective actions. First, gaining access into the political system depends on immi-grants' ability to court and maintain ties with institutional and/or state allies who can serve as access points or help to create access points into the political system using their standing and resources. But the ability to win the support of institutional or state allies in the first place could depend on many other factors, including immigrants' existing networks. Second, immigrants' capacity to engage in and sustain collective actions depends on their discursive and other kinds of resources and on cultural and political opportunities. For immigrant groups such as Hmong, who have fewer economic resources and limited political standing, discursive resources become even more important and can be mobilized as politically relevant resources during political struggles.

One of the problems facing Hmong former refugees in the 1990s is that they lacked meaningful access points into the political system, especially access into the upper echelons of the government. Hmong's historically asymmetrical relationship with the U.S. government gave them limited access points, namely via the CIA, into the U.S. political system in the 1960s and 1970s. However, given the U.S. government's secret plan in 1975 to keep displaced Hmong refugees permanently in Thailand without ever admitting them (chapter 2), it is apparent that the United States was not interested in continuing their relationship with Hmong, let alone see them as a group with legitimate political standing. Changes in the United States' bilateral and multilateral trade and military policies since the late 1980s and early 1990s coupled with the retirement or deaths of state actors (e.g., CIA officials) familiar with Hmong's military service and sympathetic to Hmong refugees' plight meant that Hmong had even fewer access points into the U.S. political system. Additionally, until the 2000s, Hmong Americans lacked descriptive representation in state-level governments. Combined, these conditions put Hmong in a politically vulnerable position. However, as I have shown, Hmong were not politically powerless. To gain access into the political system, Hmong relied on other more politically experienced organizational actors, state actors, and politically integrated ethnic actors. But these actors usually had to be activated or mobilized to do this work.

Consistent with previous research that shows that civic organizations play important roles as mobilizing structures (Wong 2006), the case studies in this book show that Hmong's civic organizations played important roles in mobilizing Hmong during each of their movements for political incorporation. Leaders and staff of Hmong's civic organizations often were the first ones to find out about new policy changes, such as when federal welfare reform was passed in 1996. They were some of the first to respond to these changes by getting together with other informed individuals and volunteers, gathering information, and writing letters to government officials or agencies on behalf of the ethnic community to express their concerns and demand responses. Some leaders and staff of civic organizations were also in the position to know what other non-Hmong civic organizations were planning to do to, such as where and when public marches and demonstrations were planned. Civic organizations such as CHAC, LVA, and the Fresno-based Hmong Community Education Task Force served multiple roles, such as meeting places, providing information, rallying community members, organizing protests, and so on. But most important of all, these civic organizations operated as ad hoc social movement organizations or took the initiative to create ad hoc social movement organizations and worked to inform and build collective consensus among ethnic individuals around shared concerns or problems. They planned letter writing campaigns, rallies, marches, and/or demonstrations, called people to inform them about these events, and found transportation for people who wanted to participate in these events. Besides serving as mobilizing structures, some civic organizations also served as important bridges between the Hmong community and other more established organizations, such as ALC, or state actors, such as Congressman Bruce Vento.

As we have seen, institutional and state allies helped Hmong access the state and the political system in ways that they might not have been able to do alone. In California, ALC, for instance, represented hundreds of vulnerable Hmong men and women who had lost their public benefits because of welfare reforms during their state hearing appeals. It filed a lawsuit in federal court on behalf of a Hmong veteran who lost his benefits. But ALC also called on its Washington-based lobbying firm, NAPALC, to lobby the U.S. Congress and to work with other political lobbying firms to lobby the White House and other departments in the executive branch. State actors such as Vento of Minnesota served as Hmong's access point into the political system, mediated Hmong's interactions with political actors in that system, and facilitated the convergence between Hmong's interest and that of the state. In Minnesota, Hmong organizations like the Minnesota branch of LVA approached and sought the help of Vento in coming up with and introducing HVNA. But beyond serving as access points into the political system, Vento (and other state allies) also helped Hmong frame and amplify their political claims.

Beyond serving as access points into the political system, sympathetic and politically skillful state allies facilitated Hmong's interactions with the political system. It mattered that state allies who possessed legitimate political standing within the political system, such as U.S. representatives Bruce Vento, Sonny Bono, Melvin Watt, Zoe Lofgren, and other elected congressmembers, were the ones articulating Hmong Americans' interests and the state's obligations (read interests). By amplifying Hmong's claims and articulating how these claims bear on the U.S. government's foreign policies and military interests, state allies were able to persuade policy makers to consider what was politically sound for the state. However, what eventually motivated policy makers to take action—to grant limited policy concessions to a former military ally in the late 1990s—probably had a lot to do with timing and broader political contexts.

Just as immigrants are embedded in contexts of exit and reception that shape their resources, opportunities, and strategic choices, the broader political contexts in which the host state is embedded can shape its opportunities and interests and the extent to which it may be persuaded to take action on certain political claims that certain groups make on the political system. I argued that Hmong's use of the military service frame during their movements for benefits restoration and naturalization accommodations (chapters 3 and 4) was persuasive in influencing policy, in part because of Hmong's unique historical relationship with the

United States and in part because it created a convergence of interests between Hmong's interests and those of the state during a time when the United States was anticipating another impending war in the Middle East, the Iraq War. As a well-known "global player" in the "international community," the United States cares as much about asserting military and economic power around the world as it does about managing its impression on the rest of the world, especially its impression as an "honorable democracy." As a colony and, later, country, the United States has been involved in wars almost continuously since the American Revolutionary War and has a long history of relying on indigenous peoples to do its fighting in major battles and wars (and then abandoning them). It was in these contexts—the U.S. government's interest in presenting itself as an honorable country and its ongoing foreign policy and military interests in the Middle East in the late 1990s and early 2000s—that the United States responded the way that it did to Hmong's collective claims, positively and with some deference to Hmong's military service claims (see chapter 4).

Besides immigrants' civic organizations and their institutional and state allies, politically integrated ethnic actors also played important roles. These are individuals who are not necessarily constituents or active participants in social movements but nevertheless possess an insider's view of the political process, which helped them to recognize important windows of political opportunities that outsiders, including movement leaders, might not have. For instance, during the Hmong veterans' movement for naturalization accommodations (chapter 4), Lee Pao Xiong, who was a resident of Minnesota and an appointed member of President Clinton's Advisory Commission on Asian-Americans and Pacific Islanders, recognized and took a series of actions on a crucial window of opportunity opened up by the House of Representatives' decision on HVNA. Xiong took quick steps to motivate action from within Senator Wellstone's office, which then led to the bill being fast-tracked (instead of stalled). Finally, Xiong was consulted and provided President Clinton with several compelling reasons to pass the bill. Had social actors like Xiong not taken the actions that they did, it is possible that Hmong veterans' movement for naturalization accommodations might not have turned out the way that it did. Gaining access into the political system, however, does not mean that a group will be able to influence the political system.

Hmong Americans also faced and continue to face the issue of being a relatively small, racialized minority group with limited resources and political standing. Although some might assume that this presents serious challenges for them in terms of their capacity to sustain collective actions, Hmong Americans were able to mobilize and sustain collective actions by doing a number of things, but especially by deploying political narratives and constructing self-incorporated political identities—in short, by strategically positioning themselves. As we have seen, Hmong drew on existing collective political narratives and tactical repertoires when they needed to make and contest political claims in the United

States. For instance, in response to the U.S. government's policy of limiting public benefits to only U.S. citizens, Hmong noncitizens constructed themselves as a
military ally to challenge the state's arbitrary categories of deserving and undeserving people. Rather than positioning themselves merely as an immigrant or
refugee group seeking benefits, Hmong positioned themselves as simultaneously
a former U.S. military ally, Hmong, and a refugee people. Along with forging this
particular political identity, Hmong drew on the narratives of the Secret War to
locate the cause of Hmong's statelessness and presence in the United States
squarely in the U.S. government's involvement in that war and its subsequent
abandonment and betrayal of Hmong (chapter 3).

These processes highlight the significance of immigrants' contexts of exit and
the important role of group formation in political incorporation. Theorists of
segmented assimilation have long recognized that immigrant groups' contexts of
exit shape the types and levels of resources they arrive with and, by extension,
their socioeconomic assimilation. Yet the kinds of discursive resources that
immigrants bring along with them and the implications that discursive resources
have for immigrants' political incorporation remain understudied. By examining
how Hmong, in response to perceived political threats and/or opportunities,
drew on their collective political narratives and deployed protest repertoires to
make claims on the political system, my study clarifies the roles that immigrants'
contexts of exit play in immigrant political incorporation.

An immigrant group's contexts of exit shape not only the material and financial resources that it arrives with but also its discursive resources—specifically,
its members' collective political narratives or the common stories that people
within a group tell about people, events, and unanticipated crises or troubles.
These collective political narratives in turn provide the raw materials upon which
social movement actors can draw to construct political identities and make
political claims to meet their needs during concrete political struggles. For
Hmong former refugees, the story of how Americans came to Laos in the 1960s,
recruited or conscripted Hmong young boys, men, and women to fight and die
in America's Secret War, and abandoned Hmong refugees in the aftermath of
that war (chapter 2) remains one of the most heart-wrenching and unforgettable
stories in their collective memory. When Hmong became stateless refugees and
prior to their international migration, Hmong refugees narrated these common
stories in their poetry, prose, and music, in their colorful story cloths, in their
audiotaped exchanges with their loved ones, and during their interviews with
refugee workers and immigration officers. While the details of individuals' stories varied, taken together they form an unmistakable collective political narrative that often begins with "Americans came to our home country" and ends
with "we became war-torn stateless people." As I have shown, in two Hmong
American–led social movements (chapters 3 and 4), movement actors drew
upon Hmong's collective political narratives of the Secret War to construct

Hmong as a U.S. military ally and to demand that the U.S. government recognize and grant special considerations to Hmong for their military service to the nation. In some other social movements, including their movement for curricular inclusion in California (chapter 5), Hmong interest groups deployed the military service frame as part of their efforts to persuade either the state or federal government to grant them recognition and/or certain benefits (Xiong 2016).

Moreover, contexts of exit can shape an immigrant group's repertoires of contention—that is, the set of collective actions, including protest tactics, that people know they can adapt and use when they want to oppose decisions or conditions they consider unjust or threatening. As people who were entangled in decades of armed conflicts and the various kinds of political identities and collective actions that armed conflicts entail, many Hmong refugees arrived with knowledge if not also experience of the tactics of recruitment, resource mobilization, and various means of making claims that bear on the interests of individuals, groups, and governments (chapter 2). As we saw in Hmong's movement for benefits restoration (chapter 3), Hmong veterans organized themselves and traveled to Washington to lobby the U.S. Congress and other government bodies. At the same time, leaders of Hmong community organizations wrote letters on their community's behalf to state officials demanding answers and corrective actions. Several Hmong older adults committed suicide in protest of welfare reforms, and others threatened to kill themselves. Hundreds of Hmong women and men throughout Central California traveled to their state capitol to join thousands of other immigrants in rallies and demonstrations against welfare reforms. At these protest events, Hmong activists and representatives of Hmong refugees called out the U.S. government and demanded better, more equitable treatment for all immigrants. Meanwhile, thousands of Hmong heads of households filed mass appeals, gathered old photographs and military and refugee documents, and used them in their testimonies in front of administrative law judges who presided over their state hearings on public benefits. While some of these repertoires of contention may be familiar to politically active Americans, some of them, especially suicide protests, are extraordinary. All these individual and collective actions require skills and, most of all, courage.

Other scholars have recognized the role of immigrants' home country experiences in shaping their political socialization and political choices. In his study of Afro-Caribbean immigrants' and African Americans' political attitudes and behaviors, Reuel Rogers (2006, 33) argues that home country attachments, experiences, and memories are "likely to have a cognitive effect on immigrants' political attitudes and behavior." This is because immigrants' home country ties, experiences, and memories provide them with "cues" or cognitive frames through which to "make judgments about politics in the early stages of incorporation" (Rogers 2006, 237). For instance, although both African Americans and Afro-Caribbean immigrants have faced racial discrimination in the United

States, Afro-Caribbean immigrants have responded differently than their native-born counterparts to racial discrimination because their home country ties provide them with the option of exiting the United States should racial barriers to their advancement become too great (Rogers 2006). Besides the difference in how Afro-Caribbean immigrants and African Americans have responded to racial discrimination, Rogers finds that members of these two groups also differ in how they viewed policy issues and defined themselves. For example, most of the Afro-Caribbeans he interviewed did not "attach the same collectivist political meanings to their racial identity as African Americans" (Rogers 2006, 247). It is quite possible that immigrants rely on cues from both the home country and the host society to make sense of their political situations and options, as Rogers (2006) suggest they do, and then draw on collective political narratives and repertoires of contention in order to engage in claims-making activities such as framing political identities and deploying tactics of protest and persuasion.

Rather than arriving as "blank slates," refugees and immigrants come as persons, families, and communities whose experiences have been conditioned by particular historical contexts. My findings suggest that for groups such as Hmong former refugees who lack financial resources, durable institutional bases, and White privilege, discursive resources are just as politically relevant as if not more relevant than financial resources for immigrants' capacity to influence the political system. My finding is consistent with past research which shows that groups such as women who have been excluded from major political arenas and therefore lack political institutional bases for making claims rely heavily on discursive resources to influence public policies (Fraser 1989; Hobson 1999).

In highlighting the significance of discursive resources, I am not claiming that other kinds of resources such as financial resources and social capital do not matter for a group's capacity to make sustained claims on the political system, because they do. As Browning, Marshall, and Tabb (1984) have shown, a group's organization and structure of resources can affect its mobilization capacity and strategic choices. Similarly, I have shown that Hmong's ethnic capital and organizational networks play important roles in Hmong's capacity to mobilize collective action. However, what is unexpected is that Hmong, whose population was relatively small and had much fewer socioeconomic resources and institutional bases than other immigrant groups, were able to not only participate in the political system but also occasionally have their interests represented in public policies. A resource-based perspective on immigrant political incorporation would have predicted Hmong to form coalitions with other immigrant and/or minority groups in order that they could aggregate the resources needed to pursue political incorporation. It would not have expected Hmong to go it alone, as they did in the social movements I examined.

Taking account of an immigrant group's contexts of exit may also help to clarify why a group might choose to pursue collective claims as an ethnic group rather than as members of a panethnic group or racial category. Focusing on conditions in the contexts of reception, Okamoto (2014) theorizes and shows convincingly that occupational segregation along racial lines can create the necessary albeit insufficient condition for panethnic formation. Since Hmong are racialized as Asian and have experienced occupational segregation alongside other Asian subgroups (namely, other Southeast Asian former refugees), we might expect Hmong to form alliances with other similarly situated Asian American groups and pursue claims as panethnic members. Yet during the past three decades Hmong Americans have often pursued political claims as an ethnic group rather than as members of a panethnic group. As we have seen, even in cases where Hmong Americans sought and received substantial help from institutional allies such as ALC and marched alongside other racialized immigrant groups, including Vietnamese and Cambodians, Hmong American movement actors did not construct or mobilize themselves as an Asian American or Southeast Asian American group. Although I do not have original data about Hmong Americans' feelings toward other ethnic groups, what we do know is that Hmong's interethnic relations prior to their international migration have ranged from peaceful coexistence to quite contentious and violent to tragic.

Past hostile or distrustful interethnic relations may encourage ethnic instead of panethnic formation. Hmong's premigration experiences have been conditioned by a long history of political oppression and marginalization at the hands of various states and ethnic groups, including Han Chinese, Vietnamese, French, Lao, Japanese, and Thai. As a minority group, Hmong have been subjected to various forms of violence, manipulation, control, and persecution. But Hmong have also rebelled against their oppressors. They have had to struggle economically and politically alongside various ethnic groups who seemed concerned primarily with advancing their own political interests rather than with building trust or solidarity—two crucial ingredients in panethnic formation (Okamoto 2014). It was not until relatively recently (after the 1970s) that Hmong, labeled as Miao in China and Meo in Southeast Asia, were able to rid themselves of the Meo straitjacket and achieve the political identity, "Hmong." In short, Hmong are no strangers to political oppression by states and majority groups and to distrust and struggles among political factions of various national and ethnic backgrounds. These experiences of factional struggles for political power and survival or, more precisely, Hmong's collective narratives of them do not simply disappear when they cross international borders. As Hmong refugees resettle in the United States and as they and their descendants interact with members of White and racial minority groups, their collective narratives as well as new experiences of interethnic interactions have implications for how they define themselves and others within the political system. Collective narratives shape Hmong individuals' sense of who they are as persons or members of groups and can serve as a lens through which they view and interpret the (in)actions of their new government and groups within U.S. society.

Besides the lack of trust and solidarity between distinct ethnic groups, the strong pressures for national origin and ethnic groups to protect their own interests in the United States may be a barrier to panethnic coalition building. Both actual and manufactured scarcity of tangible resources and opportunities may pressure groups to prioritize their own self-interests before others. Hmong Americans' residential segregation from other Asian American groups in large urban cities like the Twin Cities may be another barrier to their panethnic formation.[1] Anecdotal evidence suggests that more established Asian American actors sometimes prioritize the goals of their groups/organizations over those of Hmong; such practices may discourage Hmong actors from engaging in pan–Asian American coalitions with these actors and the groups they represent. Furthermore, Hmong's frequent use by other more established Asian Americans as the stereotypical negative "case" against the Asian model minority myth as if Hmong were a monolith and as if other Asian Americans do not also share the experiences of poverty has marked them as separate from rather than a part of the Asian American category. Whatever the actual reasons may be, it seems that panethnic formation requires more than just the condition of being racialized (Brown and Jones 2015; Okamoto 2014).

My case study lends support to the claim by Nagel (1995) that group identities are political constructions. However, merely knowing that this is the case does not help us answer the important questions posed by Brown and Jones (2015): "What institutional practices or structures lead to the contraction or expansion of group identities?" and "What are the conditions under which institutional classifications respond to group-based mobilization?"

To begin with, the findings from my case study suggest that we have no way of knowing in advance exactly which political identity or identities a group will construct in concrete political struggles. But we are not completely clueless either. A group like the Hmong can simultaneously resist government-imposed categories (e.g., noncitizens), form alliances with panethnic organizations without forging a panethnic identity, and construct and deploy a nonethnic, nonracial collective identity (e.g., military ally of the United States) but particularize it to their ethnic group or community (Hmong). However, regardless of the collective identity that a group chooses to deploy, the state has a tendency to racialize them. It is this intersection between immigrants' assertion of political identities and the state's racial ascription of them that remains understudied but deserves further empirical investigation. Brown and Jones (2015, 181) point out that despite race and immigration scholars' shared interest in understanding group formation and intergroup relations, "few analytical concepts adequately bridge both specializations." For instance, although research on panethnicity has "shed new light on the formation of group identities and mobilization, it has emerged alongside but rarely in conversation with a well-established literature on the racialization process" (Brown and Jones 2015, 182).

STATE RACIALIZATION

My findings suggest that research should pay closer attention to both processes of group identity formation and processes of ascription, especially state racialization, to uncover how these processes intersect with one another and the extent to which they shape immigrants' political incorporation. The findings of my case studies suggest that state racialization can take subtle forms, such as occurring in the language of public policies that, on their face, appear to be race-neutral in their intent and operation. These findings are consistent with past research which demonstrates the enduring presence of racial considerations and racialized consequences in public policies, including policies that claim to be free of racial prejudice (Saito 2009).

Despite its subtlety, state racialization may be more pervasive and more consequential than it seems. I have argued throughout this book that state racialization curtails immigrant groups' political standing and delimits their political incorporation. How the state (re)racializes an immigrant group or where it positions that group within the racial hierarchy of the United States can have consequences for its political incorporation. I have shown that even when Hmong movement actors tried to resist racialization by defining and incorporating themselves—for example, as political refugees or as veterans or military allies of the United States—and even when their self-incorporated political identities were taken seriously, the state, in every movement, ended up reracializing Hmong by putting them in racialized categories such as "alien," "tribe," and "Southeast Asian."

Brown and Jones (2015) argue that instead of seeing racialization and panethnicity as separate processes, racialization, or ascription in general, and panethnicity, or the formation of group identity and mobilization more generally, ought to be seen as mutually constitutive processes. They propose an ethnoracialization model of group formation that contains three premises: (1) "the ascription process intimately involves major social institutions and reflects society-specific hierarchies of power"; (2) ascription is an ongoing process as "categories around which individuals mobilize and self-identity are continually reinforced by external institutions and power structures"; and (3) "the relationship between ascription and racialization depends on the process of discursive reinterpretation" (Brown and Jones 2015, 187). My findings related to Hmong's group formation and state racialization support some of these premises, elaborate on some of them, but also complicate some of them.

First, my work lends some support to the claim by Brown and Jones (2015, 187) that racialization or ascription in general is an ongoing process and that the "process of ascription does not end with the advent of identity adoption or collective mobilization." Examining non-White immigrant groups' processes of political incorporation can help to clarify how racialization is ongoing and intertwined with the equally ongoing process of political incorporation. I have examined the role of the state in racializing immigrant groups upon or after their entry and reracializing them through subsequent public policies. This state practice of initial racialization and reracialization is one way in which racialization is an ongoing process. In Hmong's case, they were referred to by the U.S. government, following French colonialists' racialization of them, as "Indochinese," even before they first arrived on U.S. soil. Throughout the 1970s and 1980s, official documents continued to label Hmong, Lao, Cambodians, and Vietnamese as "Indochinese." In 1990, the U.S. Census Bureau officially classified Hmong as "Asians" or "Other Asians." Often lumped in the vague category, "Other Asians," Hmong and other ethnic groups along with them were made invisible in official documents about "Asians." But beyond legal classification, this book has shown that the state often reracializes Hmong. State reracialization occurs alongside the granting of limited policy concessions to groups. This (re)racialization is sometimes subtle, such as when Hmong were racialized as a "tribe," and sometimes quite overt, such as when they were labeled as "Southeast Asians." Whether subtle or overt, state racialization has consequences for Hmong's political standing.

Another way in which racialization is ongoing is that for some or perhaps most immigrant groups, where they are positioned within the "field of racial positions" by the state and public institutions in civil society is an ongoing process subject to change over time. Kim (1999) uses the phrase "racial triangulation" to refer to how Asian Americans experience both relative valorization and civic ostracism in the United States. By "relative valorization," she means that Asians, as a category, are often positioned as closer to Whites than to Blacks within the field of racial positions—an analytical field that represents multiple axes of identity/subordination. By "civic ostracism" she means that Asians are often seen as foreigners and excluded from society accordingly. This book has offered us some clues about how the state positioned Hmong Americans as it responded to their political claims from time to time. By labeling Hmong as a tribe, the state not only marked Hmong as a nonethnic group but perpetuated stereotypes about Hmong's primitiveness and unassimilability. Cast as primitive and foreigners, albeit not necessarily valorized, Hmong and their descendants continue to face forms of civic ostracism in the United States.

A year after Hmong veterans won naturalization accommodations, the United States passed the USA PATRIOT Act and in 2005 passed the U.S. REAL ID Act. These acts were part of the United States' campaign in its so-called global war on terror—a campaign that has had far-reaching consequences on various groups of people around the world, especially Muslims and Muslim Americans (Selod 2018). One of the consequences of these acts was that Hmong who fought on the side of the United States became classified as "terrorists" for having provided "material support" to a "terrorist organization."[2] As a result of this classification, Hmong refugees who were not already in the United States were barred from entry and Hmong who were applying for permanent resident status had their applications delayed in being processed.[3] In response to this racial and political ascription, Hmong Americans organized, protested, and lobbied policy makers to demand change. In December 2007, the Consolidated Appropriations Act (Public Law 110–161) finally removed Hmong from the terrorist list. However, the damage had already been done, as in June 2007 General Vang Pao, former commander of the U.S. secret army in Laos, along with several other Hmong men were charged for an alleged plot to overthrow the Lao People's Democratic Republic. Although the terrorist charges were leveled against just this group of men, many in the Hmong American community felt that the U.S. government targeted the ethnic group and betrayed Hmong once more. In these ways, ascription has been an ongoing highly consequential process for Hmong Americans.

Second, Brown and Jones (2015, 187) assert that "group identity is not primarily a function of cognition or interactions but rather depends on how individuals understand and construct the broader social fields they inhabit." I take their claim to mean that the social/cultural contexts in which individuals are embedded can shape their framing of group identity and collective claims more generally, but social actors have agency in reinterpreting and resisting dominant frames. If this understanding is accurate, I agree with them. As I have shown in this book, Hmong American movement leaders framed claims in terms of intergenerational crises, cultural crises, military service, and/or national honor. They did so not because they are blind to other kinds of framing or because they accept dominant explanations about the causes and consequences of social phenomena. On the contrary, they recognized the cultural and political contexts in which they and targets are embedded and the discursive constraints under which they must operate. They chose and deployed claims that were more consistent with existing dominant discourses than not. By constructing and advancing discourses (e.g., service and sacrifice for and loyalty to the nation) that worked within rather than against existing dominant discourses (e.g., national honor), Hmong and their allies persuaded the racial state to take them and their claims seriously (chapter 4). But Hmong were certainly also capable of reframing dominant discourses, as we saw in Hmong American professionals' movement to incorporate Hmong history into the California public school curriculum (chapter 5). For instance, rather than accept the media's framing of Hmong communities as embroiled in cultural crises, Hmong American women professionals reframed the issues in terms of racism and discrimination within American society, setting a new agenda that emphasized the need for representation of Hmong history in public schools and acknowledgement of Hmong's contributions to the United States. These findings suggest that immigrants' broader cultural contexts shape their discursive opportunities/options for the framing of group identity and collective claims.

However, Brown and Jones's premises seem to speak more to the first of their original questions but less so to the second question: what are the conditions under which institutional classifications respond to group-based mobilization? I do not have the data to answer this question either, but I propose that a slight modification to the question might lead to fruitful future research. Instead of asking about whether or when "institutional classifications" respond to group-based mobilization, we might ask a more general question: what are the conditions under which the state might respond positively to a particular group identity mobilized by racialized social actors?

The fact that the United States is a racial state with strong capitalist tendencies has implications for immigrants' collective mobilization and the state's responses to them. As Fred Block (1977) has pointed out, the state has a strong tendency to serve the interests of the capitalist class even though it is not necessarily run by a class-conscious ruling class and even though those who manage the state apparatus ("state managers") are not necessarily capitalists or members of the same social class. As many scholars remind us, despite the rhetoric about "color blindness" and "equal treatment" under the law, systemic racism exists in most U.S. social institutions and serves to maintain White privilege and non-White disadvantage and subordination (Feagin and Elias 2013; Harris 1993; Omi and Winant 1994). While in some branches of the state, such as the legislative branch, there is growing racial and gender diversity, most state managers are still predominantly White men. This condition or social arrangement (state managers being predominantly White and having strong capitalist tendencies; systemic racism existing in most social institutions) probably maintains the state's biases toward particular ethnoracial groups (Oliver 2017) and constrains disadvantaged groups' framing options. While this condition does not necessarily compel disadvantaged groups to work only within acceptable political discourses, it probably discourages them from framing claims that are likely to be construed by state managers as antithetical or threatening to capitalist interests. As opposed to Whites who enjoy White privilege, minority individuals and groups cannot simply expand or contract identities at will and expect that the state will take them seriously. They still have to be attentive to what are considered politically acceptable political narratives and to be strategic about which kinds of group identities will likely lead to the granting of compromises.

In some situations, it may be possible to affect the state—such as persuade it to respond positively to a collective identity constructed by racialized social actors—by creating the conditions that enable interest convergence (Bell 1980) to occur. Put differently, my conjecture is that the state may be more likely to respond positively to a particular group identity and its associated political narratives if and when such identity and narratives are seen as consistent with the state's interests, whatever those may be during any particular historical period. The state's interests, of course, can shift and change according to time and place. There may be periods during which the state simply does not have immigrants' or particular classes of immigrants' best interests in mind. In such periods, we can expect immigrants to continue to mobilize themselves to seek social justice and tangible resources by interacting with the political system. However, regardless of the political identities that they construct and deploy as part of claims making, we might expect the racial state to continue to homogenize and marginalize them.

IMMIGRANT AND REFUGEE RIGHTS IN THE POST-9/11 AND DONALD TRUMP ERA

In the United States, strong rhetoric around national security and defense has existed for quite some time. The U.S. response to the events of September 11, 2001, has led to an increasingly volatile and hostile environment for existing and prospective immigrants from Latin America and Asia. President George W. Bush's 2002 National Security Strategy proclaims, "America's experience as a great multi-ethnic democracy affirms our conviction that people of many heritages and faiths can live and prosper in peace." At the same time, it declares, "The United States has long maintained the option of preemptive actions to counter a sufficient threat to our national security. . . . To forestall or prevent such hostile acts by our adversaries, the United States will, if necessary, act preemptively" (White House 2002). Donald Trump's campaign intensified the rhetoric of national security, and after his election as U.S. president, he declared that "past leaders" had "lost sight of America's destiny" and "greatness" and "left our borders wide open."[4] What is happening to immigrants and refugees and their rights within the contexts of a strong rhetoric around national security/defense, especially as we are seeing it play out during the Trump era and the ongoing global COVID-19 pandemic?

Immigrants' freedom of movement and their human and civil rights are increasingly threatened or violated by the policies of the racial state. In January 2017, Trump signed a number of executive orders on border security, interior enforcement, and refugees and visa holders that have had far-reaching and violent impacts on the lives and rights of immigrants and refugees. Trump's Border Security and Immigration Enforcement Improvements executive order contains several sections that undermine human rights. These include authorizing the construction of a wall on the "southern border," increasing enforcement along the U.S.-Mexico border, expanding the use of detention, and limiting asylum seekers' access to asylum by expanding the use of expedited removal throughout the country as opposed to within one hundred miles of the border. His executive order on interior enforcement, Enhancing Public Safety in the Interior of the United States, among other things, forbids "sanctuary" jurisdictions from receiving federal grants, authorizes more state and local officials to enforce federal immigration laws, increases the number of Immigration and Customs Enforcement (ICE) agents by ten thousand, and expands the priority list of noncitizens subject to deportation.

These policies have led to the detention of tens of thousands of migrants, including about seventy thousand migrant children in 2019 and fifteen thousand migrant children in 2020.[5] Most adult migrants are being detained in privately run immigrant prisons.[6] Members of migrant families are often detained and violently separated at the border, and children, including infants and toddlers, are shipped to and kept at Office of Refugee Resettlement shelters or other places, such as hotels, away from their parents.[7] Not only are people being held in immigrant prison and jails for longer periods of time compared to previous years, but documented abuses in these prisons and jails have been frequent and wide-ranging.[8] Of concern to immigrant and civil rights groups is the very real possibility that immigrants' constitutional rights, especially their due process rights, are being violated. The Supreme Court ruling in *Jennings v. Rodriguez* leaves open the question of whether indefinite detention of a person without offering him or her a hearing violates the Constitution. To most immigrants and their advocates, it is quite clear that indefinite detention without a hearing is unconstitutional (Arulanantham and Tan 2018).

Trump's executive order on refugees, titled Protecting the Nation from Terrorist Attacks by Foreign Nationals, among other things, suspended the issuance of visas to nationals from Iran, Iraq, Libya, Somalia, Sudan, Syria, and Yemen, reduced the number of refugees admitted to the United States in fiscal year 2017 from 110,000 to 50,000, suspended the Refugee Admissions Program for 120 days, and banned the resettlement of Syrian refugees indefinitely (Center for Migration Studies n.d.). The list of countries selected for suspension suggests that this policy is targeting Muslim immigrants. Despite legal challenges to Trump's executive orders for violating various constitutional rights and despite the findings of at least two district courts that these policies were motivated by anti-Muslim sentiment, the Supreme Court has ultimately upheld Trump's authority to implement them. Between March and June 2020, partly in response to the global COVID-19 pandemic, Trump has signed additional executive orders to ban additional nationals (e.g., North Korea, Myanmar, Nigeria, Sudan, etc.), halt immigration for months, and suspend new work visas for foreign workers in a wide variety of jobs, including skilled workers, seasonal workers, and students on work-study summer programs.[9]

In short, immigrants' and refugees' human and civil rights have been severely diminished in the Trump era. The ongoing global COVID-19 pandemic and the racial state's largely ineffective responses to it have put immigrant workers and their families at great health risk. An estimated six million immigrants are essential workers in a number of industries, ranging from health care to retail, manufacturing, and agriculture.[10] Even though the Occupational Safety and Health Act gives all workers the right to safe and healthy working conditions and requires employers to provide workplaces that are free of known hazards that could harm employees, it does not currently have policies that specifically address protection from COVID-19 in the workplace, nor does it currently conduct any COVID-19-related inspections at workplaces, including health care settings. In states such as California, immigrants have been disproportionally impacted by COVID-19. According to the state's Department of Public Health, although Latinos make up 39 percent of the California population, they constitute 60 percent of COVID-19 infections and 48 percent of deaths.[11]

In the past century and a half, immigrants racialized as Asians and Asian Americans stereotyped as immigrants have been subjected to racially motivated violence and exclusion, racial discrimination and subordination, and racial surveillance and persecution of various kinds (Kurashige 2016; Lee and Zia 2001; Selod 2018; Takaki 2000). In recent years, the much more openly racist attitudes, statements, and actions by racist political figures toward Americans of Asian descent have made them even more vulnerable to attacks and exclusion. In the ongoing COVID-19 pandemic, people racialized as Asian continue to be stereotyped by the state and some public institutions as disease carriers, perpetuating the long-standing racist stereotype of Asians as dangerous "yellow perils" to the Western world (Li and Nicholson 2020). These racist stereotypes have led to various acts of anti-Asian violence and hate crimes around the country (Gover, Harper, and Langton 2020; Tessler, Choi, and Kao 2020).[12] Clearly, nativism and racism persist in American society. Nativism and racism will probably continue to be significant barriers to immigrants' and minority groups' political incorporation. What is less clear is the extent to which Asian Americans will be able to overcome these barriers. Some groups have begun to mobilize in response to anti-Asian violence; however, it is too soon to tell whether or what kinds of impact their mobilizations will have on public policy.

CONCLUSION

Like all other immigrant groups, Hmong are an immigrant group with its own unique contexts of exit and reception. Their unique contexts of exit and reception have conditioned their resources, opportunities, and strategic actions and shaped their process of political incorporation in U.S. society. Recognizing that no single model of immigrant political incorporation can account for all the complexities of immigrant groups' actions and interactions with political systems or the outcomes of these interactions, I have developed the Strategic Ethnic Collective Action model of immigrant political incorporation as a framework for thinking about the roles of and dynamic interactions between immigrant collective agency and state racialization in shaping immigrants' political incorporation. How each immigrant group or, rather, how mobilized segments of immigrant groups plan and carry out collective action will vary depending on their resources, opportunities, and strategies, but collective action is crucial to immigrant groups' ability to participate in the political system and occasionally have their interests represented in public policies. While the particular collective action frames that Hmong used, such as the military service frame, may be unique to them, the use of framing to mobilize collective consensus and motivate collective action on social problems is not necessarily unique, as social movement actors and scholars know. Also, Hmong's use of outside institutions and state allies to create access points into the political system is not necessarily a unique tactic. What is unique is that once access points were created, Hmong American movement actors sustained their collective actions by continuing to construct and deploy political identities, maintaining alliances across and between their network of ethnic organizations and institutional and state allies and coming up with a variety of ways to make claims on their targets.

Although the racial state will probably racialize and reracialize different immigrant groups differently depending on political circumstances, state interests, and immigrant groups' relationships with the state, state racialization will continue to reinforce and be reinforced by systemic racism. As long as systemic racism persists within the political system, immigrant minority groups' prospects of achieving full political incorporation will be very minimal if not nonexistent. The persistence of a racialized economic and political hierarchy in the United States has led Rodney Hero (1992) to characterize the U.S. political system as practicing "two-tier pluralism." America's political system is a two-tier pluralism system, Hero contends, because Latinos and other ethnic minority groups "have largely been relegated to a lower social and political tier or arena. Despite the equal legal and political status of Latinos formally, distinct factors and processes have led to systematically lower political and social status" (Hero 1992, 29). Given current political contexts and dominant discourses in the United States, we can expect that immigrant and refugee groups from Asia and Latin America will continue to be racialized and that racialization will continue to have social, economic, and political consequences for them. That is, some immigrant groups may continue to be positioned as inferior to Whites, be defined as foreigner as opposed to insider, and be cast as threatening or dangerous rather than nonthreatening or friendly. We can expect Asian Americans and Latinos to continue to resist negative racialization as they continue to pursue political incorporation in the United States. Collective resistance will likely differ from one immigrant group to another according to time and place.

Hmong's story is both unique and an important lesson to other marginalized, racialized, and economically strapped immigrant groups. Against tremendous odds, Hmong former refugees managed to participate in and influence public policies. They were able to do so in part by mobilizing a network of ethnic organizations that, in turn, mobilized ethnic participants and served as bridges between the ethnic community and other institutional and state actors. These institutional and state allies, in turn, helped to create access points into the political system. State allies and politically integrated ethnic actors sometimes also facilitated interest convergence between challengers and the state. Rather than distancing themselves from others, Hmong fought for social justice alongside other immigrants. Rather than distancing themselves from Asian Americans, Hmong allied with and received substantial support from Asian American organizations. But Hmong also actively drew on their collective political narratives to construct and position themselves as a unique ethnic group. Keenly aware of the historical racial discrimination against racial minorities and racialized immigrants and the systemic racism that persists, Hmong political actors continue to do everything in their power to challenge U.S. historical amnesia, create access points into the upper echelons of the U.S. political system, and fight for their rightful place in their new homeland.

ACKNOWLEDGMENTS

I am indebted to a number of people and institutions without whose generous help and support this book would not have been possible. Although I will not be able to mention everyone who has made a lasting positive impact on my thinking and writing, I am indebted to everyone who has lent me support, guidance, or encouragement in one form or another and whom I have had the fortune to know as mentors, colleagues, and friends.

Immigrant Agency would not have been possible without the Hmong men and women, activists, professionals, veterans, students, and former refugees whose experiences and acts of courage this book has tried to reconstruct, interpret, and represent. I benefited tremendously from the expertise and insights of Yee (Vaming) Xiong and Pai (Mai Kou) Yang, who were key leaders in Hmong's movements for benefits restoration and Hmong's movement for curriculum inclusion, respectively. Vaming and Mai Kou generously shared their experiences as activists and public servants, and they went above and beyond to provide me with crucial original documents that I could not have accessed otherwise. I also benefited from the expertise and insights of Lee Pao Xiong, who was instrumental in the outcome of Hmong veterans' movement for naturalization accommodations. Lee Pao was the former president and CEO of the Urban Coalition and a member of President Clinton's Advisory Commission on Asian-Americans and Pacific Islanders. I also benefited immeasurably from the insights of Hmong veterans, including many who are my relatives and some who are no longer here with us. They have taught me a great deal about courage in the face of despair, about the consequences of war, and about the preciousness of life. I am grateful to Wameng Moua, editor of *Hmong Today,* for freely providing and granting me permission to use his photograph on the cover of my book.

A single book can never sufficiently represent let alone thoroughly convey the hardships, sacrifices, and struggles that Hmong men and women have had to endure, the hopes and dreams they aspire toward, or the difference that they have made to their communities and societies. But I hope that the histories, analyses, and voices that I have provided in *Immigrant Agency* offer a glimpse into Hmong men and women's remarkable courage and agency of the past thirty years. I hope that this book will encourage sociologists and other scholars to dig deeper and wider into how social forces such as colonization, imperialism, and wars and their numerous tragic consequences have profoundly impacted the conditions of Hmong and other human populations and their place in the world. Although this book focuses on Hmong's political incorporation in the United States, this is not the only thing or destination that matters to them.

I am deeply indebted to Min Zhou for her continuous support over the past eighteen years of my academic career. Min's encouragement inspired me to finish this book. The important concepts of contexts of exit and contexts of reception that I draw on to understand Hmong refugees' capacity for and contexts of political mobilization in this book emerged out of the seminal works of Alejandro Portes, Rubén Rumbaut, and Min Zhou. The enormous, distinguished contributions that they have made to the discipline of sociology and field of immigration and refugee studies need no introduction.

A few people read the manuscript from the beginning. Their sound advice and strong encouragements helped me improve and finish *Immigrant Agency*. I am grateful to the three anonymous reviewers from Rutgers University Press who read my book manuscript and provided highly insightful, meaningful, and constructive comments that helped me revise and strengthen the manuscript. I am grateful to Michael Thornton for always being there whenever I needed help and advice. I benefited immeasurably from our conversations on collective agency and race. Mike also read my book manuscript and provided me with invaluable comments and advice for how to shape and develop the book. I am grateful to Pamela Oliver for always agreeing to read and provide insightful comments on my work, including my theoretical framework on immigrant political incorporation and my paper on Hmong's movements for benefits restoration. I thank Mike and Pam for their mentorship, guidance, and friendship over the years.

I am grateful to the UCLA Department of Sociology, the UCLA Institute of American Culture, and the UCLA Asian American Studies Center for providing research funding which enabled me to collect some of the data used in this book. The Nellie Y. McKay fellowship from the University of Wisconsin–Madison also provided me with time to write. I thank the participants of the UW Department of Sociology's Race and Ethnicity workshop who provided helpful comments on my papers on Hmong American protest and political contexts. I also thank the inquisitive friendly audience during my presentation of my theoretical framework of immigrant political incorporation at the annual meeting of the American Sociological Association in Seattle a few years ago. Finally, I owe a debt of gratitude to my Hmong American colleagues of the Critical Hmong Studies Symposium at the University of California, Merced, who inspired me to think more deeply about the relationships between colonialism, imperialism, war, and Hmong's acts of resilience and resistance in the contexts of ongoing geopolitics.

It has been a complete joy working with the first-rate production team at Rutgers. I am grateful to my acquiring editor Jasper Chang for believing in this book project and for his support from the beginning of this project to its publication. I thank Cheryl Hirsch and Alissa Zarro for their excellent support throughout the book's production process and Joseph Dahm for his meticulous copyediting help.

During the writing of this book, I benefited from the comfort, energy, and support of my friends and family. Lee Pao Xiong generously shared his experience and expertise as a former public servant, helped me to locate sources of information, and was always willing to share his insights about U.S. and interethnic politics. Yee Chang generously shared his expertise on U.S. and Midwestern politics, and he was always willing to listen to my questions and engage in further conversations about topics related to U.S. politics. I am grateful to everyone in my and my wife's extended family in California, Minnesota, and Wisconsin who showered my children, wife, and I with love and support over the years. I am forever grateful to my mother and father, Shoua Her and Nhia Pao Xiong, who, in the aftermath of the devastating war in their former homeland, risked their lives once more by crossing the Mekong River and endured the consequences of statelessness alongside hundreds of thousands of other Southeast Asian refugees for over a decade so that they could bring us, their children, to the United States. My father lost his mother when he was just two years old. He was drafted into the Secret War when he was sixteen. He lost his father when he was twenty-three and lost his country when he was twenty-eight. His story, like the story of so many other Hmong veterans, teaches us how precious family is. My wife, Mary Moua, and my children made many sacrifices for our family so that I could have time to write (and eat). I thank them for their unconditional love. It is to my parents, wife, and children that I dedicate this book.

NOTES

1. IMMIGRANT AGENCY

1. To clarify, groups need not have achieved "full incorporation" (e.g., have their interests completely or overwhelmingly represented in public policy, enjoy privileged political standing, have ample capacity to make sustained claims on the political system) for them to be disincorporated. To the extent that political incorporation occurs for an immigrant group, it will occur in degrees.

2. By degree, I mean variation in terms of both the amount or level (lesser or greater) and kind (e.g., having more influence in some domains or arenas of the society than in other domains or arenas).

3. The U.S. census 2010 shows that 91 percent of Hmong Californians (86,989) live in the eighteen counties of the Central Valley (Butte, Colusa, Fresno, Glenn, Kern, Kings, Madera, Merced, Placer, Sacramento, San Joaquin, Shasta, Stanislaus, Sutter, Tehama, Tulare, Yolo, and Yuba).

4. A cost of living comparison was made between several metro areas using data from the Council for Community and Economic Research (C2ER), available at http://www.bankrate .com/calculators/savings/moving-cost-of-living-calculator.aspx.

5. Although Japanese composed the largest Asian subgroup (with 6,471 persons), there were already 590 Vietnamese living in Fresno County (Reder et al. 1984, 2).

6. S. Moua, personal communication, Fresno, CA, December 28, 2009.

7. In 1990, the Fresno inner city encompassed or overlapped with the following census tracts: 1–7, 13, 20–28, and 32–37. In the 2000 census, some of these tracts were divided into two or three, hence the twenty-eight tracts.

8. The "Zos Vib Nais" neighborhoods correspond approximately with census tracts 29.02, 27, and 28, which contained 2,070, 551, and 1,035 Hmong persons in 1990, respectively.

9. P. Her, personal communication, Fresno, CA, May 14, 2009. Summerset Village is located in census tract 34 of Fresno County—specifically block group 4, between N. Angus and Fresno streets.

10. Parc Grove Commons, "Income Guidelines," www.parcgrovecommons.com/ income_guide lines.htm.

2. HISTORY AND CONTEXTS OF EXIT

1. Until the 1990s, very few Hmong villages possessed personal telephones or vehicles.

2. Opium was the main cash crop in Southeast Asia. Indeed, opium was traded and monopolized in much of the Eastern and Western world during that historical period.

3. Laotian Hmong call the country of Laos *tebchaws Los Tsuas*. They call Laotians *neeg Los Tsuas*; Lao, *Nplog*, Kmhmu, *Mab Khub Mub*, and Iu Mien, *Co*. Hmong use the term *mab sua* to refer to all non-Hmong.

4. Population censuses before the 1960s lumped together Hmong and Iu Mien (historically categorized as Meo and Yao, respectively).

5. It is unknowable how many Hmong sided with the Americans, how many went to the Pathet Lao, and how many held or tried to hold a "neutral" position (not to be confused with

the formal neutralist position). Depending on writers' reconstructions of history, the population that sided with the Americans could range from most Hmong to a majority of Hmong.

6. Nhia P. Xiong, personal communication, Marysville, CA, March 10, 2010.

7. Greenstein and Immerman (1992, 577–578) write that "three weeks before his January meeting with Kennedy" and during his meeting "with a group of his top foreign policy advisers," President Eisenhower made the following remarks: "We cannot let Laos fall to the Communists even if we have to fight—with our allies or without them." Furthermore, Eisenhower expressed his willingness to use force in Laos in this statement: "We cannot stand by and allow Laos to fall to the Communists. The time may soon come when we should employ the Seventh Fleet, with its force of marines" (1992, 578).

8. Based on Leary's (1999) account, the CIA's plan for the creation of the secret army was approved during President Eisenhower's term in office (1953–1961), prior to President Kennedy's term in office (1961–1963).

9. See CBS, "Laos: The Not So Secret War" (1970), https://www.youtube.com/watch?v =huf8bxSDiy4.

10. See National Archives, "Pentagon Papers," https://www.archives.gov/research/pentagon -papers.

11. The descriptor "warrior" runs throughout Jane Hamilton-Merritt's *Tragic Mountains*. G. K. Ovington's *Birth Jacket* describes Hmong as a "fiercely independent people" who had an "ingrained historical animosity towards the Vietnamese" (2008, 195–197).

12. President Lyndon B. Johnson Executive Order 11414, "Adjusting the Rates of Monthly Basic Pay for Members of the Uniformed Services" (Washington, DC: Government Printing Office).

13. Stephen Magagnini, "Hmong Veterans of CIA's Secret War in Laos Honored at California Capitol," *Sacramento Bee*, May 16, 2016 (stating that Hmong guerrilla soldiers were paid $1.50– 2.00 a month).

14. Magagnini, "Hmong Veterans." Xiong recalls clearly that, in his group, Hmong army privates were paid 2,700 kips ($4.00) per month, while sergeants were paid 3,000 kips ($4.50) per month. Higher ranking officers were paid more. Hmong battalion commanders (majors) were paid about 40,000–50,000 kips ($60–$75) per month.

15. In this passage, the acronym AID refers to the U.S. Agency for International Development, MASF refers to Military Assistance Service Funded, and CAS refers to controlled American source.

16. Translated from "Txhua tug txiv neej 15 txog 65 xyoos ces luag yeej kom mus [ua tub rog] tib si. Luag tsis nug tias puas kam li." N. Xiong, personal communication, Marysville, CA, February 15, 2010.

17. John Howard, "Hmong Who Fought for CIA to Lose Food Stamps," *Telegraph Herald*, November 2, 1997.

18. Barry Lando and Mike Wallace, "Our Secret Army," *60 Minutes*, CBS, March 4, 1979.

19. Carl Strock, "The Long March," *New Republic*, May 9, 1970.

20. I thank Lee Pao Xiong, director of the Center for Hmong Studies, for providing me with these figures from the Jerry Daniels Collection, Center for Hmong Studies, Concordia University.

21. Lee Lescaze, "Laotians Waiting in Thai Camps for Chance to Fight Again," *Washington Post*, March 26, 1979.

22. Barry Lando and Mike Wallace, "Our Secret Army," *60 Minutes*, CBS, March 4, 1979.

23. Tou Cheng Lo, personal communication, Fresno, California, December 26, 2016.

24. Ban Vinai was not unique in being located near the Thai border. Most other refugee camps for Burmese, Laotian, and Cambodian refugees were also located near the Thai border with Burma, Laos, and Cambodia.

25. Particular sections (e.g., center 9) of Ban Vinai were built on top of a cemetery. Hmong eyewitnesses attest that some of the graves contained the remains of deceased Hmong and that a few Hmong made the difficult decision to relocate the remains of their relatives.
26. U.S. Congress, House, "Refugees from Indochina" (1975), serial 43, p. 538.
27. U.S. Congress, Senate, "Midyear Consultation on Refugee Programs" (1987), serial J-100–29, p. 56.
28. Seth Mydans, "California Says Laos Refugee Group Is a Victim of Leadership's Extortion," *New York Times*, November 7, 1990.
29. Warren Brown, "Refugee Plan Would Hurt Laos Tribe, Hill Critics Say," *Washington Post*, March 24, 1979; Brian Sullivan, "Mysterious Deaths of Tribesmen Reported," Associated Press, February 6, 1981; "Excerpts from State Department Report on Chemical Warfare; Study Asserts Lethal Toxins Were Used in 3 Asian Countries," *New York Times*, March 23, 1982.
30. Margy McCay, "Family Hangings Trouble Other Laotian Refugees," Associated Press, January 26, 1980.
31. Wayne King, "New Life's Cultural Demons Torture Laotian Refugee," *New York Times*, May 3, 1981; Robert A. Hamilton, "For Refugees from Southeast Asia, Adapting Is a Slow Road," *New York Times*, January 14, 1990.
32. Roy Beck, "The Ordeal of Immigration in Wausau," *Atlantic Monthly*, April 1994.
33. As late as 2009, Doctors Without Borders / Médecins Sans Frontières reported that forced repatriation was occurring against 5,000 Hmong in the Huai Nam Khao camp in northern Thailand.
34. Nra Lee Her, personal communication, Stockton, CA, May 15, 2010.
35. Specifically, of 1,755,268 Southeast Asian refugees, the United States took in 930,153 (53 percent), China 263,000 (15 percent), Canada 154,264 (9 percent), Australia 136,157 (8 percent), and France 126,897 (7 percent).

3. CAMPAIGN FOR JUSTICE

1. Using data from the U.S. Current Population Survey, the National Center for Education Statistics reports that, in 1990, 6.4 percent of Whites, 27.2 percent of Blacks, 17.2 percent of Hispanics, 12.8 percent of Asians and Pacific Islanders, and 24.3 percent of American Indians received some form of public assistance. https://nces.ed.gov/pubs2012/2012026/tables/table_32.asp.
2. Virginia Ellis, "Hmong Seek Exemption from Food Stamp Cuts," *Los Angeles Times*, November 2, 1997.
3. Vaming (Yee) Xiong, personal communication, October 19, 2017.
4. Yee Xiong and Donna Wolfe, letter to the office of Governor Pete Wilson, "Hmong Community Comments on 45 Day Public Review of HR 3734" (November 14, 1996).
5. Yia Lor, personal communication, October 23, 2017.
6. Lao Veterans of America, http://www.laoveterans.org.
7. Vaming (Yee) Xiong, personal communication, October 19, 2017.
8. Carol Morello, "Aid Cutoff Driving Immigrants to Suicide," *Philadelphia Inquirer*, May 25, 1997.
9. "Immigrants Seek Easing of Welfare Cuts: Rally at Capitol Draws Some 2,000 Protestors," *Sacramento Bee*, March 19, 1997.
10. Press release, "Immigrant Lobby Day and Justice and Dignity for Sacramento's Working Poor," March 18, 1997.
11. T. T. Nhu, "Immigrants Plan Capitol Protest," *San Jose Mercury News*, May 28, 1997.
12. Daniel Sneider, "Reforms Begin to Cut Off Dollars to US Immigrants," *Christian Science Monitor*, April 1, 1997.

13. Deborah Hastings, "Hmong Women's Suicide Puts Spotlight on Welfare Problems," *Los Angeles Times*, February 22, 1998.

14. Deborah Hastings, "A Suicide Highlights Welfare Worries of CIA War Veterans," Associated Press, February 16, 1998.

15. Virginia De Leon and Jim Camden, "The Land of Broken Promises, the Hmong, Brave Fighters in Vietnam Now Falling Victim to U.S. Welfare Cuts," *Spokesman Review*, June 22, 1997.

16. Carol Morello, "Aid Cutoff Driving Immigrants to Suicide," *Philadelphia Inquirer*, May 25, 1997.

17. Morello, "Aid Cutoff Driving Immigrants to Suicide"; Clifford Levy, "In Mayor's Race, Clash on Workfare and immigrant's Suicide," *New York Times*, February 23, 1997; Tim Weiner, "Many Laotians in U.S. Find Their Hopes Betrayed," *New York Times*, December 27, 1997; Steve Maganini, "Suicide Illustrates Welfare Reform's Toll among Hmong," *Sacramento Bee*, November 9, 1997; Carol Morello, "No Benefits: Cutoff Fears Spur Suicides," *Philadelphia Inquirer*, June 1, 1997.

18. Za Chong Xiong, personal communication, August 10, 2008.

19. Xiong and Wolfe, letter to Pete Wilson.

20. Xiong and Wolfe, letter to Pete Wilson.

21. Yee Xiong, written speech for state capitol rally, February 24, 1997.

22. Jodie DeJonge, "Southeast Asians Decry Torture, Killings in Laos, Seek U.S. Help," Associated Press, February 3, 1990.

23. Karla Bruner, "Hmong Pushing Welfare Relief: Fresno Group Hoping to Convince Lawmakers They Need Exemption from Possible Loss of Benefits," *Fresno Bee*, February 22, 1997.

24. Ben Barber, "Hmong Veterans to Receive Medals: Laotian People Become Refugees after Helping U.S. Fight Vietnam War," *Washington Times*, May 14, 1997; Marc Kaufman, "U.S. Honors Hmong Who Helped American Military during Vietnam War," *Philadelphia Inquirer*, May 14, 1997.

25. Kaufman, "U.S. Honors Hmong."

26. Balanced Budget Act of 1997, Public Law 105–33, §5566, 111 Stat. 251, 639–640 (1997), emphasis added.

27. Stephen Schwartz, "Food Stamp Cutoff Upheld: Benefits Denied to Hmong Who Fought for the U.S.," *San Francisco Chronicle*, March 7, 1998.

28. Agricultural Research, Extension, and Education Reform Act of 1998—Conference Report (May 12, 1998) (Washington, DC: Government Publishing Office).

4. BATTLE FOR NATURALIZATION

1. The Hmong Veterans' Naturalization Act, a bill "to expedite the naturalization of aliens who served with special guerrilla units in Laos" (H.R. 4513), was introduced in the House, 101st Congress.

2. The cosponsors of H.R. 4513 included Walter Fauntroy (D-DC), Chester Atkins (D-MA, 5th Congressional District), Jim Bates (D-CA, 44th), Gary Condit (D-CA, 15th), Robert Dornan (R-CA, 38th), William Frenzel (R-MN, 3rd), Benjamin Gilman (R-NY, 22nd), Frank Horton (R-NY, 29th), Henry Hyde (R-IL, 6th), Jill Long Thompson (D-IN, 4th), Robert Matsui (D-CA, 3rd), Charles Pashayan (R-CA, 17th), Martin Sabo (D-MN, 5th), Patricia Schroeder (D-CO, 1st), Gerald Sikorski (D-MN, 6th), and Henry Waxman (D-CA, 24th). The cosponsors of S. 2687 included William Bradley (D-NJ), James Jeffords (R-VT), Frank Murkowski (R-AK), and James Sanford (D-NC).

3. Bernard Weinraub, "Senate Votes Funds for More Refugees," *New York Times*, June 26, 1979.

4. Dirk Johnson, "Hmong Refugees Find Adjustment to U.S. Painful," *New York Times*, July 25, 1988.

5. Lee Pao Xiong, personal communication, Saint Paul, MN, July 2020.

6. Philip Smith, "Letter to Congressman Henry Hyde, Chair of Judiciary Committee, regarding Hmong Veterans' Naturalization Act of 1999," *Congressional Record* 146, pt. 6 (2000): 8904–8906.

7. Lao Veterans of America, http://www.laoveteransofamerica.org/.

8. The Hmong naturalization bills that were introduced in 1990, 1991, 1994, and 1995 apparently never made it pass the House and Senate committees or subcommittees to be included in hearings or debates.

9. Jimmy Carter, "The President's News Conference" (March 24, 1977), http://www.presidency.ucsb.edu/ws/?pid=7229.

10. This is language similar to those who argue against "free welfare handouts." Krikorian made these claims during the congressional hearing on the Hmong Veterans' Naturalization Bill of 1997.

11. Wangyee Vang, prepared statement (see U.S. Congress 1997).

12. Vang, prepared statement.

13. I gathered versions of these claims in the course of my observations, informal discussions, interactions, and interviews with ordinary Hmong persons, veterans, leaders, community activists, etc. These claims can also be found in Hmong music and poetry (folk ballads and songs). More recently, they are also found in protest slogans. The mass media also have helped to construct and/or report on some of these claims.

14. During the congressional hearing, the phrase "Hmong people" was used six times and "Hmong refugees" five times.

15. The *Oxford English Dictionary* (3rd ed., 2002) defines "militarization" as "the action of making military in character or style; spec. transformation to military methods or status, esp. by the provision or expansion of military forces and other resources." It defines "militarism" as "military attitudes or ideals, esp. the belief or policy that a country should maintain a strong military capability and be prepared to use it aggressively to defend or promote national interests. Also: a political condition characterized by the predominance of the military in government or administration or a reliance on military force in political or diplomatic matters."

16. Just months after the congressional hearing on HVNA occurred, the crisis in the Middle East intensified; and in December of 1998, the United States and Britain were engaged in bombing campaigns against Iraq. This military campaign was known as Operation Desert Fox and occurred between December 16 and 19, 1998.

17. By "substantive political incorporation," I mean that a group's interests are frequently articulated and well represented in policy making.

18. Hmong Veterans' Naturalization Act of 2000, *Congressional Record*, May 2, 2000, H2359–H2362.

19. "A Man of the People—Bruce Vento's Legacy Etched by Service," *Saint Paul Pioneer Press*, February 3, 2000.

20. Lee Pao Xiong, personal communication, Saint Paul, MN, July 2020.

21. Laura Lynn Efurd obituary, *Honolulu Star-Advertiser*, July 29, 2018.

22. Lee Pao Xiong, personal communication, Saint Paul, MN, July 2020.

23. Hmong Veterans' Naturalization Act of 2000, Public Law 106–207, May 26, 2000 (114 Stat. 316).

24. William J. Clinton, "Statement on Signing the Hmong Veterans' Naturalization Act of 2000" (May 26, 2000), https://www.presidency.ucsb.edu/documents/statement-signing-the-hmong-veterans-naturalization-act-2000.

25. Ben Barber, "Hmong Veterans to Receive Medals: Laotian People Became Refugees after Helping U.S. Fight Vietnam War," *Washington Times*, May 14, 1997.

26. "Laos Hmong Leader Denied Arlington Burial," *BBC News*, February 5, 2011.

5. MOVEMENT FOR INCLUSION

1. Assembly Bill 78, July 10, 2003 (chap. 44, statutes of 2003).
2. Gene I. Maeroff, "Rising Immigration Tide Strains Nation's Schools," *New York Times*, August 21, 1983.
3. Wayne King, "New Life's Cultural Demons Torture Laotian Refugee," *New York Times*, May 3, 1981; Robert A. Hamilton, "For Refugees from Southeast Asia, Adapting Is a Slow Road," *New York Times*, January 14, 1990.
4. Based on census 2000 enumeration, the total number of Hmong in Fresno, California (MSA) was 22,456. The total population in Fresno, California (city) was 427,652. Of this number, non-Hispanic Whites composed 30.0 percent, Blacks 8.3 percent, American Indians / Alaska Natives 1.7 percent, Asians and Pacific Islanders 12.8 percent, and Hispanics/Latinos 46.9 percent. See U.S. Census Bureau, "Census 2000, State and County QuickFacts," http:// quickfacts.census.gov/qfd/states/06/0627000.html.
5. Anne Dudley Ellis, "Lost in America," *Fresno Bee*, August 11, 2002.
6. Office of Refugee Resettlement, "State Letter #02-38: Executive Summary" (U.S. Department of Health and Human Services, 2002).
7. Office of Refugee Resettlement, "State Letter #02-38."
8. Ellis, "Lost in America."
9. Ellis, "Lost in America."
10. Ellis, "Lost in America."
11. Ellis, "Lost in America."
12. Pai Yang, personal communication, Fresno, CA, July 2020.
13. Fresno Unified School District website, http://www.fresno.k12.ca.us/divdept/stafed /titleiii/page/ab78.htm.
14. Pai Yang, personal communication, Fresno, CA, July 2020.
15. Legislative Counsel of California, "Complete Bill History, Bill Number A.B. No. 78 (Reyes)," http://www.leginfo.ca.gov/.
16. Legislative Counsel of California, "California Legislature, 2003–2004 Regular Session. Assembly Bill No. 78. Amended in Assembly June 17, 2003."
17. Legislative Counsel of California, "Bill Number: AB 78 Introduced Bill Text," California Legislature's Public Access Computer, ftp://www.leginfo.ca.gov/pub/03-04/bill/asm/ab _0051-0100/ab_78_bill_20021223_introduced.html.
18. Doua Vu, personal communication, Fresno, CA, July 25, 2011.
19. The Hmong Veterans' Naturalization Act of 2000 was officially known as Public Law 106–207. According to the U.S. Department of Justice, "The Hmong Veterans' Naturalization Act of 2000, which became law on May 26, 2000, provides an exemption from the English language requirement and special consideration for civics testing for certain refugees from Laos applying for naturalization. This benefit is limited to no more than 45,000 eligible refugees from Laos who were admitted to the United States as refugees from Laos pursuant to Section 207 of the INS." See http://www.ailc.com/publicaffairs/factsheets/Hmong.htm.
20. Christopher Vang, "Hmong Role in History Must Be in Schoolbooks," *Fresno Bee*, April 26, 2003.
21. Felicia Cousart Matlosz, "Bill Urges Teachers to Address Contribution in Vietnam Lessons," *Fresno Bee*, December 31, 2002.
22. Doua Vu, personal communication, Fresno, CA, July 25, 2011.
23. Pai Yang, personal communication, Fresno, CA, July 2020.
24. Yee Vang, personal communication, Fresno, CA, April 2009; also see Hmong Student Inter-Collegiate Coalition email listserv, HSIC_@yahoo.com.

25. Kaoly Yang, "History of the Assembly Bill 78," http://www.hmongcontemporaryissues
.com/archives/HistoryBill78.html.
26. This is based on reports from my interviewees who live in these cities or know other relatives who live in these cities.
27. Vang, "Hmong Role in History."
28. Formed in 1927, the "California School Employees Association is the largest classified
school employees union in the United States, representing nearly 220,000 school support staff
throughout California." CSEA, "About CSEA," http://members.csea.com/memberhome
/AboutUs/AboutCSEA/tabid/115/Default.aspx. Formed in 1932, the "AFSCME is the
nation's largest and fastest growing public services employees union with more than 1.6 million active and retired members." AFSCME, "We Are AFSCME," http://www.afscme.org
/union/about. The membership of the Lao Veterans, Inc., formed in 1998, includes significant
numbers of Hmong men and women "who served in combat and combat support roles" during the Secret War in Laos. http://www.laoveterans.com. Legislative Counsel of California,
"California Assembly Committee on Education, Hearing on AB 78" (March 19, 2003).
29. Legislative Counsel of California, "Senate Rules Committee, Committee Analysis of AB
78" (June 11, 2003). According to its website, "The California Federation of Teachers is the
statewide affiliate of the American Federation of Teachers." Founded in 1919, the "CFT represents over 120,000 educational employees working at every level of the education system in
California, from Head Start to the University of California." http://www.cft.org/index.php
/at-a-glance.html.
30. The information in this paragraph was gathered through the author's own observations as
he was part of the email listservs of the HSIC and other Hmong college student organizations.
31. Srida Moua, Members of Hmong Student Inter-collegiate Coalition (HSIC), Petition to
Senator John Vasconcellos and the California Senate Education Committee: "Support
Assembly Bill 78 (Reyes)—Hmong Curriculum," http://www.PetitionOnline.com/s12m34
/petition.html.
32. To increase readability, I have made slight modifications to the punctuation and grammar
in this excerpt. The original texts come from Kao-ly Yang, "History of the Assembly Bill 78,"
http://www.hmongcontemporaryissues.com/archives/HistoryBill78.html.
33. Other scholars have used the term "historical amnesia" to refer to the government's or
public's purposeful forgetting of past political events or histories of particular groups of
people. Selective forgetting is used as a way to support certain political agendas: anti–
affirmative action or color-blind policies and/or to perpetuate certain myths: equal opportunity exists for all regardless of race, class, gender, etc. Educational institutions, from public
elementary schools to universities, engage in and reproduce the practice of selective historical
amnesia.
34. Legislative Counsel of California, "California Assembly Committee on Education, Hearing on AB 78" (March 19, 2003), 1–2.
35. Paoze Thao, email in a message forum, June 1, 2003.
36. The state's second major response that followed this initial response was the Senate Committee on Education's suggestion to erase Hmong from the bill. The final state response was
actual erasure of Hmong from AB 78.
37. Lee Romney, "Bill Spurs Bitter Debate over Hmong Identity," Los Angeles Times, May 24,
2003.
38. Apparently, Thao was referring to the May 24, 2003, Los Angeles Times article "Bill Spurs
Bitter Debate over Hmong Identity."
39. According to the American Civil Liberties Union, "Proposition 187 sought, among other
things, to require police, health care professionals and teachers to verify and report the

immigration status of all individuals, including children." In June 1999, California's governor Gray Davis "initiat[ed] a request for mediation to resolve the appeal of Proposition 187." This mediation resulted in the voiding of major parts of Prop. 187. Source: American Civil Liberties Union, "CA's Anti-Immigrant Proposition 187 Is Voided, Ending State's Five-Year Battle with ACLU, Rights Groups" (July 29, 1999), http://www.aclu.org/immigrants-rights/cas-anti -immigrant-proposition-187-voided-ending-states-five-year-battle-aclu-righ.

40. Proposition 209 amended the California Constitution by adding Section 31 to Article I. Section 31 read, in part, "The state shall not discriminate against, or grant preferential treatment to, any individual or group on the basis of race, sex, color, ethnicity, or national origin in the operation of public employment, public education, or public contracting" (California Constitution, Article I, § 31 (a)).

41. Proposition 227 is formally titled "English Language Education for Immigrant Children." California Education Code Chapter 3 §§ 300–340.

42. Within Fresno County, the percentages of those who voted for Prop. 187, Prop. 209, and Prop. 227 were 66 percent, 61 percent, and 63 percent, respectively (Jones 1994, 109; 1996, 34; 1998, 84).

6. RACIALIZED POLITICAL INCORPORATION AND IMMIGRANT RIGHTS

1. Yang Sao Xiong and Mark E. Pfeifer, "The Suburbanization and Residential Segregation of Southeast Asians in the Twin Cities" (manuscript, University of Wisconsin–Madison).

2. Rachel Swarns, "Provision of Antiterror Law Delays Entry of Refugees," *New York Times*, March 8, 2006.

3. Joe Orso, "Bill Reverses Terrorist Classification for Hmong," *La Crosse Tribune*, January 3, 2008.

4. Donald J. Trump, Address on National Security Strategy (Washington, DC, December 18, 2017).

5. Christopher Sherman, Martha Mendoza, and Garance Burke, "US Held Record Number of Migrant Children in Custody in 2019," Associated Press, November 12, 2019; Office of Refugee Resettlement, "Unaccompanied Children Facts and Data" (U.S. Department of Health and Human Services, Office of Refugee Resettlement, 2021).

6. Freedom for Immigrants, "Detention by the Numbers" (2018), https://www.freedomforim migrants.org/detention-statistics.

7. Southern Poverty Law Center, "Family Separation under the Trump Administration—A Timeline" (2020), https://www.splcenter.org/news/2020/06/17/family-separation-under -trump-administration-timeline.

8. Freedom for Immigrants, "Detention by the Numbers."

9. Nick Miroff, Maria Sacchetti, and Tracy Jan, "Trump to Suspend Immigration to U.S. for 60 Days, Citing Coronavirus Crisis and Jobs Shortage, but Will Allow Some Workers," *Washington Post*, April 21, 2020; Michael D. Shear and Marian Jordan, "Trump Suspends Visas Allowing Hundreds of Thousands of Foreigners to Work in the U.S.," *New York Times*, June 22, 2020.

10. National Employment Law Project, "A Resource for Workers and Their Advocates" (National Employment Law Project, National Immigration Law Center, and OSH Law Project, 2020).

11. Wendy Fry and Alexandra Mendoza, "Immigrants, Hit Hard by the Pandemic, Are Sending Even More Money Back to Mexico," *Los Angeles Times*, September 8, 2000.

12. Robby Berman, "COVID-19 and the Surge in Anti-Asian Hate Crimes," *Medical News Today*, August 2, 2020.

REFERENCES

Ablavsky, Gregory. 2018. "'With the Indian Tribes': Race, Citizenship, and Original Constitutional Meanings." *Stanford Law Review* 70:1025–1076.

Abourezk, James. 1977. "The Congressional Veto: A Contemporary Response to Executive Encroachment on Legislative Prerogatives." *Indiana Law Journal* 52:323–343.

Ahern, Thomas L. 2006. *Undercover Armies: CIA and Surrogate Warfare in Laos.* Washington, DC: Central Intelligence Agency.

Amenta, Edwin, Chris Bonastia, Tina Fetner, and Michael Young. 2002. "Challengers and States: Toward a Political Sociology of Social Movements." *Research in Political Sociology* 10:47–83.

Anderson, Benedict. 1983. *Imagined Communities: Reflections on the Origin and Spread of Nationalism.* London: Verso.

Anthony, Victor B., and Richard R. Sexton. 1993. *The War in Northern Laos: The United States Air Force in Southeast Asia (Unclassified Version).* Washington, DC: Center for Air Force History, U.S. Air Force.

Arulanantham, Ahilan, and Michael Tan. 2018. "Is It Constitutional to Lock Up Immigrants Indefinitely?" New York: American Civil Liberties Union. www.aclu.org/blog/immigrants-rights/immigrants-rights-and-detention/it-constitutional-lock-immigrants.

Barney, George L. 1961. *The Meo of Xieng Khouang Province.* Los Angeles: University of California, Los Angeles, Department of Anthropology.

Bell, Derrick A. 1980. "Brown v Board of Education and the Interest-Convergence Dilemma." *Harvard Law Review* 93:518–533.

Benford, Robert. 1997. "An Insider's Critique of the Social Movement Framing Perspective." *Sociological Inquiry* 67(4):409–430.

Benford, Robert D., and David A. Snow. 2000. "Framing Processes and Social Movements: An Overview and Assessment." *Annual Review of Sociology* 26:611–639.

Biggs, Michael. 2013. "How Repertoires Evolve: The Diffusion of Suicide Protest in the Twentieth Century." *Mobilization: An International Quarterly* 18(4):407–428.

Block, Fred. 1977. "The Ruling Class Does Not Rule: Notes on the Marxist Theory of the State." *Socialist Revolution* 33:6–28.

Bloemraad, Irene. 2006. "Becoming a Citizen in the United States and Canada: Structured Mobilization and Immigrant Political Incorporation." *Social Forces* 85(2):667–695.

Bonilla-Silva, Eduardo. 1997. "Rethinking Racism: Toward a Structural Interpretation." *American Sociological Review* 62(3):465–480.

———. 2004. "From Bi-Racial to Tri-Racial: Towards a New System of Racial Stratification in the USA. *Ethnic and Racial Studies* 27(6):931–950.

Brown, Hana, and Jennifer A. Jones. 2015. "Rethinking Panethnicity and the Race-Immigration Divide: An Ethnoracialization Model of Group Formation." *Sociology of Race and Ethnicity* 1(1):181–191.

Browning, Rufus P., Dale Rogers Marshall, and David H. Tabb. 1984. *Protest Is Not Enough: The Struggle of Blacks and Hispanics for Equality in Urban Politics.* Berkeley: University of California Press.

———. 1986. "Protest Is Not Enough: A Theory of Political Incorporation." *PS: Political Science & Politics* 19(3):576–581.

Buckingham, William. 1982. *Operation Ranch Hand: The Airforce and Herbicides in Southeast Asia, 1961–1971*. Washington, DC: U.S. Air Force.

Castle, Timothy N. 1999. *One Day Too Long: Top Secret Site 85 and the Bombing of North Vietnam*. New York: Columbia University Press.

Center for Migration Studies. n.d. "President Trump's Executive Orders on Immigration and Refugees." New York: Center for Migration Studies. https://cmsny.org/trumps-executive -orders-immigration-refugees.

Chacon, Ramon D. 1986. "A Case Study of Ghettoization and Segregation: West Fresno's Black and Chicano Community During the 1970s." Working Paper Series No. 12. Stanford, CA: Stanford Center for Chicano Research.

Chan, Sucheng. 1994. *Hmong Means Free: Life in Laos and America*. Philadelphia: Temple University Press.

Chantavanich, Supang, Marisa Phupinyokul, Philip Finch, and Saikaew Tipakorn. 1992. "The Lao Returnees in the Voluntary Repatriation Programme from Thailand." Occasional Paper Series no. 003. Bangkok: Institute of Asian Studies, Chulalornkorn University.

Chantavanich, Supang, and Paul Rabe. 1990. "Thailand and the Indochinese Refugees: Fifteen Years of Compromise and Uncertainty." *Southeast Asian Journal of Social Science* 18(1):66–80.

Chesser, Judy L. 1997. "The Personal Responsibility and Work Opportunity Reconciliation Act and SSI Eligibility for Noncitizens." *In Defense of the Alien* 20:14–22.

Chiu, Monica. 2004–2005. "Medical, Racist, and Colonial Constructions of Power in Anne Fadiman's *The Spirit Catches You and You Fall Down*." *Hmong Studies Journal* 5:1–36.

Chung, Angie Y. 2007. *Legacies of Struggle: Conflict and Cooperation in Korean American Politics*. Stanford, CA: Stanford University Press.

City of Fresno. 2008. "Inner City Areas: Approved by City Council Per Res. No. 93–368 and 96–277." Fresno, CA: Planning and Development Department.

Cohen, Ronald. 1978. "Ethnicity: Problem and Focus in Anthropology." *Annual Review of Anthropology* 7:379–403.

Collet, Christian, and Pei-te Lien. 2009. *The Transnational Politics of Asian Americans*. Philadelphia: Temple University Press.

Cook, John T. 1998. "The Food Stamp Program and Low-Income Legal Immigrants." *Nutrition Reviews* 56(7):218–221.

Cordero-Guzmán, Hector, Nina Martin, Victoria Quiroz-Becerra, and Nik Theodore. 2008. "Voting with Their Feet: Nonprofit Organizations and Immigrant Mobilization." *American Behavioral Scientist* 52(4):598–617.

Crain, Mark, and Robert D. Tollison. 1979. "The Executive Branch in the Interest-Group Theory of Government." *Journal of Legal Studies* 8(3):555–567.

Culas, Christian, and Jean Michaud. 2004. "A Contribution to the Study of Hmong (Miao) Migrations and History." Pp. 61–96 in *Hmong-Miao in Asia*, edited by N. Tapp, J. Michaud, C. Culas, and G. Y. Lee. Chiang Mai, Thailand: Silkworm Books.

Diamond, Norma. 1995. "Defining the Miao." Pp. 92–116 in *Cultural Encounters on China's Ethnic Frontiers*, edited by S. Harrell. Seattle: University of Washington Press.

Downing, Bruce T., Douglas P. Olney, Sarah R. Mason, and Glenn L. Hendricks. 1984. "The Hmong Resettlement Study." Minneapolis: University of Minnesota, Southeast Asian Refugee Studies Project Center for Urban and Regional Affairs.

Duffy, John. 2007. *Writing from These Roots: Literacy in a Hmong-American Community*. Honolulu: University of Hawaii Press.

Dunham, George R., and David A. Quinlan. 1990. *U.S. Marines in Vietnam: The Bitter End, 1973–1975*. Washington, DC: U.S. Marine Corps.

Dunnigan, Timothy, Douglas P. Olney, Miles A. McNall, and Marline A. Spring. 1996. "Hmong." Pp. 191–212 in *Refugees in America in the 1990s*, edited by D. W. Haines. Westport, CT: Greenwood.

Fadiman, Anne. 1997. *The Spirit Catches You and You Fall Down: A Hmong Child, Her American Doctors, and the Collision of Two Cultures*. New York: Farrar, Straus and Giroux.

Feagin, Joe R. 2006. *Systemic Racism: A Theory of Oppression*. New York: Routledge.

Feagin, Joe R., and Sean Elias. 2013. "Rethinking Racial Formation Theory: A Systemic Racism Critique." *Ethnic and Racial Studies* 36(6):931–960.

Ferree, Myra Marx. 2003. "Resonance and Radicalism: Feminist Framing in the Abortion Debates of the United States and Germany." *American Journal of Sociology* 109:304–344.

Fine, Gary Alan. 1995. "Public Narration and Group Culture: Discerning Discourse in Social Movements." Pp. 127–143 in *Social Movements and Culture*, edited by H. Johnston and B. Klandermans. Minneapolis: University of Minnesota Press.

Fraser, Nancy. 1989. "Talking about Needs: Interpretive Contests as Political Conflicts in Welfare-State Societies." *Ethics* 99(2):291–313.

Fujiwara, Lynn. 2005. "Immigrant Rights Are Human Rights: The Reframing of Immigrant Entitlement and Welfare." *Social Problems* 52(1):79–101.

———. 2008. *Mothers without Citizenship: Asian Immigrant Families and the Consequences of Welfare Reform*. Minneapolis: University of Minnesota Press.

Gale, Dennis E. 1984. *Neighborhood Revitalization and the Postindustrial City: A Multinational Perspective*. Lexington, MA: Lexington Books.

Gamson, William A., and David S. Meyer. 1996. "Framing Political Opportunity." Pp. 275–290 in *Comparative Perspectives on Social Movements: Political Opportunities, Mobilizing Structures, and Cultural Framings*, edited by D. McAdam, J. D. McCarthy, and M. N. Zald. New York: Cambridge University Press.

Gans, Herbert J. 1999. "The Possibility of a New Racial Hierarchy in the Twenty-First Century United States." Pp. 371–390 in *The Cultural Territories of Race: Black and White Boundaries*, edited by M. Lamont. Chicago: University of Chicago Press.

Getrich, Christina M. 2008. "Negotiating Boundaries of Social Belonging: Second-Generation Mexican Youth and the Immigrant Rights Protests of 2006." *American Behavioral Scientist* 52(4):533–556.

Gold, Stephen J. 2004. "From Jim Crow to Racial Hegemony: Evolving Explanations of Racial Hierarchy." *Ethnic and Racial Studies* 27(6):951–968.

Goldstein, Martin E. 1973. *American Policy toward Laos*. Cranbury, NJ: Associated University Presses.

Goldstone, Jack A., and Charles Tilly. 2001. "Threat (and Opportunity): Popular Action and State Response in the Dynamics of Contentious Action." Pp. 179–194 in *Silence and Voice in the Study of Contentious Politics*, edited by R. Aminzade, J. A. Goldstone, D. McAdam, E. J. Perry, W. H. J. Sewell, S. Tarrow, and C. Tilly. Cambridge: Cambridge University Press.

Gover, Angela R., Shannon B. Harper, and Lynn Langton. 2020. "Anti-Asian Hate Crime During the COVID-19 Pandemic: Exploring the Reproduction of Inequality." *American Journal of Criminal Justice* 45:647–667.

Government of Lao PDR. 2006. "Results from the Population and Housing Census 2005." Vientiane: Steering Committee for Census of Population and Housing.

Greenstein, Fred I., and Richard H. Immerman. 1992. "What Did Eisenhower Tell Kennedy about Indochina? The Politics of Misperception." *Journal of American History* 79(2):568–587.

Greer, Christina M. 2013. *Black Ethnics: Race, Immigration, and the Pursuit of the American Dream*. Oxford: Oxford University Press.

Gunn, Geoffrey C. 1986. "Shamans and Rebels the Ba'chai (Meo) Rebellion of Northern Laos and North-West Vietnam (1918–1921)." *Journal of the Siam Society* 74:107–121.

Hafner, James A. 1985. "Lowland Lao and Hmong Refugees in Thailand: The Plight of Those Left Behind." *Disasters* 9(2):83–91.

Haines, David. 1996. *Refugees in America in the 1990s: A Reference Handbook*. Westport, CT: Greenwood.

Hardina, Donna, Jane Yamaguchi, Xong Moua, Molly Yang, and Phoua Moua. 2003. "Competition and Cooperation among Organizations Serving an Ethnic Community: The Case of the Hmong Suicide Prevention Task Force." Paper presented at the Annual Conference of the Association for Research on Nonprofit Organizations and Voluntary Action, Denver.

Harris, Cheryl I. 1993. "Whiteness as Property." *Harvard Law Review* 106(8):1707–1791.

Hein, Jeremy. 1993. *States and International Migrants: The Incorporation of Indochinese Refugees in the United States and France*. Boulder, CO: Westview.

Herman, Edward S., and Noam Chomsky. 2002. *Manufacturing Consent: The Political Economy of the Mass Media*. New York: Pantheon Books.

Hero, Rodney E. 1992. *Latinos and the U.S. Political System: Two-Tiered Pluralism*. Philadelphia: Temple University Press.

Hobson, Barbara. 1999. "Women's Collective Agency, Power Resources, and the Framing of Citizenship Rights." Pp. 149–178 in *Extending Citizenship, Reconfiguring States*, edited by M. Hanagan and C. Tilly. Lanham, MD: Rowman & Littlefield.

Hochman, Adam. 2019. "Racialization: A Defense of the Concept." *Ethnic and Racial Studies* 42(8):1245–1262.

Hochschild, Jennifer L., Jacqueline Chattopadhyay, Claudine Gay, and Michael Jones-Correa. 2013. *Outsiders No More? Models of Immigrant Political Incorporation*. New York: Oxford University Press.

Hochschild, Jennifer L., and John H. Mollenkopf, eds. 2009a. *Bringing Outsiders In: Transatlantic Perspectives on Immigrant Political Incorporation*. Ithaca, NY: Cornell University Press.

———. 2009b. "Modeling Immigrant Political Incorporation." Pp. 15–30 in *Bringing Outsiders In: Transatlantic Perspectives on Immigrant Political Incorporation*, edited by J. L. Hochschild and J. H. Mollenkopf. Ithaca, NY: Cornell University Press.

Hochschild, Jennifer L., and Vesla Weaver. 2007. "Policies of Racial Classification and the Politics of Racial Inequality." Pp. 159–182 in *Remaking America: Democracy and Public Policy in an Age of Inequality*. New York: Russell Sage Foundation.

Hwang, Victor. 2002. "The Hmong Campaign for Justice: A Practitioner's Perspective." *Asian Law Journal* 9:83–115.

Ireland, Patrick R. 1994. *The Policy Challenge of Ethnic Diversity: Immigrant Politics in France*. Cambridge, MA: Harvard University Press.

Jacobs, Brian W. 1996. "No-Win Situation: The Plight of the Hmong—America's Former Ally." *Boston College Third World Law Journal* 16:139–166.

Jasper, James M. 2004. "A Strategic Approach to Collective Action: Looking for Agency in Social-Movement Choices." *Mobilization: An International Journal* 9(1):1–16.

———. 2012. "Introduction: From Political Opportunity Structures to Strategic Interaction." Pp. 1–33 in *Contention in Context: Political Opportunities and the Emergence of Protest* edited by J. Goodwin and J. Jasper. Stanford, CA: Stanford University Press.

Jasso, Guillermina, and Mark Richard Rosenzweig. 1990. *The New Chosen People: Immigrants in the United States*. New York: Russell Sage Foundation.

Jefferys, Kelly. 2006. "Annual Flow Report on Refugees and Asylees: 2005." Washington, DC: Department of Homeland Security.

Jenks, Robert Darrah. 1994. *Insurgency and Social Disorder in Guizhou: The "Miao" Rebellion, 1854–1873*. Honolulu: University of Hawaii Press.

Jesilow, Paul, and Machiline Xiong. 2007. "Constructing a Social Problem: Suicide, Acculturation, and the Hmong." *Hmong Studies Journal* 8:1–43.

Jones, Bill. 1994. *November 8, 1994 General Election*. Washington, DC: U.S. Congress.

———. 1996. *November 5, 1996 General Election*. Washington, DC: U.S. Congress.

———. 1998. *June 2, 1998 Primary Election*. Washington, DC: U.S. Congress.

Jung, Moon-Ho. 2011. "Seditious Subjects: Race, State Violence, and the U.S." *Journal of Asian American Studies* 14(2):221–247.

Jung, Moon-Kie. 2009. "The Racial Unconscious of Assimilation Theory." *Du Bois Review* 6(2):375–395.

Jung, Moon-Kie, and Yaejoon Kwon. 2013. "Theorizing the US Racial State: Sociology Since Racial Formation." *Sociology Compass* 7(11):927–940.

Kang, Jerry. 2004. "Denying Prejudice: Internment, Redress, and Denial." *UCLA Law Review* 51:933–1013.

Khamvongsa, Channapha, and Elaine Russell. 2009. "Legacies of War: Cluster Bombs in Laos." *Critical Asian Studies* 41(2):281–306.

Kim, Claire Jean. 1999. "The Racial Triangulation of Asian Americans." *Politics and Society* 27(1):105–138.

———. 2003. *Bitter Fruit: The Politics of Black-Korean Conflict in New York City*. New Haven, CT: Yale University Press.

Kivisto, Peter. 2003. "Social Spaces, Transnational Immigrant Communities, and the Politics of Incorporation." *Ethnicities* 3(1):5–28.

Koopmans, Ruud. 2004. "Migrant Mobilisation and Political Opportunities: Variation among German Cities and a Comparison with the United Kingdom and the Netherlands." *Journal of Ethnic and Migration Studies* 30(3):449–470.

Koopmans, Ruud, and Susan Olzak. 2004. "Discursive Opportunities and the Evolution of Right-Wing Violence in Germany." *American Journal of Sociology* 110(1):198–230.

Kriesi, Hanspeter, Ruud Koopmans, Jan Willem Duyvendak, and Marco G. Guigni. 1995a. *New Social Movements in Western Europe: A Comparative Analysis*. Minneapolis: University of Minnesota Press.

———. 1995b. *The Politics of New Social Movements in Western Europe*. Minneapolis: University of Minnesota Press / University College London Press.

Kundstadter, Peter. 1985. "Health of Hmong in Thailand: Risk Factors, Morbidity and Mortality in Comparison with Other Ethnic Groups." *Culture, Medicine and Psychiatry* 9:329–351.

Kurashige, Lon. 2016. *Two Faces of Exclusion: The Untold History of Anti-Asian Racism in the United States*. Chapel Hill: University of North Carolina Press.

Lai, James S. 2011. *Asian American Political Action: Suburban Transformations*. Boulder, CO: Lynne Rienner.

Lao Statistics Bureau. 2015. *Results of Population and Housing Census*. Vientiane: Ministry of Planning and Investment.

Leary, William M. 1995. "The CIA and the 'Secret War' in Laos: The Battle for Skyline Ridge, 1971–1972." *Journal of Military History* 59(3):505–517.

———. 1999. "CIA Air Operations in Laos, 1955–1974: Supporting the 'Secret War.'" Langley, VA: U.S. Central Intelligence Agency, Center for the Study of Intelligence.

Lee, Gary Yia. 1982. "Minority Policies and the Hmong." Pp. 199–219 in *Contemporary Laos: Studies in the Politics and Society of the Lao People's Democratic Republic*, edited by M. Stuart-Fox. St. Lucia: University of Queensland Press.

————. 2000. "Bandits or Rebels? Hmong Resistance in the New Lao State." http://members .ozemail.com.au/~yeulee/Topical/bandis%20or%20rebels.html.

————. 2004. "Transnational Adaptation: An Overview of the Hmong of Laos." Pp. 441–456 in *Hmong-Miao in Asia*, edited by N. Tapp, J. Michaud, C. Culas, and G. Y. Lee. Chiang Mai, Thailand: Silkworm Books.

————. 2007. "Diaspora and the Predicament of Origins: Interrogating Hmong Postcolonial History and Identity." *Hmong Studies Journal* 8:1–25.

Lee, Gary Yia, and Nicholas Tapp. 2010. *Culture and Customs of the Hmong*. Santa Barbara, CA: Greenwood.

Lee, Mai Na M. 2005. "The Dream of the Hmong Kingdom: Resistance, Collaboration, and Legitimacy under French Colonialism." PhD diss., Department of History, University of Wisconsin–Madison.

————. 2015. *Dreams of the Hmong Kingdom: The Quest for Legitimation in French Indochina, 1850–1960*. Madison: University of Wisconsin Press.

Lee, Wen Ho, and Helen Zia. 2001. *My Country versus Me: The First-Hand Account by the Los Alamos Scientist Who Was Falsely Accused of Being a Spy*. New York: Hyperion.

Leeker, Joe F. 2010a. "Air America in Laos II—Military Aid Part I." In *The History of Air America*. Richardson: University of Texas at Dallas.

————. 2010b. "Air America in Laos II—Military Aid Part II." In *The History of Air America*. Richardson: University of Texas at Dallas.

Lemoine, Jacques. 2005. "What Is the Actual Number of the (H)Mong in the World?" *Hmong Studies Journal* 6:1–8.

————. 2008. "To Tell the Truth." *Hmong Studies Journal* 9:1–29.

Li, Yao, and Harvey L. Nicholson. 2020. "When 'Model Minorities' Become 'Yellow Peril'—Othering and the Racialization of Asian Americans in the COVID-19 Pandemic." *Sociological Compass* 15(2):1–13.

Light, Ivan Hubert. 2006. *Deflecting Immigration: Networks, Markets, and Regulation in Los Angeles*. New York: Russell Sage Foundation.

Literacy and Language Program, Southeast Asian Refugee Studies Project and Lao Family Community. 1985. "The Hmong Resettlement Study." Vol. 1. Washington, DC: Office of Refugee Resettlement. https://files.eric.ed.gov/fulltext/ED267151.pdf.

Lobban, Richard A., and Carolyn Fluehr-Lobban. 1976. "'Tribe': A Socio-Political Analysis." *Ufahamu: A Journal of African Studies* 7(1):143–165.

Long, Lynellyn. 1993. *Ban Vinai, the Refugee Camp*. New York: Columbia University Press.

Lopez Jerez, Montserrat. 2019. "Colonial and Indigenous Institutions in the Fiscal Development of French Indochina." Pp. 110–136 in *Fiscal Capacity and the Colonial State in Asia and Africa, 1850–1960*, edited by E. Frankema and A. Booth. Cambridge: Cambridge University Press.

Martinez, Lisa M. 2008. "'Flowers from the Same Soil': Latino Solidarity in the Wake of the 2006 Immigrant Mobilizations." *American Behavioral Scientist* 52(4):557–579.

Massey, Douglas S. 2009. "Racial Formation in Theory and Practice: The Case of Mexicans in the United States." *Race and Social Problems* 1(1):12–26.

Massey, Douglas S., and Nancy A. Denton. 1993. *American Apartheid: Segregation and the Making of the Underclass*. Cambridge, MA: Harvard University Press.

Massey, Douglas S., and Karen A. Pren. 2012. "Unintended Consequences of US Immigration Policy: Explaining the Post-1965 Surge from Latin America." *Population and Development Review* 38(1):1–29.

Massey, Douglas S., and Magaly Sánchez. 2010. *Brokered Boundaries Immigrant Identity in Anti-immigrant Times*. New York: Russell Sage Foundation.

Masuoka, Natalie, and Jane Junn. 2013. *The Politics of Belonging: Race, Public Opinion, and Immigration.* Chicago: University of Chicago Press.

Maxwell, Rahsaan. 2008. "Inclusion Versus Exclusion: Caribbeans in Britain and France." Pp. 134–159 in *Civic Hopes and Political Realities: Immigrants, Community Organizations, and Political Engagement,* edited by S. K. Ramakrishnan and I. Bloemraad. New York: Russell Sage Foundation.

McAdam, Doug. 1982. *Political Process and the Development of Black Insurgency, 1930–1970.* Chicago: University of Chicago Press.

McCammon, Holly J., Harmony D. Newman, Courtney Sanders Muse, and Teresa M. Terrell. 2007. "Movement Framing and Discursive Opportunity Structures: The Political Successes of the U.S. Women's Jury Movements." *American Sociological Review* 72(5):725–749.

McCarthy, John D., and Mayer N. Zald. 1977. "Resource Mobilization and Social Movements: A Partial Theory." *American Journal of Sociology* 82(6):1212–1241.

Médecins Sans Frontières. 2009. "Hidden Behind Barbed Wire: Plight of Hmong Refugees Held in Detention Camp in Northern Thailand Ignored amid Ongoing Deportations to Laos." New York: Médecins Sans Frontières.

Meyer, David S. 2003. "Political Opportunity and Nested Institutions." *Social Movement Studies* 2(1):17–35.

———. 2004a. "Opportunities and Identities: Bridge-Building in the Study of Social Movements." Pp. 3–24 in *Social Movements: Identity, Culture, and the State,* edited by D. S. Meyer, N. Whittier, and B. Robnett. New York: Oxford University Press.

———. 2004b. "Protest and Political Opportunities." *Annual Review of Sociology* 30:125–145.

Miller, Susan Lindbergh, Bounthavy Kiatoukaysy, and Tou Yang. 1992. *Hmong Voices in Montana.* Missoula, MT: Missoula Museum of the Arts.

Molina, Natalia. 2010. "'In a Race All Their Own': The Quest to Make Mexicans Ineligible for U.S. Citizenship." *Pacific Historical Review* 79(2):167–201.

Moon, Debra. 2003. *Chico: Life and Times of a City of Fortune.* Charleston, SC: Arcadia.

Morrison, Gayle. 1999. *Sky Is Falling: An Oral History of the Cia's Evacuation of the Hmong from Laos.* Jefferson, NC: McFarland.

———. 2013. *Hog's Exit: Jerry Daniels, the Hmong, and the CIA.* Lubbock, TX: Texas Tech University Press.

Mortland, Carol A., and Judy Ledgerwood. 1987. "Secondary Migration among Southeast Asian Refugees in the United States." *Urban Anthropology and Studies of Cultural Systems and World Economic Development* 16(3/4):291–326.

Mottin, Jean. 1980. *History of the Hmong.* Bangkok: Odeon Store.

Munger, Ronald Grant. 1987. "Sudden Death in Sleep of Laotian-Hmong Refugees in Thailand: A Case-Control Study." *American Journal of Public Health* 77(9):1187–1190.

Murdoch, John B. 1974. "The 1901–1902 'Holy Man's' Rebellion." *Journal of the Siam Society* 62(1):47–66.

Murphy, Raymond. 1988. *Social Closure: The Theory of Monopolization and Exclusion.* New York: Oxford University Press.

Nagel, Joane. 1995. "American Indian Ethnic Renewal: Politics and the Resurgence of Identity." *American Sociological Review* 60(6):947–965.

Ngai, Mae M. 1998. "Legacies of Exclusion: Illegal Chinese Immigration during the Cold War Years." *Journal of American Ethnic History* 18(1):3–35.

———. 2004. *Impossible Subjects: Illegal Aliens and the Making of Modern America.* Princeton, NJ: Princeton University Press.

Nguyen, Manh Hung, and David Haines. 1997. "Vietnamese." Pp. 34–56 in *Case Studies in Diversity: Refugees in America in the 1990s,* edited by D. W. Haines. Westport, CT: Greenwood.

Nguyen, Van Hanh. 1995. "The Refugees of Southeast Asia." Pp. 317–332 in *The Asian-American Almanac: A Reference Work on Asians in the United States*, edited by S. B. Gall and I. Natividad. Detroit: Gale Research.

Okamoto, Dina G. 2003. "Toward a Theory of Panethnicity: Explaining Asian American Collective Action." *American Sociological Review* 68(6):811–842.

———. 2014. *Redefining Race: Asian American Panethnicity and Shifting Ethnic Boundaries.* New York: Russell Sage Foundation.

Oliver, Pamela E. 2017. "The Ethnic Dimensions in Social Movements." *Mobilization: An International Quarterly* 22(4):395–416.

Omi, Michael, and Howard Winant. 1994. *Racial Formation in the United States: From the 1960s to the 1990s.* New York: Routledge.

———. 2013. "Resistance Is Futile? A Response to Feagin and Elias." *Ethnic and Racial Studies* 36(6):961–973.

Ong, Aihwa. 2003. *Buddha Is Hiding: Refugees, Citizenship, the New America.* Berkeley: University of California Press.

Ong, Paul M., and Evelyn Blumenberg. 1994. "Welfare and Work among Southeast Asians." Pp. 113–138 in *The State of Asian Pacific America: Economic Diversity, Issues & Policies*, edited by P. M. Ong. Los Angeles: LEAP Asian Pacific American Public Policy Institute and UCLA Asian American Studies Center.

Østergaard-Nielsen, Eva. 2003. "The Politics of Migrants' Transnational Political Practices." *International Migration Review* 37(3):760–786.

Ovesen, Jan. 2004. "All Lao? Minorities in the Lao People's Democratic Republic." Pp. 214–240 in *Civilizing the Margins: Southeast Asian Government Policies for the Development of Minorities*, edited by C. R. Duncan. Ithaca, NY: Cornell University.

Ovington, G. K. 2008. *Birth Jacket.* Victoria, BC: Trafford Publishing.

Parker, James E. 1995. *Covert Ops: The Cia's Secret War in Laos.* New York: St. Martin's.

Parrott, Thomas M., Lenna D. Kennedy, and Charles G. Scott. 1998. "Noncitizens and the Supplemental Security Income Program." *Social Security Bulletin* 61(4):3–31.

Patler, Caitlin. 2018. "'Citizens but for Papers': Undocumented Youth Organizations, Anti-deportation Campaigns, and the Reframing of Citizenship." *Social Problems* 65:96–115.

Perea, Juan F. 1997. *Immigrants Out! The New Nativism and the Anti-immigrant Impulse in the United States.* New York: New York University Press.

Pfeifer, Mark E., and Serge C. Lee. 2000. "Hmong Population, Demographic, Socioeconomic, and Educational Trends in the 2000 Census." Pp. 3–11 in *Hmong 2000 Census Publication: Data and Analysis.* Washington, DC: Hmong National Development and Hmong Cultural and Resource Center.

Pfeifer, Mark E., John Sullivan, Kou Yang, and Wayne Yang. 2012. "Hmong Population and Demographic Trends in the 2010 Census and 2010 American Community Survey." *Hmong Studies Journal* 13(2):1–31.

Pholsena, Vatthana. 2002. "Nation/Representation: Ethnic Classification and Mapping Nationhood in Contemporary Laos." *Asian Ethnicity* 3(2):175–197.

———. 2006. *Post-war Laos: The Politics of Culture, History and Identity.* Singapore: Institute of Southeast Asian Studies.

Polletta, Francesca, and James M. Jasper. 2001. "Collective Identity and Social Movements." *Annual Review of Sociology* 27:283–305.

Portes, Alejandro, and Rubén Rumbaut. 1990. *Immigrant American: A Portrait.* Berkeley: University of California Press.

Portes, Alejandro, and Min Zhou. 1992. "Gaining the Upper Hand: Economic Mobility among Immigrant and Domestic Minorities." *Ethnic and Racial Studies* 15(4):491–522.

————. 1993. "The New Second Generation: Segmented Assimilation and Its Variants." *Annals of the American Academy of Political and Social Science* 530:74–96.

Quincy, Keith. 2000. *Harvesting Pa Chay's Wheat: The Hmong and America's Secret War in Laos*. Spokane: Eastern Washington University Press.

Quisumbing King, Katrina. 2018. "Institutionalized Ambiguity in Legal Status: Managing Citizenship in the U.S. Imperial Rule of the Philippines." SocArXiv, June 13.

Reder, Stephen, Mary Cohn, Shur Vang Vangyi, Dang Vang, and Thongsay Vang. 1984. "The Hmong Resettlement Study: Site Report: Fresno, California." Washington, DC: U.S. Department of Health and Human Services, Office of Refugee Resettlement.

Reese, Ellen. 2011. *They Say Cut Back, We Say Fight Back! Welfare Activism in an Era of Retrenchment*. New York: Russell Sage Foundation

Rhie, Anne Y. 1994. "The Dilemma of Refugees: Lessons from the Thai Experience." MA thesis, Naval Postgraduate School, Monterey, CA.

Robbins, Christopher. 1987. *The Ravens: The Men Who Flew in America's Secret War in Laos*. New York: Crown.

Robinson, W. Courtland. 2004. "The Comprehensive Plan of Action for Indochinese Refugees, 1989–1997: Sharing the Burden and Passing the Buck." *Journal of Refugee Studies* 17(3):319–333.

Rogers, Reuel Reuben. 2006. *Afro-Caribbean Immigrants and the Politics of Incorporation: Ethnicity, Exception, or Exit*. Cambridge: Cambridge University Press.

Romero, Mary. 2008. "Crossing the Immigration and Race Border: A Critical Race Theory Approach to Immigration Studies." *Contemporary Justice Review* 11(1):23–37.

Rosenblatt, Lionel. 2015. "How the Hmong Came to Be in the U.S." Saint Paul, MN: Center for Hmong Studies.

Rumbaut, Rubén G., and Kenji Ima. 1988. "The Adaptation of Southeast Asian Refugee Youth: A Comparative Study." Washington, DC: Office of Refugee Resettlement.

Saenz, Rogelio, and Karen Manges Douglas. 2015. "A Call for the Racialization of Immigration Studies: On the Transition of Ethnic Immigrants to Racialized Immigrants." *Sociology of Race and Ethnicity* 1(1):166–180.

Saito, Leland T. 2009. *The Politics of Exclusion: The Failure of Race-Neutral Policies in Urban America*. Stanford, CA: Stanford University Press.

Saperstein, Aliya, Andrew M. Penner, and Ryan Light. 2013. "Racial Formation in Perspective: Connecting Individuals, Institutions, and Power Relations." *Annual Review of Sociology* 39:359–378.

Schanche, Don A. 1963. "An American Hero: The Exclusive Story of How an American Farmer Has Devoted His Life to a One-Man Crusade for Freedom and Democracy in the War-Torn Communist-Infiltrated Laos." *Congressional Record* 119(14).

Selod, Saher. 2018. *Forever Suspect: Racialized Surveillance of Muslim Americans in the War on Terror*. New Brunswick, NJ: Rutgers University Press.

Sherman, Spenser. 1985. "Waking Up on the Moon: The Hmong in America." Washington, DC: Alicia Patterson Foundation.

Singer, Audrey. 2004. "Welfare Reform and Immigrants: A Policy Review." Pp. 21–34 in *Immigrants, Welfare Reform, and the Poverty of Policy*, edited by P. Kretsedemas and A. Aparicio. Westport, CT: Praeger.

Smalley, William A., Chia Koua Vang, and Gnia Yee Yang. 1990. *Mother of Writing: The Origin and Development of a Hmong Messianic Script*. Chicago: University of Chicago Press.

Snow, David A., and Robert D. Benford. 1988. "Ideology, Frame Resonance, and Participant Mobilization." *International Social Movement Research* 1:197–217.

————. 1992. "Master Frames and Cycles of Protest." Pp. 133–155 in *Frontiers in Social Movement Theory*, edited by A. D. Morris and C. M. Mueller. New Haven, CT: Yale University Press.

Steinberg, Marc W. 1998. "Tilting the Frame: Considerations on Collective Action Framing from a Discursive Turn." *Theory and Society* 27(6):845–872.

———. 1999. "The Talk and Back Talk of Collective Action: A Dialogic Analysis of Repertoires of Discourse among Nineteenth-Century English Cotton Spinners." *American Journal of Sociology* 105(3):736–780.

Stuart-Fox, Martin. 1995. "The French in Laos, 1887–1945." *Modern Asian Studies* 29(1):111–139.

———. 1997. *A History of Laos.* Cambridge: Cambridge University Press.

Summers Sandoval, Tomás F. 2008. "Disobedient Bodies: Racialization, Resistance, and the Mass (Re)articulation of the Mexican Immigrant Body." *American Behavioral Scientist* 52(4):580–597.

Takaki, Ronald T. 2000. *Iron Cages: Race and Culture in 19th-Century America.* New York: Oxford University Press.

Tapp, Nicholas. 2005. "Hmong Diaspora." Pp. 103–113 in *Encyclopedia of Diasporas: Immigrant and Refugee Cultures around the World,* edited by C. R. Ember, M. Ember and I. A. Skoggard. New York: Springer.

Tarrow, Sidney. 1993. "Modular Collective Action and the Rise of the Social Movement: Why the French Revolution Was Not Enough." *Politics and Society* 21:647–670.

———. 1994. *Power in Movement: Social Movements, Collective Action and Politics.* Cambridge: Cambridge University Press.

Taylor, Verta, and Nella Van Dyke. 2004. "'Get Up, Stand Up': Tactical Repertoires of Social Movements." Pp. 262–293 in *The Blackwell Companion to Social Movements,* edited by D. A. Snow, S. A. Soule, and H. Kriesi. Malden, MA: Blackwell.

Tessler, Hannah, Meera Choi, and Grace Kao. 2020. "The Anxiety of Being Asian American: Hate Crimes and Negative Biases during the COVID-19 Pandemic." *American Journal of Criminal Justice* 45:636–646.

Thao, Paoze. 2004. "The Mong American Families." *Mong Journal* 2:1–23.

———. 2008. "Cultural Transitions and Adjustment: The Experiences of the Mong in the United States." Pp. 34–51 in *Emerging Voices: Experiences of Underrepresented Asian Americans,* edited by H. Ling. New Brunswick, NJ: Rutgers University Press.

Thompson, Larry Clinton. 2010. *Refugee Workers in the Indochina Exodus, 1975–1982.* Jefferson, NC: McFarland.

Tilly, Charles. 1977. "Repertoires of Contention in America and Britain, 1750–1830." Working Paper Series no. 151, Center for Research on Social Organization.

———. 1998. *Durable Inequality.* Berkeley: University of California Press.

———. 2008. *Contentious Performances.* Cambridge: Cambridge University Press.

Torres, María de los Angeles. 1999. *In the Land of Mirrors: Cuban Exile Politics in the United States.* Ann Arbor: University of Michigan Press.

Treitler, Vilna Bashi. 2015. "Social Agency and White Supremacy in Immigration Studies." *Sociology of Race and Ethnicity* 1(1):153–165.

Tuan, Mia. 1998. *Forever Foreigners or Honorary Whites? The Asian Ethnic Experience Today.* New Brunswick, NJ: Rutgers University Press.

Umbach, Kenneth W. 1997. "A Statistical Tour of California's Great Central Valley." http://www.library.ca.gov/crb/97/09/index.html.

United Nations High Commissioner for Refugees. 1996. "Update on Regional Developments in Asia and Oceania." Vol. EC/46/SC/CRP.44 (August 19). http://www.unhcr.org/3ae68cf94.pdf.

U.S. Bureau of the Census. 1983. "1980 Census of Population: General Population Characteristics." Washington, DC: Government Printing Office.

———. 1990. "Census of Population and Housing, 1990." New York: Social Explorer.

————. 1993a. "1990 Census of Population: Asians and Pacific Islanders in the United States, CP-3-5." Washington, DC: Government Printing Office.

————. 1993b. "We the Americans: Asians." Washington, DC: Government Printing Office.

————. 1995. "Census of Population and Housing, 1990 (United States): Public Use Microdata Sample: 5-Percent Sample [Computer File], 3rd ICPSR Release No. 9952." Ann Arbor, MI: Inter-university Consortium for Political and Social Research.

————. 2010. "Census of Population and Housing, 2010." New York: Social Explorer.

U.S. Congress. 1983. "Annual Refugee Consultation—Hearing before the Subcommittee on Immigration and Refugee Policy of the Committee on the Judiciary, House of Representatives." Washington, DC: U.S. Government Publishing Office.

————. 1997. "Hmong Veterans' Naturalization Act of 1997; and Canadian Border Boat Landing Permit Requirements—Hearing before the Subcommittee on Immigration and Claims of the Committee on the Judiciary, House of Representatives, 105th Congress." Washington, DC: U.S. Government Publishing Office.

U.S. Department of Agriculture. 2003. "Non-Citizen Requirements in the Food Stamp Program." Washington, DC.

U.S. Department of State. 1998a. "Foreign Relations of the United States 1969–1976, Vietnam, July 1970–January 1972, Document 4." Foreign Relations of the United States VII.

————. 1998b. "Foreign Relations of the United States 1969–1976, Documents on East and Southeast Asia, 1973–1976, Document 403." Foreign relations of the United States E-12.

————. 1998c. "Foreign Relations of the United States 1969–1976, Documents on East and Southeast Asia, 1973–1976, Document 404." Foreign Relations of the United States E-12.

————. 1998d. "Foreign Relations of the United States 1964–1968, Laos, Document 1. 10523." Foreign Relations of the United States XXVIII.

————. 1998e. "Foreign Relations of the United States 1961–1963, Laos Crisis." Foreign Relations of the United States XXIV.

————. 1998f. "Foreign Relations of the United States 1969–1976, Vietnam, July 1970–January 1972, Document 215." Foreign Relations of the United States VII.

Van Dyke, Nella, and Holly J. McCammon. 2010. *Strategic Alliances: Coalition Building and Social Movements*. Minneapolis: University of Minnesota Press.

Vang, Chia Youyee. 2019. *Fly until You Die: An Oral History of Hmong Pilots in the Vietnam War*. New York: Oxford University Press.

Vang, Christopher Thao. 2016. *Hmong Refugees in the New World: Culture, Community, and Opportunity*. Jefferson, NC: McFarland.

Wada, Takeshi. 2012. "Modularity and Transferability of Repertoires of Contention." *Social Problems* 59(4):544–571.

Wain, Barry. 1981. *The Refused: The Agony of the Indochina Refugees*. New York: Simon & Schuster.

White House. 2002. *The National Security Strategy of the United States of America*. Washington, DC: White House.

Williams, Rhys H. 1995. "Constructing the Public Good: Social Movements and Cultural Resources." *Social Problems* 42(1):124–144.

Wolfinger, Raymond E., and Steven J. Rosenstone. 1980. *Who Votes?* New Haven, CT: Yale University Press.

Wong, Carolyn. 2017. *Voting Together: Intergenerational Politics and Civic Engagement among Hmong Americans*. Stanford, CA: Stanford University Press.

Wong, Janelle. 2006. *Democracy's Promise: Immigrants and American Civic Institutions*. Ann Arbor: University of Michigan Press.

———. 2013. "Immigrant Political Incorporation: Beyond the Foreign-Born versus Native-Born Distinction." Pp. 95–104 in *Outsiders No More? Models of Immigrant Political Incorporation*, edited by J. L. Hochschild, J. Chattopadhyay, C. Gay, and M. Jones-Correa. New York: Oxford University Press.

Wong, Janelle, Pei-Te Lien, and M. Margaret Conway. 2005. "Group-Based Resources and Political Participation among Asian Americans." *American Politics Research* 33:545–576.

Xiong, Yang Sao. 2013. "An Analysis of Poverty in Hmong American Communities." Pp. 66–105 in *Diversity in Diaspora: Hmong Americans in the Twenty-First Century*, edited by M. Pfeifer, M. Chiu, and K. Yang. Honolulu: University of Hawaii Press.

———. 2016. "The Centrality of Ethnic Community and the Military Service Master Frame in Hmong Americans' Protest Events and Cycles of Protest, 1980–2010." *Hmong Studies Journal* 17:1–33.

———. 2020. "Hmong Americans Are Up for Grabs in the 2020 Presidential Election." AAPI Data.

Xiong, Yang Sao, and Michael Thornton. 2021. "Framing Racial Position and Political Standing: Hmong Americans in the Wisconsin State Journal and the Chico Enterprise-Record." *Ethnicities* 21(1):42–61.

Yang, Dao. 1972. "Les Difficultés Du Développement Économique Et Social Des Populations Hmong Du Laos." PhD diss. Université de Paris.

———. 1975. *Les Hmong Du Laos Face Au Développement*. Vientiane, Laos: Edition Siaosavath.

———. 1993. *Hmong at the Turning Point*. Minneapolis: WorldBridge Associates.

Yang, Kou. 2000. "The Passing of a Hmong Pioneer: Nhiavu Lobliayao (Nyiaj Vws Lauj Npliaj Yob), 1915–1999." *Hmong Studies Journal* 3:1–5.

Yukich, Grace. 2013. "Constructing the Model Immigrant: Movement Strategy and Immigrant Deservingness in the New Sanctuary Movement." *Social Problems* 60(3):302–320.

Zasloff, Joseph J. 1973. "Laos 1972: The War, Politics and Peace Negotiations." *Asian Survey* 13(1):60–75.

Zepeda-Millán, Chris. 2017. *Latino Mass Mobilization: Immigration, Racialization, and Activism*. Cambridge: Cambridge University Press.

INDEX

Page numbers in italics refer to tables, figures, or maps.

ABOUT THE AUTHOR

YANG SAO XIONG is an assistant professor in the School of Social Work and the Program in Asian American Studies at the University of Wisconsin–Madison. He holds a PhD in sociology from the University of California, Los Angeles. His research examines the collective agency and political incorporation of immigrants with a particular focus on Hmong former refugees in the United States. He teaches courses on social movements, race and ethnicity, Hmong American experiences, and immigrants and refugees.